The Triumph of Abraham's God

THE TRIUMPH OF ABRAHAM'S GOD

The Transformation of Identity in Galatians

BRUCE W. LONGENECKER

ABINGDON PRESS
NASHVILLE

THE TRIUMPH OF ABRAHAM'S GOD

Published in Great Britain by T&T Clark Ltd,
59 George Street, Edinburgh EH2 2LQ, Scotland

This edition published under license from T&T Clark Ltd by
Abingdon Press.

Library of Congress Cataloging-in-Publication Data

Longenecker, Bruce W.
    The triumph of Abraham's God : the transformation of identity
in Galatians / Bruce W. Longenecker.
        p.   cm.
    Includes bibliographical references.
    ISBN 0–687–03537–6
    1. Bible. N.T. Galatians—Theology.   I. Title.
BS2685.2.L66   1998
227'.406—DC21   98–18437
                                                                          CIP

Typeset by Fakenham Photosetting Limited, Fakenham, Norfolk, UK
Printed and bound in Great Britain by Page Bros, Norwich

To Beth and Dave
'What's past is prologue'

(Shakespeare, *The Tempest*, 2.1.258)

Contents

Acknowledgements

The writing of this book has taken place in a context of support from several different sectors. Special thanks must go to those who have gone out of their way to sponsor my well-being at Tyndale House. In particular, Dr Bruce Winter has encouraged me throughout the writing process. Also, my great appreciation goes to the New Testament team at the Faculty of Divinity, University of Cambridge, for the stimulation that they provide at the highest level: Professor Morna Hooker, Dr Markus Bockmuehl, Dr James Carleton Paget, and Dr Andrew Chester. For having read an early draft from start to finish, I thank Professor Graham Stanton and Dr John Barclay, whose suggestions have introduced improvements at many points. Any sparkle within these pages is probably due to the influence of my wife, Fiona Bond.

Abbreviations

Abbreviations for biblical books are conventional. The abbreviations used for other primary literature appear below, as do those pertaining to the secondary literature cited in the Bibliography.

Apocrypha

Jud.	Judith
Wis. Sol.	Wisdom of Solomon
Sir.	Ecclesiasticus (Sirach)
Bar.	Baruch
1 Macc.	1 Maccabees

Old Testament Pseudepigrapha

1 En.	1 Enoch
2 En.	2 Enoch
2 Bar.	2 Baruch
Apoc. Abr.	Apocalypse of Abraham
Jub.	Jubilees
Bib. Ant.	Pseudo-Philo, *Biblical Antiquities*
3 Macc.	3 Maccabees
4 Macc.	4 Maccabees
Pss. Sol.	Psalms of Solomon

Dead Sea Scrolls

CD	Covenant of Damascus
1QS	Rule of the Community
1QH	Thanksgiving Hymns
1QpHab	Pesher on Habakkuk

Philo

Abr.	On Abraham
Aet.	On the Eternity of the World
Decal.	On the Decalogue
Det.	The Worse Attacks the Better
Flacc.	To Flaccus
Heres	Who is the Heir?
Somn.	On Dreams
Spec. Leg.	On the Special Laws
Vit. Cont.	On the Contemplative Life

Josephus

Ant.	Jewish Antiquities
Vita	The Life

Rabbinic Literature

b. Ber.	Babylonian Talmud, *Berakoth*
b. Šabb.	Babylonian Talmud, *Šabbat*
b. Yom.	Babylonian Talmud, *Yoma*
m. 'Abot.	Mishnah, *Pirke Aboth*
m. Kid.	Mishnah, *Kiddushin*
Gen. Rab.	Midrash Rabbah, *Genesis Rabbah*

Greek and Latin Literature

Metaph.	Aristotle, *Metaphysics*
C. Lept.	Demosthenes, *Against Leptines*
Diss.	Epictetus, *Discourses*
Nat. Hist.	Pliny, *Natural History*
Quaest. conviv.	Plutarch, *Table Talk*
Inv. et od.	Plutarch, *On Envy and Hatred*
Id.	Theocritus, *Idylls*

Early Church Fathers

Protrept.	Clement of Alexandria, *Exhortation to the Greeks*

Serials Appearing in the Bibliography

ANRW	*Aufstieg und Niedergang der Römischen Welt*
BHT	Beiträge zur historischen Theologie

BZNW	Beihefte zur *Zeitschrift für die neutestamentliche Wissenshaft*
CECNT	Critical and Exegetical Commentary on the New Testament
EKK	Evangelisch-katholischer Kommentar zum Neuen Testament
GAP	Guides to the Apocrypha and Pseudepigrapha
HDR	Harvard Dissertations in Religion
HTKNT	Herders theologischer Kommentar zum Neuen Testament
IVPNT	Inter-Varsity Press New Testament Commentary
JSNTS	Journal for the Study of the New Testament Supplement Series
JSPS	Journal for the Study of the Pseudepigrapha Supplement Series
NICNT	New International Commentary on the New Testament
NIGTC	New International Greek Testament Commentary
NovTS	Novum Testamentum Supplement Series
SBLDS	Society of Biblical Literature Dissertation Series
SBLSBS	Society of Biblical Literature Sources for Biblical Study
SNTSMS	Society for New Testament Studies Monograph Series
SSEJC	Studies in Scripture in Early Judaism and Christianity
SP	Sacra Pagina
THKNT	Theologischer Handkommentar zum Neuen Testament
WBC	Word Biblical Commentary
WMANT	Wissenschaftliche Monographien zum Alten und Neuen Testament
WUNT	Wissenschaftliche Untersuchungen zum Neuen Testament

Introduction

This book has been a great pleasure to write. It is always something of a luxury to consider the intricate worldview of great historical figures, and many have found Paul to be among that class. This is not to suggest that it is a simple thing to analyse Paul's extant writings, let alone the worldview that lies behind and informs them; it has even been suggested on occasion that Paul's own arguments are themselves inconsistent, and that his whole theological programme is based on problematic premises.[1] While recognising the difficult features of Paul's letter to the Galatians, this book seeks to draw together the features that act as the structural foundations for Paul's reflections on Christian identity in the light of God's transforming power.

This book has not been written with a single readership in mind. Contemporary scholarship on Paul and his letter to the Galatians has influenced its content and interests significantly, and I hope to have made profitable contributions to Pauline study at various points throughout the book. Nonetheless, I have consciously avoided writing simply for academics and professional theologians. In attempting to express something of Paul's theological and social project in Galatians, I have sought

---

[1] So especially Räisänen, 1983. Boers writes: 'what gives coherence to Paul's thought is contradiction at its most fundamental level' (1988: 63, emphasis removed; cf. Boers, 1994: 32, 218). Sanders has proposed a similar view (e.g., 1983), but is sympathetic to creative tensions in Paul, stating: 'Paul was a religious genius, perhaps the most creative and productive figure of religious history whom we can still study at first hand, through his own writings ... Paul had bigger fish to fry than systematic consistency' (1996: 117).

to avoid both an overly-technical presentation on the one hand and trivialising over-simplifications on the other.

Whatever contribution might be made herein, I do not perceive it to be restricted to scholarly circles, hoping that ecclesiastical professionals and laity, theological students and others might find benefit in this exploration of Galatians. But it would be inappropriate to imply that the study of Galatians might only be of interest to Christian readers or to historians of early Christianity (whatever their religious persuasion). In our contemporary pluralist society, personal and social identities are fostered in relation to a broad canvas of diverse cultural backgrounds and contingencies. In our day, concerns for human solidarity are mixed with the hard realities of cultural differences and incompatibilities; cultural particularity meets with a wide continuum of often conflicting currents, from social imperialism and ideological triumphalism on the one hand, to undisciplined tolerance on the other. In this context, some have recently sought to give consideration to Paul's ecclesiastical vision as an instructive resource for considering the problems and possibilities, the strengths and weaknesses, of a multicultural enterprise.[2] Similarly, in a day when individualism seems to have been a primary influence in the shaping of so much of modern western society, the corporate dynamic of Paul's theology might prove to be an important resource for contemporary reflection. In fact, whereas in the sixteenth century Martin Luther was 'seized' by Galatians for what he found it to say about justification by faith, it was the precision of Paul's corporate imaging that has taken hold of my imagination as a consequence of reading Galatians closely in our contemporary culture.

The letter to the Galatians, then, can be read for different purposes. For the academic historian, it can shed important light on the beginnings of the early Christian movement and the relationship between Christianity and Judaism. For the committed Christian, it can enhance understanding of Christian faith and nurture relationship with God. And for the modern analyst of culture, whether professional or otherwise, it

---

[2] For example, see Boyarin, 1994; Barclay, 1996a.

can stimulate reflection on dynamics of contemporary social plurality and identity. In fact, all three aspects have been important in my own study of Galatians.

Regardless of one's starting point in reading the pages that follow, the reader will encounter several features that have motivated my writing, and I envisage the following features of this book to be brought together in a fashion distinctive from the secondary literature currently available. First, the eschatological or (so-called) 'apocalyptic' dimension of Paul's thought is highlighted; Paul's conviction concerning the obliteration of one 'world' and its replacement by another lies at the very heart of his programme in Galatians, and is arguably fundamental to the whole of Pauline theology. Eschatological eruption is not for Paul about the introduction of a new religious configuration on to the scene of world history. Instead, it is about God's triumph over competing suprahuman forces, about God's invasion into the order of this world in order to set things aright in a new sphere of existence where God's reputation as the cosmic sovereign is vindicated.

This aspect, highlighted in chapter 3, is linked to all other features of this book. Chapters 5 and 6 consider the way in which Paul imagines God's triumph in Christ to relate to God's dealings in history – with Israel (chapter 5) and in relation to the law (chapter 6). Chapters 4 and 7 consider Paul's understanding of the triumph of God in relation to Christian moral identity, as God's transforming power becomes embodied within individual and corporate behaviour. As we will see, for Paul this transformation itself is a prerequisite for valid Christian readings of scripture among the Galatian Christian communities. So too, the theme of God's triumph is linked in chapter 5 to the motif of the 'faithfulness of Christ' – a motif which, in this writer's view, is crucial to the theological and corporate enterprise that Paul envisages in Galatians.[3]

Apart from the final chapter ('Concluding Observations'), the shortest chapters herein are the first two, which introduce

---

[3] Cf. Meeks: the faithfulness of Christ 'is a foundational element of Paul's theologizing in the letters to Galatia and Rome' (1993: 160). Martyn goes further: The faithfulness of Christ 'is crucial to an understanding not only of Galatians, but also of the whole of Paul's theology' (1993a: 142).

two situations important for our engagement with Paul's letter to the Galatians. The first chapter focuses on significant issues currently at the forefront of scholarly interest in Galatians. Then, in order to capture some of the original resonances of Paul's case, the second chapter reconstructs the situation that provoked Paul to write his letter in the first place.

In the process of reading this book, it is hoped that Galatians will be seen not simply as a text that sheds light on first-century concerns about Christian self-definition against a background of Jewish traditional theology. This letter from a controversial Christian Jew, who planted Christian churches throughout the Graeco-Roman world of the Mediterranean basin, is not without relevance to the concerns of our modern world. It is a text that gives a recipe for healthy social relationships, including corporate diversity, solidarity and responsibility. But it is first and foremost a theological text, rather than an anthropological or sociological handbook, and God is depicted as the essential ingredient in the recipe for personal and social wellbeing. For, as Paul envisages things in Galatians, beyond the sphere of God's sovereignty in Christ, humanity is under the influence of forces that shatter solidarity and introduce chaotic and destructive impulses; such a scenario runs counter to Paul's view of God as the one who created the world as a place of goodness and productivity. Accordingly, God's triumphal invasion in Christ creates a sphere of divine sovereignty that results in positive and productive human relationships. And I believe it is here where contemporary Christian theology can benefit from recapturing Paul's theological vision, especially in what it suggests about Christian moral identity.

1

The Triumph of God and Salvation History in Galatians

1. The Problem of 'Apocalyptic' Theology in Galatians

Like A. Schweitzer and E. Käsemann in earlier generations,[1] J. C. Beker has more recently been vocal in describing Paul's gospel as fundamentally 'apocalyptic' in nature, involving 'the dawning victory of God' and 'the imminent redemption of the created order, which he has inaugurated in Christ'.[2] In Paul's apocalyptic theology, the enemies of God are not a social entity, a political dynasty, or a national overlord, but 'those ontological powers that determine the human situation within the context of God's created order', identified by Paul as the powers of 'death, sin, the law, and the flesh'.[3] Paul's is a theology of hope, centred on 'the coming triumph of God over all the evil powers which pollute and threaten his good creation'.[4] While Paul transforms traditional forms of an apocalyptic worldview, his theology finds its organisational centre in this apocalyptic scenario of the imminent, cosmic triumph of God over opposing spiritual forces.

Beker's use of the word 'apocalyptic' is set firmly within the context of the *future* subjugation of the world to God; while the processes of divine victory are recognised to have already been set in motion in the ministry of Jesus Christ, Beker finds Paul's emphasis to be toward the future establishment of God's

[1] Schweitzer, 1931; Käsemann, 1969a; 1969b.
[2] 1980: ix. For reviews of scholarship on Paul's 'apocalyptic' theology, see Johnson, 1989: 4–23; Matlock, 1996.
[3] 1980: 145.
[4] 1993a: 157.

sovereignty and the vindication of God's name. Everything in Paul's theological arsenal takes its cue from this future-oriented worldview. For Beker, this is the organisational centre of Paul's theology which finds expression in his letters in various 'surface' terminologies that address particular concrete situations. In Beker's terms, the coherence of Paul's gospel is found in a set of interrelating symbols, which he develops this way or that according to the needs of the situation addressed; the future-oriented 'apocalyptic worldview', however, is not merely one of many symbols, but is the 'master symbol' under which all other symbols converge.

When he turns to Galatians, however, Beker finds this scheme to be jeopardised since there (notwithstanding Paul's comments in 5.5 and 6.8) Paul evidences little interest in the future manifestation of God's triumph. Instead, the focus in Galatians is on the eschatological present.[5] Beker thinks that this theological anomaly has resulted from the situational demands which have suppressed the future orientation of Paul's gospel; Paul's case in Galatians emerges not from the deep master symbols of his apocalyptic worldview, but from the surface level of a situational polemic. In a sense, Paul has been thrown off his theological balance, being forced to construct a theological argument in ways unnatural to him, due to the need to refute those who are stirring up trouble among his Galatian converts. According to Beker, Paul's primary purpose in Galatians 'is to oppose the Judaizers, and *in the process of radicalizing their position, he radicalizes his own*'.[6] It is for this reason, says Beker, 'that the apocalyptic future with its basis in the resurrection of Christ does not receive its proper emphasis' in Galatians.[7]

This is a stimulating option. Galatians is thought to be a curious anomaly in relation to the rest of the Pauline literature, which is thought to be axiomatically informed by apocalyptic motifs of God's future reclamation of the world. But exceptions and anomalies are curious things, and have the potential to unravel synthesising schemes. In this case, if one contingent

---

[5] The same absence of future orientation applies also to 2 Corinthians; see Thrall, 1982: 269.

[6] 1980: 57, emphasis mine.

[7] 1980: 58.

expression of Paul's thought shows little interest in what is supposedly fundamental to his thought, the problem might lie not with the particularities of the situation, but with one's reconstruction of the core of Paul's theological perspective. That is, perhaps a future-oriented worldview is not the coherent centre of Paul's thought-world, but is instead a contingent expression of something still more fundamental, or at least more nuanced.

Following on from Beker, J. Louis Martyn has also addressed the issue of the apocalyptic nature of Galatians.[8] Admitting that Galatians exhibits none of the motifs of an imminent apocalyptic climax that marks out 1 Corinthians 15, Romans 8, and 1 Thessalonians 4, Martyn makes much of the pervasive contrast of two opposing worlds, a cosmological dualism of sorts which is 'clearly apocalyptic'.[9] In the death of Christ, God has performed a 'newly-creative act' in which a new sphere of existence is established; 'the cosmos in which he [Paul] previously lived met its end in God's apocalypse of Jesus Christ'.[10] Consequently, a new cosmic warfare is now evident between two clashing forces: the Spirit and the flesh. These are not two phenomena inhabiting one single world; instead, they are the primal forces that drive two antagonistic and rival worlds. Martyn explains their relationship by coining the term 'apocalyptic antinomy', explaining it in the following fashion:

> the Spirit and the Flesh ... are two opposed orbs of power, actively at war with one another *since* the apocalyptic advent of Christ and of his Spirit. The space in which human beings now live is a newly invaded space, and that means that its structures cannot remain unchanged.[11]

All this transpires as a consequence of the crucifixion of Christ, suggesting, as a corrective to Beker's future apocalyptic, that 'the focus of Paul's apocalyptic lies not on Christ's parousia, but rather on his death ... Paul's perception of Jesus' death is, then, fully as apocalyptic as is his hope for Jesus' parousia'.[12]

[8] See, for instance, his articles of 1985, 1991 and 1993a.
[9] 1985a: 416.
[10] 1985a: 417.
[11] 1985a: 417 (= 1997: 121).
[12] 1985a: 420–21.

From this brief survey, we see how Beker and Martyn hold different positions in their assessments of Paul's apocalyptic worldview. For Beker, this feature is compromised in Galatians, where there is little future-orientedness; for Martyn, this feature is not compromised in Galatians but is focused on the event of Christ's death, in which a new creation has already taken hold.

Despite the differences of emphasis in Beker and Martyn,[13] their heavy emphasis on the 'apocalyptic' contours of Paul's gospel is broadly appreciated by many Pauline professional students.[14] For them, the driving force behind Paul's theological presentations is the invasion of God into the world in order to subjugate forces that run contrary to God's will and to set relationships aright. Behind any concerns for ethics, ecclesiology, pneumatology, christology, and the like, lies a theology that focuses on God as the cosmic overlord of creation. Theology of this sort is fundamentally 'theodicy' – that is, a defence of God's reputation as the one in control of this world, despite any appearances to the contrary. Pauline theodicy describes how God's sovereignty remains intact despite threats from opposing forces. It focuses on the divine reclamation and rectification of the cosmos, something inaugurated in Christ, driven on by the Spirit and completed eventually when God becomes 'all in all' (1 Cor. 15.28). At heart, then, Paul's gospel is not simply about soul-saving, involving ethical or doctrinal teaching. Such features are contained within a larger theological programme, one that concerns the warfare between God and the forces that are stacked up in hostility to God's beneficent reign over the world. This warfare is carried out not just in the future when hostility to God is completely eradicated,[15] but at every stage in the drama of reconciling the world in Christ to God.

---

[13] Beker has since noted that Martyn's analysis improves on his own; see his 1980: xix–xx in all reprints since 1984; and 1986b: 598.

[14] So, e.g., Rowland, 1985: 207–214; Soards, 1987: 163–72.

[15] The Pauline literature depicts several forms of eradication. The eradication of opposition involves the destruction of the powers of Death and Sin in a passage like 1 Corinthians 15 (15.21–28, 54–57), whereas in Colossians 1 it takes the form of reconciliation of opposition (1.15–20).

2. The Problem of Salvation History in Galatians

The above discussion has taken us some way into a much related subject that has seen a good deal of literature dedicated to it – that is, the question of whether and to what extent Paul's presentation in Galatians is the product of a theology of God's saving purposes in relation to Israel. Does Paul in this letter recognise the people of Israel to be the covenant people of God, as he does for instance in other letters (e.g., Rom. 3.1–2; 9–11)? And if so, to what extent does Paul's programme in Galatians envisage the new world as the result of God's working in history through and with this ethnic people? Here again, Beker and Martyn hold stimulating positions.

In Beker's work, Paul's apocalyptic worldview presupposes a covenant relationship between God and God's people Israel. The future triumph of God is the time in which God's covenant faithfulness to Israel will be vindicated. This is true of apocalyptic conviction in general, which addresses poignantly felt issues, such as: Is God the cosmic sovereign if God's people are downtrodden? Is the God who created this world still in control of this world, when those God loves suffer? Such theological conundra have set the theological agenda for the people of Israel at various points in their history, especially in times of foreign domination and oppression. When Israel is subjugated by others, the reputation of Israel's God is threatened; their subjugation by hostile foreign powers might testify to the subjugation of their covenant God by hostile divine powers.

Issues of this sort are evident in many of the ancient Jewish apocalyptic texts (e.g., Daniel; 4 Ezra; 2 Baruch), which themselves have strong (but not exclusive) roots in Jewish prophetic literature. In both apocalyptic and prophetic material, one of the most enduring responses to this issue lays the blame for Israel's desperate condition on Israel herself, due to the sins of her people (cf. Ezek. 39.23). But regardless of the explanation for Israel's oppressed condition, the expectation that God would ultimately act to set things right for Israel was rife and commonplace, as prophetic, apocalyptic, and Jewish sectarian material demonstrates well. When God comes to restore the world to order and set things right, Israel will once and for all be recognised as God's chosen and beloved covenant people.

In Beker's view, Paul's future-oriented apocalyptic gospel incorporates these same dynamics. It 'expresses the conviction that, in the death and resurrection of Jesus Christ, the Covenant-God of Israel has confirmed and renewed his promises of salvation to Israel and to the nations, as first recorded in the Hebrew Bible'.[16]

Beker also maintains, however, that while this inter-connectedness of covenant faithfulness and cosmic sovereignty lies at the heart of Paul's gospel, it has nonetheless broken down in his letter to the Galatians. This is due not merely to the absence of future-apocalyptic in Galatians, but also, and almost as a consequence, to the absence of a full-blooded appreciation of salvation history. Whereas those who were stirring up trouble in Galatia were stressing the continuity of salvation history, allowing them to find circumcision as essential to covenant membership in the people of God, Paul was forced to stress the discontinuity of history, thereby highlighting the new phenomenon of faith. In this way, just as he had been forced to compromise his future-oriented gospel, so Paul has compromised his convictions about God's working throughout history. Beker writes:

> The peculiar logic of the argument shows that the salvation-historical thrust of the Abraham story can be used by Paul against the Judaizers only if he centres the story Christocentrically (Christ as the exclusive seed) and therefore discontinuously ... Because the Judaizers stress the continuity in salvation-history between Abraham, Torah, circumcision, and Christ, Paul can use the Abraham story only in terms of discontinuity.[17]

This has important ramifications for Paul's understanding of salvation history since Abraham cannot be presented in Galatians as the father of the Jewish people (as he is, for instance in Rom. 4.12, 16; 9.5; 11.28–29). Instead, according to Beker:

> Abraham can only be maintained in salvation-history as a figure of

[16] 1982: 30. Beker explores this theme in Paul's letter to the Romans in particular; 1986a.
[17] 1980: 51.

promise ... The 'Jewish' dispensation of circumcision and the Torah has only been a curse and an obstacle ... an interloper that inserted itself illegitimately between the promise to Abraham and its exclusive fulfillment in Christ.[18]

The Torah did, however, serve a function within history, but not as the legal corpus and social constitution of the covenant people of God. Instead, the Torah is depicted as:

a divine necessity in salvation-history, for it represents the dark but necessary foil for the coming of faith ... In Christian hindsight, the law was given by God to increase the trespasses, so that it might be the prison and taskmaster that highlights the coming of faith.[19]

In this, and only this, sense can it be said that the law is depicted in Galatians as 'an inalienable part of salvation-history'.[20] Nonetheless, lacking altogether is a fully-developed view of salvation-history, in which God has been at work in and through his people, leading up to a grand eschatological climax with the advent of the Messiah.

Martyn makes a similar point, and even more strenuously. While employing the term 'apocalyptic', Martyn severs this term from any notion of salvation history:

[I]n this text the covenantal promise [to Abraham] is precisely *not said* to have commenced a history that subsequently served as the context into which Christ was born ... [T]here is no indication in this passage that before that point [Christ's advent] there was something that could be identified as the history of a corporate people of God created by the power of that promise.[21]

Repeatedly Martyn argues that Paul's presentation in Galatians involves 'the end of *Heilsgeschichte*', that Paul's gospel there has no 'linear *pre*-history', that it includes no affirmation of 'a salvific linearity prior to the advent of Christ', and that there is in Galatians 'no indication of a covenant-created people of God during the time of the Law'.[22] Paul 'passes clean by ... the

---

[18] 1980: 51.
[19] 1980: 55.
[20] 1980: 55.
[21] 1991: 173, emphasis his.
[22] 1991: 174. Cf. Martyn, 1993b: 141 n. 13 (= 1997: 164 n. 10), 145–47 (= 1997: 168–71), 151.

history of Israel in order to speak of the eschatological purpose of God'.[23] So he states:

> Galatians shows us a Paul who does not accept 'covenant' as a term indicating a fundamental building block of his theology. However disappointing it may be to have to say so, this apostle is not a covenantal theologian ... Neither does he present as his theology a form of *Heilsgeschichte* in which Christ is interpreted in line with Israel's history.[24]

According to Martyn, then, in Galatians the apocalyptic death of Christ initiates the history of the new creation in which salvation is operative; salvation history is created by, and subsequent to, the eschatological invasion of God in Christ.

So, Martyn and Beker hold similar positions when assessing Paul's understanding of salvation history. For Beker, any concept of salvation history has been compromised, although history has at least demonstrated that salvation lies somewhere other than the law. For Martyn, salvation history is devoid of any reference before that eschatological event, having nothing whatsoever to do with God's new creation which owes its being not to the culmination of some historic movement set in motion long ago but to a completely novel invasion of God in Christ.

Not all would accept the view that salvation history has been compromised in Galatians, however. Since the matter of salvation history in Galatians will be an important focus for the present study, it will be helpful to contrast the positions of Beker and Martyn with the positions of others who find that Paul, even in this letter, maintains strong lines of continuity between God's past dealings with Israel and God's present dealings with those in Christ. Two scholars who advocate positions of this sort, for instance, are J. D. G. Dunn and N. T. Wright. Both of these scholars develop their arguments from a

---

[23] 1991: 176.
[24] 1991: 179. Martyn: '[C]ovenant is one of the Teachers' [agitators'] themes, not one Paul has introduced on his own' (1993b: 140 = 1997: 163). Dunn, who is frequently cited by Martyn as holding views against which Martyn is arguing, seems more recently to grant a significant concession to Martyn on this score (1996a: 319 and 319 nn. 18–19).

particular understanding of the character of Judaism in Paul's day – a matter that needs consideration not simply for the issue immediately at hand, but also for broader issues that run throughout this study. To this matter we now turn our attention, after which the positions of Dunn and Wright will be set out.

3. The Character of Judaism in Paul's Day

If scholars hold widely diverging views on the role of salvation history in Galatians, the same is true of scholarly views on the nature of Judaism in Paul's day. In general interpreters tend to gravitate towards one of two positions: the one finds Judaism to have been legalistic, and the other finds it to have been covenantal.

It is necessary to trace out the basics of these two positions, for two reasons in particular: (1) as noted above, those who have recently advocated strong lines of salvation historical continuity in Galatians have relied heavily on variations of the covenantal position to do so; (2) the text of Galatians is frequently illuminated when considered against the backdrop of mainstream forms of Jewish practice and thought. In order to illustrate the two contrasting viewpoints, the position of R. Bultmann will represent a typical 'legalistic' position, while that of E. P. Sanders will represent a typical 'covenantal' position.

At the heart of Bultmann's understanding of Early Judaism lies a contrast with its 'Old Testament heritage'. The latter is said to have been sustained by the notion of relationship 'conceived in terms of a covenant',[25] in which God graciously acted to bring into existence a specially chosen nation: 'Israel is perpetually dependent upon the grace of God, while her election is beyond her control.'[26] In Bultmann's estimate, however, by Paul's day this covenantal pillar of Jewish identity had long since broken down. Bultmann's assessment of Early Judaism is carried out under the subtitle 'Jewish Legalism'. He depicts Israel as having 'cut herself adrift from history' and as

[25] 1956: 35.
[26] 1956: 38.

living somewhere 'outside history',[27] the consequence being that 'God was no longer bound to his people'.[28]

Bultmann outlines three consequences of this conviction. First, and most significantly, the law 'was no longer primarily an historical record of God's dealings with his people, but a book of divine law',[29] regulating not only morality but ritualism in every area of life. This led to the creation of detailed and trivial regulations which went 'to the point of absurdity'.[30] Consequently, 'Jewish morality became over-scrupulous and pettifogging'.[31] Any redeeming qualities of Jewish religion had, by this time, degenerated to the point that relationship with God was viewed in purely legalistic terms. Accordingly, an attitude of works-righteousness emerged, which postulated that accumulated merit points 'might serve to atone for breaches of the law'.[32]

Second, and in the light of this legalistic view of salvation, perceptions of God became modified: 'The legalistic conception of obedience produced an equally legalistic conception of divine retribution … God had to make the punishment fit the crime.'[33] Justice, therefore, became an eschatological concept in which God, in the next age, would punish the wicked and reward the righteous according to their works.

Third, because the eschatological judgement was thought to be determined on the basis of merit, two distinct attitudes arose. Some Jews adopted a smug, self-confident attitude. Due to their own good works, they thought themselves better than the sinners who lacked a sufficient number of good works. Others, however, recognised the uncertainty of salvation by works. As Bultmann writes:[34]

> Who could be sure he had done enough in this life to be saved? Would his observance of the Law and his good works be sufficient?

[27] 1956: 60.
[28] 1956: 61.
[29] 1956: 62, elaborated throughout 62–67.
[30] 1956: 65.
[31] 1956: 67.
[32] 1956: 69.
[33] 1956: 69.
[34] 1956: 70.

> For in the day of judgement all his good works would be counted up
> and weighed, and woe to him if the scales fell on the side of his evil
> deeds.

Of course, one could repent of wrongdoing, but since he was
powerless to do good, 'the only way out was by penitential
prayer in which God's forgiveness was implored'.[35] Ultimately,
however, even repentance degenerated into a work used to
secure salvation before God. Thus, Bultmann concludes by
saying: 'In the end the whole range of man's relationship with
God came to be thought of in terms of merit.'[36]

Bultmann's portrait has come under fierce attack, not least
in the work of E. P. Sanders. Sanders has been instrumental in
breaking the stranglehold of the legalistic portrait of Early
Judaism, even if his work has not won unanimous assent. He
contends that, in contrast to the view of Bultmann, Jewish
covenantal self-identity remained as vibrant as ever in Paul's
day. Most forms of Early Judaism were marked out by an
awareness of Israel's election by a gracious God who entered
into covenant relationship with Israel. Performance of the law
was not motivated by the anxious desire to score more good
points than bad ones, but by the concern to preserve the
covenant already established by God's initiating mercy upon
Israel. According to Sanders, the notion that grace precedes
demand 'is as clear in non-Christian Jewish literature as it is in
the letters of Paul', since in Jewish literature 'God's grace always
emerges as the most important point' in any theological analysis
of salvation.[37]

For Sanders, the 'pattern of religion' in Early Judaism is best
described as 'covenantal nomism', a term devised to demonstrate that observance of the law ('nomism') remained firmly
within a covenantal context. An eight-point definition elaborates the pattern of covenantal nomism:[38]

(1) God has chosen Israel and (2) given the law. The law implies

---

[35] 1956: 70.
[36] 1956: 71. In all this, Bultmann follows the lead of his teacher, Bousset, 1906.
[37] 1992: 278 and 273 respectively.
[38] Sanders, 1977: 422. He defends, elaborates, and nuances this further in
Sanders, 1992: 262–78.

both (3) God's promise to maintain the election and (4) the requirement to obey. (5) God rewards obedience and punishes transgression. (6) The law provides for means of atonement, and atonement results in (7) maintenance or re-establishment of the covenantal relationship. (8) All those who are maintained in the covenant by obedience, atonement and God's mercy belong to the group which will be saved ... [E]lection and ultimately salvation are considered to be by God's mercy rather than human achievement.

Sanders' definition of covenantal nomism is thought by many to have captured the theological motivations and convictions that animated most forms of Judaism in Paul's day. But there are significant numbers who dissent, and who do so largely on the basis of an understanding of Paul. Debate continues unabated as to whether the proposed covenantal character of Judaism can be defended in the light of some of Paul's comments about the law. Is a form of Jewish covenantal nomism (or preferably, ethnocentric covenantalism) really apparent behind a text like Galatians, used for centuries by Christians to denounce legalism and religions of sterile works-righteousness? Or have traditional interpretations of Paul and his letters been somewhat skewed by the influence of issues and debates of later times – debates that have little resemblance to the issues with which Paul was concerned? Does a different, and perhaps more accurate, understanding of Early Judaism as covenantally motivated bring to the fore aspects of Paul's text which otherwise remain at the periphery? To what extent does a covenantal Judaism render some of Paul's theological presentations problematic?

Issues of this sort are given significant consideration in the following chapters, and are addressed specifically in chapter 8 below. In order for discussion of these matters to be considered with greater ease at the relevant points, it will help to declare my own position at this point, at least on the matter of the form of religion that was informing the programme of the Galatian agitators. On this score I am in agreement with C. K. Barrett, who finds 'the theology of the Judaizers ... to tally in some remarkable ways (though not in every way) with the covenantal nomism of E. P. Sanders'.[39] That is, behind Paul's strident stand against

---

[39] Barrett, 1985: 44.

gentiles being forced to live like Jews (2.14) lies not an infiltration of legalistic works-righteousness but the emergence of a form of covenantalism wherein ethnic identity was promoted as an important component of salvation. The agitators' case would have followed along these lines: Having enjoyed God's initial acceptance of them in Christ, the gentile Christians now needed to be brought into full membership with God's covenant people by observing the practices of the law that marked out ethnic Israel. The question that concerned the Galatian Christians, then, was not so much, 'How can I get saved, by works or by faith?' Instead, their interests were focused on the identity of the people of God, and whether God's salvific blessings could be fully enjoyed without observing the stipulations laid out in the scriptures given by God to Israel. Fundamentally, then, the issue alive in Galatian Christianity was the issue highlighted above: the relationship between what God has done in Christ and what God had already done in and with Israel.

If the agitators drew lines to connect God's dealings in the past with those of the present, we have seen that, in Beker's and Martyn's view, Paul drew lines to separate the two. But Beker and Martyn represent only one side in the contemporary debate. Others, like Dunn and Wright, find that Paul also drew strong lines of continuity between God's past and present dealings, just different lines than the ones drawn by the agitators. The proposals of Dunn and Wright, dependant on an understanding of Early Judaism as primarily covenantal in motivation, can now be briefly summarised.

4. Affirmations of Salvation History in Galatians

One of Martyn's debating partners on the matter of salvation history in Galatians is J. D. G. Dunn.[40] Dunn maintains that what Paul critiques in Galatians is not a Christian form of legalism but a Christian form of traditional Jewish covenantalism: 'Galatians is Paul's first sustained attempt to deal with the issue of covenantal nomism within the new movement we call

---

[40] See, for instance, Martyn, 1991. Dunn's position is here reconstructed from his works dedicated to the theology of Galatians specifically (1991a; 1993b).

Christianity.'[41] What Paul perceived to be wrong with traditional Judaism was its extreme form of ethnocentrism, whereby the identity of the people of God was associated with practices exclusively Jewish. Such a view posed a serious threat to Paul's mission to the gentiles. Consequently, along the way, Paul articulated his gospel in terms of freedom from the law on the basis of faith. His claim that righteousness is by faith rather than works of law was intended to undermine the need for gentiles to observe the stipulations of the law which pertained solely to the people of Israel; by 'works of law', Paul meant to signify the practices that 'were widely regarded as characteristically and distinctively Jewish'.[42] But, according to Dunn, this did not involve the rejection of the law *per se*, but only a misunderstanding of the law that equated righteousness with Jewish identity. While the traditional *form* of covenantal nomism is retained by Paul, the traditional *content* is not; Paul reinterpreted covenantal nomism by infusing it with new substance.

The result, according to Dunn, was a new type of covenantal nomism, characterised especially by two significant features. First, it affirmed the law in its proper role as the expression of God's purpose and will, while excluding the ethnic exclusivity that had become attached to it. Second, it affirmed the history of God's dealings with Israel as the precursor of God's intervention in Christ, whereupon the covenant purpose of blessing the nations through Abraham became realised. Since the era of history has changed, so membership within the covenant is now open to the gentiles as well as Jews. Gentiles can enter into the covenant relationship that had previously been enjoyed solely by the people of Israel. Faith in Christ is the means whereby gentiles come to 'share in the benefits of God's covenant with Israel', along with those Jews who themselves believe in Christ.[43] This inclusion of all the nations within covenant relationship is what Israel's God had intended to happen with the dawning of the eschatological era of salvation

---

[41] 1991a: 138, emphasis removed.

[42] 1990: 191; emphasis removed. For an early articulation of this view in the contemporary study of Paul, see Wright, 1978.

[43] 1991a: 130. Elsewhere Dunn heralds the 'story of Israel' as an axiomatic feature of Paul's theology (1994: 427).

history. The people of Israel had enjoyed that special position prior to Christ, but had succumbed to the view that they alone were to be God's people. In Galatians, Paul forges a case which locates universal salvation in Christ within the context of God's covenant relationship with Israel, doing so in such a way that the gentiles are shown to enter the arena of Israel's unfolding covenant history.

Similar in intent, although with different features, is the argument of N. T. Wright. According to him, Galatians is animated by the traditional Jewish hope that the God of Israel would one fine day be recognised by all as the sovereign of the world; this was an expectation 'about the enthronement of Yhwh and the dethronement of pagan gods; about the victory of Israel and the fall of Babylon; about the ... consequent coming of peace and justice.'[44] (As we shall see in §6.5, Wright gives a finer point to all this, articulating it in terms of a theology of Israel being in extended exile before the coming of Christ.)

Against this background, when Paul talks in Gal. 4.8–9 about Christians being released from bondage to false gods and having come to know and be known by the true God, he is speaking of Israel's God having routed 'the idols of the nations' and confronting 'the powers of the spurious gods'.[45] In a word:

> The Pharisee [Paul] ... had been zealous for the one true god, looking for his victory over paganism on behalf of his ethnic people Israel, [and] had become convinced that the victory had after all been won in Christ, and that the one true god was thereby revealed.[46]

Having encountered the resurrected Jesus at the right hand of God, Paul recognised him to reside in the exalted place reserved for Israel in the new age. Accordingly, he came to believe that the eschatological hopes of and for Israel had been already fulfilled by and in her Messiah.[47] The pre-Christian Paul

[44] 1994: 227. Wright's position is here reconstructed from his works dedicated to elucidating the theology of Galatians specifically (1994 especially; cf. also 1991a: 137–74).
[45] 1994: 230.
[46] 1994: 231.
[47] 1994: 231–32.

had believed that the sovereign God would act to fulfil his covenant to Israel, and that consequently the new world order would be ushered in; the Christian Paul maintained the same association of convictions, but found them transformed by the belief that God had already acted in Christ to fulfil the covenant, resulting in the 'new creation'. Consequently, gentiles 'are now summoned to share in the blessings of Israel's "age to come"',[48] a share that is through faith in Christ rather than any practices of law that differentiate Jews and gentiles. The sovereignty of Israel's God corresponds to faith unrestricted by any fetters; any other distinguishing marks 'speak of other loyalties and other allegiances' and 'imply that other powers are still being invoked'.[49] By faith, gentiles enter into the eschatological stage of Israel's history, at which point God's sovereignty over competing deities is revealed in Christ. In this way, Wright argues for 'the essentially apocalyptic nature of Paul's covenant theology, and vice versa'.[50]

Explanations such as those of Dunn and Wright offer a much different picture of Paul's view of salvation history in Galatians than those of Beker and Martyn. And this important feature of Paul's presentation in Galatians will be given consideration in later chapters of this book. The questions involved are these: Is the new creation the capstone (prior to the parousia) of all that God had been doing through and with Israel, as Dunn and Wright suggest? Or is it unrelated to Israel and her history, being a novel phenomenon that emerges only from God's eschatological intervention rather than a prior historical linearity, as Beker and Martyn suggest? Or might there be another option? Such matters await further consideration of Paul's understanding of Israel's history (chapter 5 below) and of the purpose and function of the law (chapter 6 below).

5. The Agenda of this Study

We have outlined the attempts of four significant interpreters to explain the relationship in Galatians of God's eschatological

[48] 1994: 232.
[49] 1994: 236.
[50] 1994: 237.

intervention and salvation history. In the chapters that follow, Paul's apocalyptic gospel will be explored in its rich complexity, first of all examining the theological underpinning that gives cohesion to his presentation in Galatians. So in chapter 3 below ('The Establishment of the New World'), consideration will be given to (1) Paul's overarching worldview, focused as it is on God's triumphant activity in Christ in relation to competing suprahuman forces, (2) the concrete results of that triumph, and (3) the mechanics whereby the benefits of divine triumph become operative for those in Christ. Chapter 4 ('Eschatological Moral Identity') sketches the contours of Paul's perception of moral identity, demonstrating how he envisages the triumph of God to become embodied and advertised within transformed patterns of Christian social behaviour. This chapter is placed early on, to combat the impression that moral identity is secondary to Paul's theological concerns in Galatians – an impression frequently given in secondary literature whenever 'ethics' is placed toward the end of the table of contents.

The question that we have seen posed above concerns how God's triumph in Christ relates to God's covenant relationship with Israel. Chapter 5 addresses that matter ('Christ, Israel, and Covenant Theology'). There, we highlight a feature of Paul's thought which falls somewhere between the positions (outlined above) of Beker and Martyn on the one hand and of Dunn and Wright on the other. This feature also embraces the theme of Christ's faithfulness, a theme that Paul employs to great theological advantage in forging a particular brand of Christian covenant theology. Such matters lead to the concerns of chapter 6 ('The Law, Abraham, and Christ'), where we consider Paul's often puzzling statements about the purpose(s) of the law in general and in relation to the people of Israel specifically.

Chapter 7 ('Eschatological Transformation Embodied') demonstrates the way in which Paul identifies different players in the Galatian situation to be animated by different suprahuman forces, whether Christ and his Spirit or the demonic spirits of the departed. This is an important matter for Paul, since it carries with it hermeneutical significance and should guide the Galatians in their understanding of who in the situation is interpreting scripture aright. Paul presupposes that scriptural interpretation requires the prior embodiment of Christ within the interpreter if interpretation is to have proper validity for guiding the Galatian communities. In this way, the scriptures that were originally given to Israel (Gal. 3.19) can be read for Christian benefit in the way that Paul reads them, rather than the way the agitators are reading them. As such, even Paul's interpretative techniques (illustrated in chapter 6) result from God's triumph animating his life.

The final chapter ('Concluding Observations') brings together some of the features of Paul's thought identified in this book, and addresses some academic and theological issues that are pertinent today.

A note about terminology: In what follows, the adjective 'apocalyptic' that appears so frequently in the work of Beker and Martyn and many others will be replaced by the adjective 'eschatological'. This is because of some debate about the appropriateness of the former term, due to complex methodological considerations that need not concern us here.[51] Although the adjective 'apocalyptic' might have more merit than its severest critics allow, the adjective 'eschatological' may do just as well for our purposes, referring to the way in which God has acted, continues to act, and will ultimately act decisively, establishing a world set right that will, in the end, include all things without remainder. Such eschatological activity, whether it be in the past (e.g., the death and resurrection of Christ), the present (e.g., the giving of the Spirit) or the future (e.g., the eradication of hostile forces), involves conflict, as opposing powers seek to thwart God's attempts to set things right. If we are to avoid the term

---

[51] See, for instance, Witherington, 1992: 16–20; Matlock, 1996. See also Keck's nuanced view, 1984. This debate in Pauline study replicates a similar one about the genre 'apocalypse', apocalyptic eschatology and apocalyptic movements in Early Judaism; see, for instance, Collins, 1991; Rowland, 1982. In the aftermath of debate on the use of the term, Beker writes: 'This nomenclature may well evoke erroneous associations. However, my interest does not lie in the nomenclature of apocalyptic, but rather in casting Paul's theology as a radical theology of hope nourished primarily, as Keck rightly stresses, by "the perspective of discontinuity"' (1993a: 157, citing Keck, 1984: 241).

'apocalyptic', the term 'eschatological' will be used to refer to this conceptual arena.

Before undertaking this study of Paul's theological presentation in Galatians, it will be helpful to reconstruct in some detail the issue that Paul addresses in that letter, and to paint a general portrait of those who were causing so much trouble for Paul and his gospel. The next chapter considers these important preliminary matters.

2

The Influence of Agitators in Galatian Christianity

If, as we have seen, some recent interpreters of Paul find his letter to the Galatians to have little emphasis on saving history prior to Christ, a similar view was held by some Christians of Paul's own day. They found his gospel to be deficient in its depiction of God's historical dealings with the people of Israel. Some of these Christians, whom we refer to as 'agitators' (οἱ ταράσσοντες, 1.7; cf. 5.10), were actively engaged in offsetting this imbalance in Paul's message. They were influencing the gentile Christians in Galatia in ways that went beyond what Paul calls 'the truth of the gospel' (2.5, 14). Whereas they seem to have paraded their case as a fuller and more accurate gospel, Paul found their message to have perverted the gospel altogether. In order to capture the full dynamics of Paul's presentation in Galatians, it will be helpful to consider the way in which he characterises the agitators throughout Galatians, and to ascertain as clearly as possible their own interests and convictions.

1. Identifying the Agitators

Paul talks about the agitators, and of others like them, in every chapter of his letter. Right at the beginning of his letter, instead of thanking God for his addressees as was his standard practice, he speaks rather of his astonishment that they are in the process of abandoning the God of grace and the gospel, due to the influence of some who are stirring up trouble by promulgating a mutation of the one, true gospel (1.6–7). Paul had encountered people of a similar ilk previously in his ministry, as he recounts in 2.4–5, recalling a time when some 'false' Christians manoeuvred their way into a position in which to manipulate 'the truth of the gospel'. In Paul's view, their interests simply promoted slavery, in contrast to the freedom that is in Christ Jesus.

In 3.1 Paul speaks again of the agitators themselves as having 'bewitched' (ἐβάσκανεν) the Galatians. While it is unlikely that the agitators were actually engaged in magical rites and demonic rituals in order to have their effect over the Galatian Christians, the word nonetheless signals that Paul envisaged the current situation of his addressees as involving the influence of spiritual powers. Paul frequently evidences the view that people's lives are caught up in a matrix of spiritual forces of one kind or another, whether they be forces for good (e.g., the Spirit, righteousness, grace) or for ill (e.g., the powers of Sin and Death). If the Galatians' experience of the Spirit had been put in jeopardy, this cannot have been due merely to the influence of human beings, but must include also spiritual powers of some kind within that process.[1] As we will see in chapter 7 below, Paul's charge of bewitchment (or better, 'injury with the evil eye') emerges from a worldview in which aspects of the concrete world are associated in one way or another with suprahuman powers. Paul was convinced, however, that those who were troubling the Galatians would themselves come face to face with the ultimate spiritual power, the God of judgement (5.10).[2]

The passages that most reveal Paul's understanding of the agitators' motivation are 4.17 and 6.12–13. In 4.17 he speaks of them alluring the Galatians, or literally being zealous for them (ζηλοῦσιν), in order that the Galatians might be zealous for the agitators themselves (ζηλοῦτε). Two things need to be noted about this verse. First, mention of the agitators' zeal is qualified by the expression 'with improper motives' (οὐ καλῶς). This is explained further to mean that the agitators hope to dissociate the Galatians from Paul himself in order that the Galatians

---

[1] See especially Neyrey, 1988; J. H. Elliott, 1988; 1990.

[2] I take τὸ κρίμα here to be an eschatological judgement by God, rather than an ecclesiastical judgement.

might declare their allegiance to the agitators. It could be said that Paul too had sought out the Galatians, as he implies in 4.18, but he qualifies this immediately with the assurance that his motivation was wholly proper (καλόν). Denigration of the agitators' character is an important aspect of Paul's critique. The same is true in 6.12–13, and more explicitly so in this case. There Paul highlights the agitators' selfish motivations: they are seeking only to 'make a good showing in the flesh' in order that 'they might boast about your flesh' (6.12–13). This suggests that, in Paul's view anyway, they sought to heighten their own influence and reputation by coercing the Galatians to fall in line with their instruction. While Paul too expected the Galatians to fall in line with his own instruction, the word 'flesh' (σάρξ) that appears twice in these verses earths the agitators' motivation in things that are contrary to the gospel, whereas Paul's own motivations are to promote only that in which he boasts: 'the cross of our Lord Jesus Christ' (6.14), rather than himself.

The second important feature to note about the verb 'to be zealous' in 4.17 is the way that it carries suggestive meaning in relation to the literature and traditions of Judaism. 'Zeal' is frequently cited as the quality or character that motivated famous Jews of Israel's history to preserve the distinctiveness of Israel's covenant identity, in conformity to the law and against the influx of pagan influences and practices, even to the point of death.[3] This may well be what Paul refers to when he speaks in Rom. 9.30–10.3 of Israel's pursuit of the 'law of righteousness' in connection with their 'zeal for God' and interest in 'their own righteousness'. The issue Paul has in mind in these verses is the definition of covenant membership along exclusively national lines.[4] It was out of this same matrix of law, righteousness and zeal that Paul's pre-Christian concerns and lifestyle flowed. So in Phil. 3.6, he speaks of his former zeal as having been translated into the action of persecuting the

---

[3] See, for instance, Jud. 9.4; Jub. 30.1–20 (esp. 30.18); Num. 25.10–13 (esp. 25.11); Sir. 45.23–24; 1 Macc. 2.19–28 (esp. 2.24, 26–27); 2.49–68 (esp. 2.50, 54, 58); 4 Macc. 18.12; Josephus, *Ant.* 12.271.
[4] See, for instance, Dunn, 1988: 576–98; Wright, 1991: 238–44; B. W. Longenecker, 1991: 215–20.

church, and of his blameless righteousness in the ways of the law. In his Galatian letter, Paul makes use of the notion of 'zeal' to signal this same concern to protect and preserve Jewish identity, identifying himself in his own pre-Christian career as 'zealous (ζηλωτής) for the traditions of my fathers' (Gal. 1.14; cf. Acts 22.3). The appearance of the same notion ('zeal') in Gal. 4.17 allows for a subtle likening of the pre-Christian Paul to the agitators themselves (although Paul would no doubt have considered his former zeal to have been superior to theirs, as his comment in 1.14 might suggest). Their concerns are of a similar kind to those of the pre-Christian Paul.[5]

Something similar emerges in the later passage of 6.12–13, where three times there is reference to the agitators' interest in having the Galatian Christians circumcised (περιτέμνειν; cf. περιτομή in 6.15). As is clear from the literature of Early Judaism, circumcision was considered to be a foremost sign of the covenant relationship between God and the people of Israel (cf. Genesis 17), a practice that distinguished Israel from most of her pagan neighbours (e.g., Jub. 15.11–15, 23–34; 16.14). This is also well documented in Graeco-Roman sources, where circumcision is shown to be a recognised practice that marked the Jewish people off from other ethnic groups.[6] The agitators, then, were promoting a version of the Christian message whereby salvation in Christ was placed within a larger context of ethnocentric covenantal theology. That is, what God had done in Christ was understood in close relation to, and in continuity with, what God had been doing throughout the history of the Jewish people, God's covenant people. In the process, circumcision was expected of any who sought to be included among God's people.

It is difficult to know how antagonistic the agitators were towards Paul, even if he himself was intensely antagonistic towards them (e.g., he wishes in 5.12 that they would castrate themselves; cf. his name-calling in Phil. 3.2). So while Paul considered the agitators to be promoting 'another gospel' and

---

[5] See Dunn, 1993c.
[6] See Stern, 1974: §195, §281 (esp. 5.2), and §301, where the picture is filled out further with reference to dietary practices and Sabbath observance; cf. §258.

'perverting' the gospel of Christ (1.7), making them accursed (1.8–9),[7] they themselves might well have considered their message to be wholly in line with Paul's own message, even if it differed in its emphasis. This might explain Paul's comment in 5.11a: 'If I am preaching circumcision now, then why am I now being persecuted?' It is possible that the agitators were saying that Paul's gospel coincided with theirs, so that, in a sense, he really did preach circumcision. A claim of this kind would receive further vindication if, in fact, Paul continued to use circumcision within his Christian ministry as a symbol of moral and 'spiritual' transformation, as in Rom. 2.25–29 or Phil. 3.3.[8]

A similar picture emerges from 3.3, where Paul asks: 'If you started off (ἐναρξάμενοι) with the Spirit, are you now finishing (ἐπιτελεῖσθε) with the flesh?' This relationship between starting and finishing might have been the way that the agitators explained the relationship between Paul's gospel and theirs, just as the letter of James finds that 'faith is completed (ἐτελειώθη) in works' (2.22). They might have held that Paul's message of faith provides an easy introduction to the Christian community for gentiles – a 'primer' that eventually needs to be supplemented with fuller teaching about the God and people of the covenant. In this way, the agitators might have conceived of their efforts as bringing to completion what Paul's ministry started.

On the other hand, just as other early Christians were outspoken in their attacks on Paul (cf. the problems behind 2 Corinthians, especially), it may be that the agitators had also mounted a vociferous assault upon his credentials, authority and gospel. Support for this can be gleaned from Paul's highly-charged legitimisation of his apostolic ministry in Galatians 1–2, which suggests that he had been brought into disrepute by the agitators.[9] Moreover, in 2.17 Paul is likely to be repudiating the charge that his gospel transforms Christ into a 'servant of the power of Sin', a charge that may well have originated with

---

[7] Morland examines the rhetoric of cursing in Galatians (1995).

[8] Cf. Baasland, 1984: 138, 143.

[9] This view has not gone unchallenged; see, e.g., Lategan, 1988; Verseput, 1993. While Galatians 1–2 involves dynamics other than simple self-defence, I find it difficult to believe that the tone and extent of Paul's comments there can be wholly explained without recourse to a defensive posture on Paul's part.

the agitators (cf. also Rom. 3.7–8; 6.1, 15). This is antagonistic polemic that suggests that the agitators might have had as little time for Paul as he had for them.

2. Circumcision and the Observance of the Law

Consideration also needs to be given to the matter of whether circumcision was the agitators' sole concern. Were these people motivated by a single issue, or was circumcision only one element in a larger package? When taken on its own, Paul's comment in 5.3 might seem to suggest the former: 'I testify again to everyone who becomes circumcised that he is obliged to do the whole law.' Is Paul telling the Galatians something that they didn't already know? If so, the agitators might not have been concerned with performance of the law beyond the single requirement of circumcision; the Galatians had no idea that further observance would be required of them because the agitators had no interest in promoting anything other than the practice of circumcision. This would explain why circumcision is the issue that Paul specifically focuses on in various parts of the letter. Moreover, in 6.13 Paul claims that, despite their circumcision, the agitators 'do not keep (φυλάσσειν) the law'. This is frequently thought to mean that they are interested only in circumcision rather than the rest of the nomistic prescriptions.

Nonetheless, this reading of 5.3 and 6.13 is not necessarily conclusive of the matter. Notable is the way that Paul implicitly links the issue of circumcision to the issue of Jewish kosher meals (2.1–10 and 2.11–14). Moreover, he explicitly states that the Galatians are also concerned with the observance of 'days, months, seasons, and years' (4.10), a reference most likely to Jewish calendrical and Sabbath observance.[10] Even at 5.3, Paul

---

[10] Martin has challenged this view (1996) as part of a reconsideration of the Galatians' response to the agitators' gospel. According to Martin, the Galatians accepted that circumcision was necessary to true Christianity but, rather than being attracted to a circumcision gospel, they had abandoned their Christian commitment altogether. In this case, 4.10 includes no reference to Jewish calendrical observances but to pagan time-keeping schemes. I find it difficult to square Martin's view with passages like 5.2–5 (see his explanation on 117–18), and especially 4.29, which seems far more significant to Paul's case than Martin's scenario seems to allow.

goes on in the next verse to speak to those who 'would be justified by law' (5.4).[11] Similarly, Paul addresses his comments in 4.21 to 'those wanting to be under law' rather than to 'those wanting to be circumcised'.[12] In the allegory that follows (4.21–31), Paul is concerned to link Sinai with the enslaved descendants of Abraham, a rather strained claim but one which serves to discredit not simply the need for circumcision but the need to observe the Sinaitic law.

This impression is strengthened by the likelihood that Deut. 27.26, which Paul quotes in 3.10, was initially brought to the attention of the Galatian Christians by the agitators themselves; the same seems to be true also for the Hagar–Sarah allegory of 4.21–31.[13] In each case, Paul is probably reworking passages and stories from scripture that the agitators were using to support their case. A simple reading of Deut. 27.26, for example, seems to say precisely the opposite of what Paul wants to argue: 'Cursed is everyone who does not stand firm in and do everything written in the book of the law.' In all likelihood, Paul felt required to put a new spin on this scriptural passage precisely because it had already been introduced to the Galatian Christians by the agitators in order to encourage the gentile Christians to observe the law as part and parcel of their Christian commitment. If this is the case, then it is virtually inconceivable that they were concerned to promote only circumcision, when one of their crucial scriptural texts is explicit in requiring the observance of everything written in the book of the law.

Moreover, as is generally agreed, the agitators gave high priority to the figure of Abraham, the father of the Jewish people, and in Jewish traditions Abraham was frequently cited as having observed all of the law, although it was not revealed to

---

[11] Kümmel: 'Paul did not try to inform the Galatians with a fact new to them in 5.3 but to remind them again (πάλιν) of a known fact to which they had not paid sufficient notice' (1975: 300); cf. Betz, 1979: 259–61.

[12] Barclay: 'this address and the allegory which follows it would be completely valueless if none of the Galatians was seriously concerned to listen to and submit to the law' (1988: 62).

[13] See Barrett, 1982. Cf. Barclay, 1988: 91; Stanton, 1996: 108–109.

Moses until generations later.[14] We know of no ardent Jews in
Early Judaism who upheld Abraham as a central figure of Jewish
self-definition while at the same time suggesting that his
significance is limited to the observance of only some of the law.
Any precedents in Jewish tradition for reflecting on the
significance of Abraham with regard to merely partial fulfilment
of the law would have been few and far between, to say the
least.

Further still, it is a strange, unprecedented form of Judaism
that maintains circumcision to be the sole requirement for true
covenant membership at the expense of all other legal requirements. In most forms of Judaism, the law was perceived to be an
indivisible whole; a person or community is not at liberty to pick
and choose its practices, deciding which legal regulations are
and are not binding (e.g., 4 Macc. 5.20–21; m.'*Abot.* 2.1; 4.2) – a
sentiment shared by some early Christians as well (Jas. 2.10; cf.
Mt. 5.18–19).

The agitators, then, appear to have had a high interest in
circumcision specifically but not simply as a single entity apart
from the rest of the law's prescriptions. Like most Jews of their
day, the agitators probably would have seen circumcision only as
part of a much larger and comprehensive legal package. They
did not restrict their concerns to circumcision alone, even if
that was the issue that drew most of Paul's ire in his letter. When
accusing the agitators of not keeping the law despite their
circumcision, Paul's charge against the agitators in 6.13 is not
factual description, but is either a kind of accusatory rhetoric to
discredit them or a polemical charge arising from his Christian
theological presuppositions about the law and how it can be
fulfilled.[15] In either case, it cannot be used as historical evidence
to reconstruct a picture of the agitators' concerns. Even if
circumcision held priority of place in the agitators' agenda, it

---

[14] E.g., Jub. 16.28; Sir. 44.20; 2 Bar. 57.2; Philo, *Abr.* 5–6, 60–61, 275; b. *Yom.* 286;
m. *Kid.* 4.14; cf. Gen. 25.6.

[15] Barclay: 'Paul's snide remark that they do not really keep the law does not
disprove but rather, paradoxically, confirms our impression from the rest of
the letter that the agitators expected the Galatians to observe the law in
conjunction with their circumcision' (1988: 65); see his full defence of this
view, 60–68.

was not likely to be their exclusive hobby-horse. It may not be wholly accurate to describe their policy as being one of 'gradualism',[16] but it seems that they expected the gentiles to carry on with further observance of the law once they had been circumcised. We hear something similar in Justin Martyr's *Dialogue with Trypho* (8.2), where Trypho the Jew is cited as urging Justin along these lines:

> first be circumcised, then keep (as the law commands) the sabbath, the feasts and God's new moons, and, in a word, do all the things that are written in the law (τὰ ἐν τῷ νόμῳ γεγραμμένα πάντα ποίει), and then you will indeed find mercy from God.[17]

In our view, then, circumcision seems not to have been the only thing that the agitators promoted. Their sights included the comprehensive observance of the law.

3. Miscellaneous Matters

Much more could be considered in relation to the agitators, issues regularly discussed in the introductory sections of most commentaries. It might be enough to say that they were Jewish (rather than gentile) Christians (rather than non-Christians) whom Paul probably did not know, and who originated from outside the Galatian churches;[18] they were indebted to nothing other than mainstream Jewish covenantal thinking and concerns (rather than any form of gnosticism, mystery cults, etc.), and were loosely associated with the Jerusalem church, even thinking of themselves as acting in its interests (whether or not that was true); and only they were causing trouble in the Galatian Christian communities (rather than two groups of

---

[16] Sanders, 1983: 29.

[17] Compare also Josephus' account of the two-stage conversion of Izates (*Ant.* 20.38–46). The translation of Justin used here is Stanton's (1996: 105). He takes ἴσως to mean 'indeed' rather than 'perchance', as it is usually translated. Stanton frequently speaks of both 'circumcision and keeping the law' (109) as the focus of the agitators' interests.

[18] Despite Winter (1994: 123–43), whose intriguing construction of the situation in Galatia envisages problems to have arisen due to internal as opposed to external factors.

agitators). A more precise description may be possible, but it is not necessary for our purposes.

Similar matters that frequently appear in commentary introductions have also gone without discussion here: Where were the Galatian communities located (i.e., north or south Galatia)?[19] At what point in his ministry did Paul write this letter (e.g., 48–49, 53–54)? How does the event recorded in Gal. 2.11–14 relate to the record of similar events found in the book of Acts? Since these matters have no impact on the issues considered in the following chapters, they need not detain us here. Instead, it simply remains to turn our attention to the text of Galatians and its depiction of the triumph of Abraham's God.

---

[19] I believe that, as Mitchell puts it, there is 'virtually nothing to be said for the north Galatian theory' (1993: 2.3).

3

The Establishment of the New World

It is likely that Paul expected his Galatian addressees to listen to his letter several times, taking note of its argument and building up an impression that would remain with them long after the letter had been sent on to the next Galatian congregation.[1] But even on a first hearing, one cannot get too far into the letter without taking full account of the eschatological motor that drives Paul's theological programme. As we will see, Paul takes certain measures to ensure that this is the case. We do well, then, to heed his signals in order to understand his letter in the way that most accords with his own intentions.

This eschatological feature will be the focus of the present chapter. First, we will examine the way that the body of Paul's letter is framed by explicit statements concerning the establishment of a new world where divine triumph reigns (§3.1). This is set against the backdrop of Paul's understanding of the demarcation of the nations that results from human enslavement to suprahuman forces, in contrast to the universal unity that transpires in the sphere of divine sovereignty (§3.2). As a consequence of his eschatological convictions, Paul envisages intimacy with God to be a characteristic of those in Christ (§3.3), who enter into the sphere of God's eschatological triumph and intimacy by means of their union with Christ (§3.4). What ties all this together is Paul's vision of the establishment of a new sphere of existence permeated by the power of God, who has triumphed over competing suprahuman forces and united a divided world.

---

[1] Martyn: Paul assumes 'that the Galatian congregations will listen to the whole of the letter several times and with extreme care' (1995: 31 = 1997: 139).

35

1. The Eschatological Frame of Paul's Letter

There is no dispute that Paul authored the letter to the Galatians. But his normal practice of authoring letters was to have a secretary put in writing what he himself dictated or instructed to be written (cf. Rom. 16.22), after which Paul usually added some final words in closing. The author of 2 Thessalonians (whether Paul or one who writes in his name) states clearly that this practice is 'characteristic of every letter [of mine]; this is my manner of writing letters' (2 Thess. 3.17; cf. 1 Cor. 16.21–24; Phlm. 19–25; Col. 4.18; possibly Rom. 16.17–20).[2] These closing statements may vary in character, ranging from brief expressions of best wishes to elaborations or recapitulations of important themes from the letter itself.[3]

The closing of Galatians (6.11–18) falls into the latter category. It does more than simply authenticate the letter, but highlights the primary points of Paul's interests, serving as the interpretive key to the whole of the letter.[4] Paul seems to signal this himself right at the start of 6.11, where he writes: 'See with what large letters I write to you with my own hand.'[5] This not only announces to his audience that he himself now has 'pen' in hand, but also draws his hearers' attention to what he is about to say. It is Paul's way of saying, 'What I'm about to write is the matter in a nutshell.'

And that nutshell involves several important points, of which two can be noted here. First, as we have already seen (chapter 2 above), Paul's comments in 6.12–13 reveal his understanding of the agitators' motivation, which he contrasts with his own character as one who boasts not in things of the flesh but in 'the cross of our Lord Jesus Christ' (6.14a; cf. Phil. 3.3–8). Second, this abbreviated crystallisation of the primary point of his letter goes on to highlight the death of one world and the inauguration of another (6.14b–15). As in 6.12–13, so here Paul focuses

---

[2] Ancient letters frequently reveal two different styles of handwriting – that of the secretary, followed by that of the composer. The practice was not exclusively Paul's.

[3] On Pauline letter-closings, see Weima, 1993; 1994; Jervis, 1991: 132–57.

[4] See Weima, 1994: 157–74.

[5] The aorist ἔγραψα is best taken as an 'epistolary' aorist, as at 1 Cor. 5.11; 9.15; Phlm. 19, 21; cf. Rom. 15.15.

his attention on the cross (σταυρός) as the means whereby, in some of Paul's most graphic language, 'the world (κόσμος) has been crucified (ἐσταύρωται) to me and I have been crucified to the world' (6.14). To this he adds that what matters is 'new creation' (6.15).[6] The motif of Paul himself having been crucified will be considered in more detail below (§3.4). Here, however, Paul's view about the death of one world and the inauguration of another needs consideration.

What Paul has in mind when he envisages the inauguration of a new world is not, of course, the establishment of a completely new physical universe of matter – a world of cause-and-effect relationships, held together by forces of gravitational attraction at the molecular level. Instead, he envisages the establishment of a new realm of existence. It is a sphere of life wholly differentiated from the 'cosmos' that has been crucified to Paul, a domain where distinctive patterns of life are operative. As his comments in 6.14–15 highlight, Paul belongs to this new world, where different standards apply, different rules are followed, different habits formed, different ways of life practised, and a different ethos exists. The world in which he used to live was characterised by many things, one of which was a fundamental distinction between those who were circumcised and those who were not, those who observed the law of God and those who did not. But Paul has seen the death of that world and now lives in a world where that distinction is not applicable.

In order to capture a fuller sense of the distinctiveness of this new domain of life, consideration needs to be given to Paul's

---

[6] There is debate over whether this phrase has anthropological or 'cosmological' import. In the former, Paul's reference focuses on the transformation within the believer who becomes, in a sense, 'a new creature' (Witherington, 1994: 273–74); in the latter, Paul's reference highlights the termination of the previous age and the establishment of a new eschatological 'sphere of existence' into which the believer becomes incorporated (Carroll and Green, 1995: 127). The two aspects are, of course, intricately interrelated. In my view, the latter is the more likely of the two, although neither view can be held with great tenacity. Accordingly, any mention herein of a 'new world' is informed primarily by other features in Galatians (e.g., the present evil age to which Paul has been crucified implies in and of itself the establishment of another age or world), and not simply by a cosmological interpretation of καινὴ κτίσις.

understanding of life within the old domain. A clear view of this emerges from Paul's letter to the Galatians, but it will be helpful to demonstrate the point from outside Galatians initially. In his letter of introduction to Christians in Rome, for instance, Paul gives an elaborate depiction of the world that he has died to, a depiction that, although distinctive, nonetheless has several points in common with his depiction of the same in Galatians.

In the opening chapters of Romans, Paul portrays a situation in which human beings from the ranks of both gentile and Jew (the two primary social categories of Jewish perception) are shown to be sinful in their behaviour (1.18–32; 2.17–24). While they themselves are accountable for this, Paul's analysis of their condition moves towards 3.9, where he claims to have shown that 'all humanity, both Jews and also Greeks [gentiles], are under the power of Sin' (ὑφ' ἁμαρτίαν).

It is important to be clear about Paul's meaning here, since the term 'under the power of Sin' can be easily misunderstood. He does not mean to suggest that our personal sins and transgressions are so numerous and ever-increasing that they weigh us down under their heavy load. Perhaps Paul would have agreed with this in general, but it has nothing to do with his meaning in Rom. 3.9. Paul is not thinking here of errors of lifestyle that are, in a sense, carried by people on their backs, exerting pressures that are too great to bear, in the style of the character 'Christian' in John Bunyan's *The Pilgrim's Progress*. Instead, he is thinking of a kind of spiritual force, a power with intentionality that exists and holds human beings in its grip, forcing them to conform to its programme in contrast to the ways of God.[7] To distinguish this phenomenon from errors in personal conduct and lifestyle, Paul often employs the singular 'sin' (ἁμαρτία) to refer to the cosmic power of Sin that is in competition with God; plural references to 'transgressions' (παραπτώματα) and the like refer to violations of

---

[7] See Beker, 1980: 189–92. Keck writes: 'Sin is not something one does; it is rather a power which makes one do' (1984: 238). An anthropological demythologisation of this fundamental aspect in Paul's worldview can be found in, e.g., Schnelle (1996), whose discussion of Paul's anthropology suffers from the misperception that the powers of sin and death are 'anthropological terms' (41). Cf. Röhser, 1987: 142–43. See the criticisms of this kind of approach in B. W. Longenecker, 1996a.

God's will for which individuals and societies are personally or corporately responsible. While the two are intricately related and reinforce each other,[8] in Paul's thought they are also distinct phenomena. Being sensitive to this distinction allows the modern reader better access to the full complexity and dynamic of Paul's thought.

Despite its brief mention in 3.9, Paul gives further consideration to the power of Sin in other passages in Romans, especially the middle chapters.[9] In Romans 7, the power of Sin originates not within but outside of the person who speaks there. Its effect is profound as it transforms a situation of potential good into one of anxiety and despair. The person of Romans 7 is eager to please God by obeying God's law, which is 'holy, righteous and good' (7.13). The scenario looks promising. Unfortunately, however, there is another character in the situation: the power of Sin. This power moves in to have its own way. It 'seizes the opportunity' (7.8, 11), deceives (7.11) and sets up house within the person (7.17, 20), enslaving him so that the person recognises himself to be 'under the power of Sin' (ὑπὸ τὴν ἁμαρτίαν, 7.14; cf. 3.9).

Paul depicts the power of Sin here as a suprahuman cosmic power that is active in God's world, influencing God's creatures, and working to undermine God's purposes. What is ultimately at stake here is not merely the person's desperate situation, but the very reputation of God as the sovereign one. If the power of Sin can pervert God's giving of the law into an occasion to serve the perverse purposes of Sin itself, God's claim to sovereignty is at least threatened, and potentially undermined altogether. In such a desperate situation the question 'Who will deliver me?' in 7.24 carries overtones of 'Who *can* deliver me?', especially if God has been outsmarted by the power of Sin.

Of course, this is not the final word on the matter. Romans 8 begins with the confidence that God, the only one who might possibly undermine the influence of the power of Sin, has done precisely that by sending Christ into the world and, thereby,

[8] Barrett: 'sin is the inward correlative of the external tyranny, the subjection to astrological and demonic forces under which man lives ... Paul conceives the universe to have come under the control of usurping cosmic elements, and men's own existence to be dominated by flesh' (1994: 60, 104).
[9] See Sanders, 1983: 70–81.

shattering the pervasive network of evil that the power of Sin had set up in conjunction with the human 'fleshly' condition (8.3). In the final verses of Romans 8, where the first half of his letter culminates in assurances about the certainty of salvation for those in Christ, Paul itemises the kinds of things that no longer can be thought to be potential usurpers of God's sovereignty. Included in this list are such things as angels, cosmic principalities (ἀρχαί), and spiritual powers (δυνάμεις). Paul envisages a battle between suprahuman phenomena where God's reputation as the cosmic sovereign is at stake, a reputation guaranteed to emerge untarnished by means of the victory inaugurated in Christ. It is not surprising, then, to find in the letter-closing, perhaps written in his own hand (16.17–20), Paul's final instruction concerning the assurance that 'the God of peace is soon to crush Satan under your feet' (16.20).[10]

This triumph of God over powers that oppose him involves a shattering of a particular kind of 'world' that had sprung up, a sphere of life that originated when the power of Sin became effective by means of the personal sinfulness of Adam (5.12). In the second half of Romans 5, Paul describes a situation in which the power of Sin has created a vast network of sinfulness, a 'society' that affects each and every person born into it. Liberation theologians have made much of the notion of 'structural evil', highlighting how our global society has been set up in such a way that ensures and perpetuates multi-faceted injustice; these structures of our world have a way of pre-determining in broad strokes the manner of life of all those who live within them.[11]

While the merits of such a view cannot be considered here, this kind of structural analysis of evil did not originate with the liberation theologians. Paul himself articulates much the same point in Romans 5. What liberation theologians call 'structures

---

[10] With Scholer, it is best to view 16.20 not simply as 'a resolution of the situation described in 16:17–18, but [as] an independent piece of concluding apocalyptic hope' (1990: 60 n. 1).

[11] So, for instance, Camara, 1971, where economic structures of the world are identified as 'established violence'. Feminists have made the same case in relation to the structures that ensure the priority and dominance of males in most modern societies.

of evil' corresponds to some extent with what Paul calls the 'power of Sin', a controlling force that predetermines the direction, course, and possibilities of the lives of those who are born into the post-Adam 'world'. For them, only one option exists: to serve the purposes of the power of Sin by their own sin. In a sense, the power of Sin has managed to set up a system, a society, a world, in which things have an almost natural way of running contrary to the will of God. And this, of course, has ramifications concerning whose sovereignty such a 'world' advertises; a world order permeated by sinfulness is under the apparent sovereignty of the powers of Sin and Death. So Death, itself conceived of as a cosmic power (cf. 1 Cor. 15; Rom. 8.38), can be said to 'reign' (5.14, 17), just as Death's accomplice also reigns, the power of Sin (5.21; cf. 5.12).[12]

Of course, Paul does not excuse individuals for their errors of lifestyle, their transgressions, their sins. For Paul, the meta-personal, meta-cultural power of Sin works in conjunction with the personal propensity towards sinfulness (which he often speaks of as the 'flesh'). Paul envisages an integral relationship between structural and personal factors to explain the network of sinfulness that forms the basis of, the pattern for, and the ethos of the Adamic 'world' into which humans are born. In fact, it is arguable that, for Paul, people are more responsible for their lifestyle since the coming of Christ, due to the fact that another world has come into existence, another sphere of influence has been established. This new world arises out of Jesus' incarnation into a world dominated by Sin and sinfulness (as, for instance, in 8.3),[13] and is described in Romans 5 as being permeated with 'grace' (5.15, 17, 20, 21), 'righteousness' (5.16–17, 19), and 'life' (5.17–18). The final sentence of Romans 5 brings these themes together in a condensed

[12] See Hofius, 1996. He writes: 'Mit Adams "Verfehlung" = "Ungehorsam" = "Sündentat" hat die Sünde als Macht (die ἁμαρτία V. 12a.21a) Einzug in die Welt gehalten und ist sie nunmehr als Herrscherin in der Welt auf dem Plan' (182). Somewhat similarly, Dunn, 1988: 275, 287. On the cosmic power identified as Death, see M. C. de Boer, 1988.

[13] I do not share Dunn's view (1980) that Paul does not believe in the literal 'pre-existence' of Christ. The incarnation into this world of Jesus as a 'pre-existent' divine being is essential to Paul's soteriological understanding. On this, see especially the brief but *apropos* argument of Nickelsburg, 1991.

mini-statement: All this happened 'so that, just as the power of Sin is sovereign by means of the power of Death, so also the grace [of God] might be sovereign through righteousness to eternal life through Jesus Christ our Lord' (5.21). This is a 'world' or sphere in which God reigns supreme in grace.

Moreover, this new world is one in which the physical order of creation takes great delight. In Rom. 8.19-23 Paul portrays creation in anthropomorphic terms, 'groaning in travail' at present but 'waiting with eager longing' for the full establishment of this new world order, when it will be 'set free from its bondage to decay'. Here Paul seems to assume that a harmonious relationship had originally existed between the physical creation and the pre-fallen Adam. Although that harmonious relationship had taken a turn for the worse as a consequence of sinfulness, Paul believed that one day it would be restored as a consequence of God's transformation of sinners into 'sons' of God.[14] Creation waits expectantly for that day.

Two things are important to note here. First, Paul conceives of salvation on a cosmic scale. God's salvation is not simply anthropocentric but includes within its scope the whole of the physical creation. Paul's understanding of salvation operates within the context of a theology of creation, or better a theology of God as the creator. Here again we see how divine sovereignty is a fundamental matter in Paul's notion of salvation, for if God were not to set right the whole of creation, God would not be supreme. The setting right of creation is carried out in relation to the salvation of human beings who, being transformed in their manner of life, interact with creation in a manner that replicates the proper stewardship of creation. Instead of the created order being misused to promote idolatry and immorality, all as a result of sin (cf. Rom. 1.18-32), the created order will find relief from the exploitation and tyranny of sinfulness, being set right in relation to humanity's redemption in Christ.

Second, we see in this something of Paul's conception of societies or 'worlds' having a spiritual aspect which are played out in concrete fashion. That is, a society that is enmeshed in sinfulness interacts with creation in a way that demonstrates its

[14] See Wright, 1992b.

sinfulness. Paul assumes that the character of a society, its spiritual personality or identity, will be manifest in the way that that society acts in practice and has an impact on concrete realities. Throughout his letters, Paul frequently presumes a profound interrelation between the physical and 'spiritual' dimensions of a society or community; the concrete world is the arena wherein the 'spiritual' temperament is lived out. The two work together in a reinforced network wherein patterns of behaviour are almost predetermined by a prior disposition of the 'spirit', whether that spirit belongs to a single individual, an institution, a community, a culture, a society or a 'world'.[15] In Paul's way of thinking, the here and now is profoundly spiritual, in one way or another; there is a spiritual dynamic evident in the life of any culture, society and community, and in one's own social relationships and behaviour.

For Paul, then, an important question must be asked of any kind of practice, whether individual or corporate: What is the spiritual force that lies behind it? What is the spiritual atmosphere that any action testifies to and reinforces? It is this that Paul has in mind when he writes in Galatians that 'the world has been crucified to me and I have been crucified to the world' (6.14), or where he emphasises the notion of 'new creation' (6.15).[16] The two divergent worlds that Paul envisages represent two different spheres of spirituality, two opposing orbs of spiritual character, two contrasting worlds of spiritual disposition, two distinct domains of corporate and personal constitution. For Paul, the old world is of an essentially different spiritual character than the newly inaugurated world. His understanding of personal and corporate identity is not simply informed by a temporal, quantitative view about the chronological passing of time, but includes a 'qualitative' view concerning the passing from one domain into another domain, from one sphere of identity into another sphere. Accordingly, in Paul's view the concern for circumcision as a marker of identity for God's people belongs to the spiritual ethos of a domain that runs contrary

[15] See Wink's important engagement with the biblical notion of the spiritual 'powers' in his trilogy (1984; 1986; 1992).

[16] So, Mell identifies the notion of the 'new creation' (Gal. 6.15; 2 Cor. 5.17) as central to Paul's Christian anthropology (1989: 387).

to the domain of God's transforming, eschatological power (an aspect considered more fully in chapter 4 below).

Paul's robust eschatological emphasis appears not only in the letter-closing (6.11–18), but is also highlighted already in the letter-opening (1.1–5). A study of Paul's letter-openings and letter-closings reveals that these sections of his letters often underscore the features that are central to his concerns in that letter. We have already seen this to be the case with regard to the closing of Galatians, and it is true of the opening of Galatians as well.[17]

The structure of Paul's letter-opening brings this out clearly. Typical of Paul's usual letter-openings are three aspects: (1) he identifies the sender/s (himself and any others who are with him); (2) he identifies and greets the recipients; and (3) he gives thanks for his recipients. The opening of Galatians is important in two ways. First, only two of the three usual features of Paul's letter-openings appear in Galatians: the identity of the sender/s (1.1a, 2a) and the identity and greeting of the recipients (1.2b–3). What is omitted on this occasion is the thanksgiving that typifies Paul's normal writing style. This, of course, is important, since it reveals something of Paul's inner anxiety about his Galatian recipients; he has nothing to be thankful about since, in his eyes, they are flirting with apostasy.

Second, two novel features make their way into the letter-opening, which do so since they encapsulate important aspects that Paul will develop in the main body of his letter. The first of these appears in 1.1 immediately after giving his own name: 'an apostle – sent neither by human commission nor from human authorities, but through Jesus Christ and God the father'. We saw in chapter 2 (above) that Paul's apostolic authority seems to have been brought into question by the agitators who were courting the Galatian Christians. That this challenge creates an urgent threat to the gospel is evident from the way that Paul interrupts his standard form of greeting and enters into an immediate defence of his apostolic credentials. Most of the first two chapters of Galatians are dedicated to elaborating this defence.

The second feature that makes its way into the letter-opening

[17] On letter-openings, see Jervis, 1991: 65–89; Cook, 1992.

appears in 1.4. Having made mention of God our father and the Lord Jesus Christ in 1.3, Paul writes, 'who gave himself for our sins to deliver us from the present evil age, according to the will of our God and father'. It is likely that here Paul has incorporated traditional Christian material which spoke of Christ giving himself 'for our sins', and that Paul has himself glossed this tradition with the additional phrase 'to deliver us from the present evil age'.[18] This notion of the present age of evil is significant. Jewish theological traditions of Paul's day often envisage a distinct division of the ages, in which the final age to come is differentiated from the preceding age (or ages) which was (or were) marked out by evil. One Jewish author, who wrote the apocalypse 4 Ezra at about 100 C.E., repeatedly draws a contrast between these two ages or 'worlds'.[19] He speaks of 'not one age/world but two' (4 Ezra 7.50). The present age/world is said to be 'ageing and passing the strength of youth' (5.55), and the author points out the difference between the difficult 'ways of this age/world' as opposed to the safe 'ways of the future world' (7.12–13). For Paul, the two ages are defined only in relation to Christ, the one who rescues Christians from the age of evil (1.4) and has inaugurated a new sphere of existence (6.15). Through Christ, the sovereignty, supremacy and triumph of God has been demonstrated. This God of grace and peace (1.3), who is Paul's patron and commissioner, is a God of power (resurrection, 1.1) and creative innovation (deliverance from the old age, 1.4).[20]

---

[18] See, e.g., Furnish, 1993: 113; Betz, 1979: 42. For more detailed discussion of this feature in Paul, see Sanders, 1977: 463–68; Käsemann, 1971: 42–46; Beker, 1980: 182–92.

[19] The terms 'age' (αἰών) and 'world' (κόσμος) can be used synonymously in this context of thought. This is clear from Paul himself, in passages like 1 Cor. 1.20 and 3.18–19 where the two words appear together. The same is true for Paul's use of the term 'age' in 1.4 and 'world' in 6.14.

[20] The notion of resurrection itself involves the notion of the victory of God over opposition to his reign. The resurrection of the dead was perceived in Judaism to be one of the events of the eschatological day of salvation when God would stride into human history, eradicate evil and set up the rule of righteousness. Early Christians found the beginning of this event to have already taken place in the resurrection of Christ, who is the 'first-fruits' of the resurrection, as Paul says in 1 Cor. 15.23.

So it is that, in this letter-opening, Paul inserts an unexpected (and therefore important) eschatological reference that high-lights the triumph of God in the dawning of the new age, the new world which is distinguished from the evil world of old (which is nonetheless still 'present' until its final eradication). Since the same emphasis characterises his letter-closing, Gala-tians is clearly framed by an eschatological perspective that Paul expects his readers to grasp as being central to his message. This eschatological perspective appears to be the letter's convic-tional basis, which is elaborated by a series of theological arguments in the main body of the letter. This eschatological perspective has to do first and foremost with the triumph of God, a triumph that is taking effect in the establishment of a new world. It is a world where matters of circumcision and uncircumcision are irrelevant. In this way we can see clearly how, in Paul's view, the circumcision of gentile Christians impacts upon deeper theological issues pertaining to the sovereignty and triumph of God in Christ.

2. Human Enslavement, Suprahuman Competitors and National Demarcation

Having noted the way in which the frame of the letter is shot through with eschatological features, consideration can now be given to one of the primary passages where the theme of the triumph of God appears in the body of the letter. Throughout Gal. 4.1–11, Paul sets up a contrast between the past time and the present time – the same temporal distinction that informs 1.4 and 6.14–15. This contrast begins with an example from every-day life about stages in the process of maturation (4.1–2). It then continues with a theological application of that example in rela-tion to the changing of the ages (4.3–7), and finally becomes earthed in a discussion of the Galatians' own situation in relation to the eschatological era that has come into effect (4.8–11). In the first section, Paul gives an example of the child who, like a 'slave' (δοῦλος), has no rights to the inheritance of the family estate until he reaches the time of maturity. In the second sec-tion, the phrase 'when the fullness of time came' (4.4) contrasts the time of childhood, or of being 'enslaved' (δεδουλωμένοι, 4.3), with the time of sonship (4.5–7). In the third, the contrast between 'then' and 'now' (4.8–9) highlights the Galatians' new position, in distinction to the time when they did not know God but were 'enslaved' (ἐδουλεύσατε) to other spiritual beings.

Woven into this temporal distinction is the imagery of slavery, which appears in each of the three sections of this passage (as highlighted by the Greek words above). The same imagery is elaborated further in the allegory of Hagar the slave woman and Sarah the free woman only verses later (4.21–31). Evidently, then, Paul went to great lengths to portray the Galatians' pre-Christian experience as a time of enslavement.

Moreover, Paul envisages human enslavement in relation to what he calls the 'elements of the world' (στοιχεῖα τοῦ κόσμου, 4.3) or simply 'elements' (στοιχεῖα, 4.9). Dispute surrounds the meaning and origin of this word, however, and students of Paul have held significantly different views on the matter. Some find the word to refer to the elemental religious teachings and practices that permeate most societies.[21] It is unlikely that this interpretation can do full justice to the passage, however, since Paul speaks of the 'elements' as 'beings who by nature are not gods' (4.8) rather than as impersonal phenomena.[22]

---

[21] So Wink, 1986: 67–72; Moore-Crispin, 1989: 210–12; Bundrick, 1991.

[22] I take οὖσιν to be masculine ('beings') rather than neuter ('things'), unlike Martyn (1995; 1997: 125–40). Martyn thinks that 'elements of the world' refers primarily to the practice of idolatry. This poses the problem that the Jews were not generally involved in idolatrous practices, and yet Paul includes the observance of the law under the auspices of the elements. Accordingly, Martyn highlights the phrase 'of the world' as a way of removing the problem, arguing that the world Paul is referring to is the world made up of opposites, Jewish and gentile being one religious pair of polar opposites. Thus Paul can include both Jew and gentile under the rubric of the στοιχεῖα since both were oppositionally conjoined in the world that has been crucified to Paul. But does this really remove the problem? Might it not merely confuse the categories, so that one attribute (i.e., oppositional) becomes the all-encompassing characteristic and sole defining property of the head noun; the lexical meaning of στοιχεῖα becomes reduced to a single subordinate quality. (If it is correct to say that all fish swim, it is not correct to say that anything that swims is therefore a fish.) In a sense, Martyn has moved the goalposts; the issue for Martyn's interpretation is how Jewish practice could have been included by Paul under the rubric of idolatry; to say that it is oppositionally related to paganism may not ultimately be a satisfactory explanation.

Others maintain that, just as the word was used to denote the four elemental components that make up the natural world (earth, air, fire, and water),[23] so too Paul is simply referring to a bondage to the present, transient world[24] which is passing away and which is subject to sin.[25] This interpretation of Paul's meaning fits well with the details of Paul's eschatological emphasis on the changing of the ages.[26] Both Jewish and pagan lifestyle are yoked together within the sphere of things that are passing away. Here, the description of the 'elements' as being 'of the world' (τοῦ κόσμου, 4.3) links them to Paul's claim in 6.15 that in Christ he and the world (κόσμος) have nothing to do with each other, and to his comment in 1.4 that Christ has redeemed his people from the present evil age.

Nonetheless, despite its attractions, this interpretation of the 'elements' as the concrete components of the physical order seems unlikely to be what Paul has primarily in mind. This is fundamentally due to the fact that Paul nowhere links erroneous lifestyle and physical matter in a way in which the latter is said to induce the former. Proponents of this interpretation quickly move from (1) an identification of the στοιχεῖα as the physical elements of nature to (2) metaphorical imagery about the sphere of sinfulness as the context of human existence; while the metaphorical conclusion is wholly Pauline, the literal starting point is not. As we have seen (§3.1), Romans 8 suggests that Paul looked for the redemption of physical creation from the tyranny of human abuse, not the redemption of humanity from the tyranny of the physical creation. While forms of Gnosticism sought release from the enslaving effects of the

---

[23] For example, see Aristotle, *Metaph.* 3.2.2; Philo, *Heres* 134, 140, 152, 197, 226 [×3], 227; *Aet.* 107, 111; *Det.* 8; Epictetus, *Diss.* 3.13.14.

[24] Rusan, 1992; Blinzler, 1961.

[25] Thielman, 1989: 80–83.

[26] The fact that the 'elements' are identified as 'beings who by nature are not gods' is not necessarily problematic to this interpretation, since it was common for the elements of the physical world to be divinised in the Graeco-Roman world. For instance, a popular Jewish text that Paul had probably read speaks of the physical elements as being popularly thought of as 'gods that rule the world' (Wis. Sol. 13.2). Cf. Wis. Sol. 7.17; Philo, *Decal.* 53; *Vit. Cont.* 3–4; 1 En. 80.7; Clement of Alexandria, *Protrept.* 5.

physical order, Paul never subscribed to such a view. He portrays the created order itself as enslaved to decay and longing for the day of its liberation, a longing that it shares with Christians who await the redemption of their bodies (8.19–23). To be sure, there is a problem that needs sorting out in the relationship between the material world and humanity in its unredeemed manner of life. But Paul perceives the problem to arise from a matrix of influences which, while affecting the material world, does not originate there. Paul gives no indication that he himself thinks of the elements of the physical world to be overarching spiritual forces or 'gods' that define and control human destiny.

If not the physical world, Paul may have been thinking of celestial bodies exerting influence over the world of humanity. In Paul's day, the stars were frequently viewed as being governed by angels (e.g., 1 En. 60.11–22; 75.1–3; 80.1, 6–7) or as spiritual beings or angels themselves (e.g., Wis. Sol. 13.2). This background might also provide the context for Paul's comment in 4.10, where he connects his point about the enslaving 'elements' with their concern to observe the calendar with precision: 'You observe days and months and seasons and years!' In Judaism, calendrical matters are of great concern, since to be out of sync with the heavenly calendar results in the improper observance of Jewish holy days and festivals. To practise the law and maintain the covenant properly requires a strict interpretation of the movements of the stars, which participate in the heavenly spheres of life and worship.[27] While the Galatians may have worshipped the stars as divine beings prior to becoming Christians, a renewed interest in heavenly bodies may have been kindled among them by means of a completely different concern: in this case, not pagan piety but Jewish covenantal piety. If Paul's reference to the 'elements' includes a reference to heavenly bodies seen as spiritual beings, then he is depicting interest in Jewish calendrical observance to be no different from

---

[27] This is what motivated the calendrical debates in Early Judaism, as evidenced in the Book of Heavenly Luminaries (1 Enoch 72–82, esp. 82.4–6; 72.4–19), Jub. 6.23–38 (cf. 1.10, 14; 2.17–18; 4.17–18; 23.18), and various Qumran passages (CD 3.13–15; 6.18–19; 1QS 1.15–16; 10.1–7; 1QpHab 11.5–8).

the astral worship of their pagan days.[28] Since the coming of Christ, Jewish calendrical observance and pagan reverence for the stars equate to the same thing: forms of enslavement.

Parallels with 1 Corinthians 8–10 also suggest that Paul's understanding of the 'elements' involves their identification as suprahuman beings. As we have seen, in Gal. 4.8 Paul speaks of the 'elements' as 'beings who by nature are not gods' – no doubt referring to the spiritual beings that the pagans considered to be gods, even if he recasts them as something other than gods.[29] This same is evident in 1 Corinthians 8, where Paul discusses the issue of food sacrificed to idols. Although an idol may have no real existence (8.4), Paul recognises that spiritual realities are operative in the worship of idols, and goes on to state that Christian allegiance should be directed exclusively towards another spiritual reality, that is, towards the creator God:

> For although there may be so-called 'gods' (whether in heaven or upon earth) – and indeed there are many 'gods' and many 'lords' – nonetheless, our allegiance is to the one God (8.5–6a).

Paul's recognition that 'there are' spiritual beings identified by many as 'gods' is countered by his claim that these are only 'so-called' gods (λεγόμενοι θεοί). That is to say, although these beings exist, they are not worthy of the worship owed to the one God alone. The similarity with 'beings who by nature are not gods' in Gal. 4.8 is striking, and assists in a closer identification of the 'elements' of Galatians 4.[30]

It seems likely, then, that Paul considers the 'elements' to be personalised spiritual forces of some kind, supernatural beings that hold power over human beings in some fashion.[31] But more needs to be said in identifying them since, in the ancient

---

[28] Martin has challenged this generally accepted view of 4.10 (1996), but his challenge involves a whole-scale reworking of 'the Galatian situation' that is problematic. See above, chapter 2 n. 10.

[29] This is reminiscent of traditional Jewish polemic against pagan idolatry; cf. Isa. 37.19; Jer. 2.11; 5.7; 16.20.

[30] Another indication of similar concepts in these two passages is Paul's emphasis on being 'known by God'; cf. Gal. 4.9 and 1 Cor. 8.3.

[31] See especially Arnold, 1996, who demonstrates that στοιχεῖα must mean more than simply fundamental religious principles or the elemental 'stuff' of nature.

religious imagination, a plethora of divine beings of various sorts filled the suprahuman world. We can be more precise in identifying the 'elements'. From the contours of his argument in 4.1–11, it seems that Paul has in mind the tribal deities that were thought to oversee the nations on behalf of God. Other metaphors that Paul incorporates within this context all include an element of oversight and regulation; in 3.23–25 the law was likened to a 'pedagogue' (a custodial supervisor of sorts; see §6.3 below), while in 4.2 he speaks of having been under the guidance of 'guardians and trustees'. Evidently similar connotations are to be heard when Paul introduces the 'elements' in 4.3. If, as we have seen, these overseeing 'elements' are also angelic beings that hold sway over human beings in some fashion, then there is a perfect match between Paul's thoughts concerning the 'elements of the world' and Jewish traditions concerning the supervisory tribal deities.

The scriptural passage that seems to have provided the basis for Jewish speculation concerning the regulating angels of the nations is Deut. 32.8–9:

> When the Most High apportioned the nations, when he divided humankind, he fixed the boundaries of the peoples according to the number of the gods; the Lord's own portion was his people, Jacob his allotted share.

The word translated 'gods' here appears in the Greek Septuagint as 'angels of God' (ἀγγέλων θεοῦ). While the non-Jewish nations are directed and overseen by angels, such is not the case for the Jewish people, who enjoy God's own special attention and oversight. The same notion appears in the book of Sirach (second century B.C.E.): God 'appointed a ruler for every nation, but Israel is the Lord's own portion' (17.17).[32]

Although the tradition of national angels implies that they were appointed to order the life of the nations in accord with

---

[32] Under the influence of a growing angelology, this tradition could depict the archangel Michael as the angelic overlord of Israel, on behalf of God. Daniel 10 preserves this aspect of the tradition, where we hear of a stand-off between the angelic overlord (ὁ ἄρχων) of the kingdom of Persia and Michael, Israel's angel (10.13–14, 20–21).

God's will, a significant mutation of this is seen in Jubilees (second century B.C.E.), where we read:

> And he [God] sanctified them [the people of Israel] and gathered them from all the sons of man because (there are) many nations and many people, and they all belong to him, but over all of them he caused spirits to rule *so that they might lead them astray from following him* (15.31).

Here, the tradition concerning the angelic overlords of nations is given an ironic, negative twist; the tribal angels (cf. 15.32) are closely associated with 'evil spirits' and 'polluted demons' who rule over people towards destruction (Jub. 10.1–6). These demonic spirits are the army of the satanic Mastema who seeks to exercise authority over humanity and lead them astray (Jub. 10.1–9). In contrast, Israel is blessed to have God as her protector and overlord:

> But over Israel he did not cause any angel or spirit to rule because he alone is their ruler and he will protect them and he will seek for them at the hand of his angels and at the hand of his spirits and at the hand of all of his authorities so that he might guard them and bless them and they might be his and he might be theirs henceforth and forever (15.32).

The connection between God and God's people is one of intimacy in an unmediated relationship. This contrasts with the situation of the other nations, which are under the direct oversight of other spiritual forces in the course of their national life. Something similar can be seen from Deut. 4.6–8, where Moses instructs Israel to obey the statutes of the law in these words:

> You must observe them diligently, for this will show your wisdom and discernment to the peoples, who, when they hear all these statutes, will say, 'Surely this great nation is a wise and discerning people!' For what other great nation has a god so near to it as the Lord our God is whenever we call to him? And what other great nation has statutes and ordinances as just as this entire law that I am setting before you today?

Here, the distinctiveness of Israel lies in the people's observance of the law. This observance ensures Israel's relationship of intimacy with her God, a God who is 'so near'.

It is this tradition of tribal deities that best explains Paul's likening of the law to one of the 'elements of the world'.[33] Paul is reworking Jewish traditions that depict the people of the law as distinctive in both their lifestyle and intimacy with God, in contrast to the pagan nations under the oversight of tribal angels. Paul's reworking is evident in two ways: first, he locates intimacy with God in a context where nomistic practice is excluded (see §3.3 below); second, he finds the distinctive lifestyle of Israel under the law to be a variation on the theme of separate nations under the oversight of their own regulating national angels. It is not simply that the law became enlisted in the service of these national angels while remaining distinct from them.[34] Instead, Paul here views the law itself as analogous to the national angels. This seems to be due to the way that the law regulated the national life of Israel in a fashion comparable to the angelic regulation of the pagan nations.

This regulatory function of the law over the people of Israel is, of course, in complete accord with the original purposes of God in giving the law in the first place, as is clear from almost any passage randomly chosen from Deuteronomy. This is also clear from any number of passages from Jewish literature, not least Pseudo-Philo (first century C.E.), who speaks of the law as providing the distinctive 'rules for our race' (*Bib. Ant.* 12.2) whereby Jewish society was properly ordered. Passages such as this frequently depict observance of the law as marking Israel out as distinctive from the other nations, a theme that is frequently coupled with the notion of the pollutedness of other nations.[35] Whereas Pseudo-Philo revels in the fact that God has

---

[33] See, e.g., Howard, 1979: 66–82; Wright, 1991: 179; 1994: 233; Dunn, 1991a: 136–37; 1993b: 88–92. Wink provides a good overview of this tradition (1984: 26–32).

[34] As Arnold suggests (1996: 68); cf. Hong, 1993: 164. Rightly Martyn: 'in some fashion or other the Law *is* one of those elements' (1995: 17 = 1997: 126, emphasis his; cf. 1995: 27 = 1997: 135). In Romans 7, however, the law is, of course, distinct from the power of Sin that claims the law for its own purposes.

[35] For example, Jub. 22.16; 23.24; Pss. Sol. 2.1, 17.15, 23; *Bib. Ant.* 7.3; 12.4; 2 Bar. 82.5; 4 Ezra 6.56.

given 'rules' to regulate the life of Israel, Paul sees this to be no different from the divine institution of angelic beings to regulate the life of the pagan nations.

It is important to notice the shift in tone from Gal. 4.3 to 4.8–9. When he first includes the law among the 'elements' in 4.3, there is a sense in which this function of the law served a proper purpose, supervising the people of Israel and nurturing their 'up-bringing' before the time of Christ. The Jewish people were 'under law' (ὑπὸ νόμον) prior to the coming of Christ (3.25; 4.5) in the same fashion that a Graeco-Roman boy from a prestigious family was kept under the influence of a supervisor (ὑπὸ παιδαγωγόν, 3.25; cf. 3.24) or of guardians and trustees (ὑπὸ ἐπιτρόπους . . . οἰκονόμους, 4.2). But when the boy 'comes of age', the influence of such people becomes unnecessary, unhealthy and perverse. So too, with the coming of Christ, with the coming of 'the fullness of time' (4.4), such supervisory overseers no longer have any proper role in relation to God's people. Accordingly, a more negative portrait of the law is noticeable in 4.8–9. If the gentile Christians in Galatia were to observe the law, they would not be marking themselves out as the distinctive people of God; instead, they would simply be returning to the sphere of life from which Christ redeemed them – a world regulated and controlled by suprahuman agents, whom Paul calls 'weak and beggarly' in contrast to the overwhelming power of the sovereign God.

While supervisory angels were to be a means whereby God oversaw the whole world, in practice such a purpose deteriorated – or so we might be led to believe from statements attributed to Paul elsewhere in the New Testament. These same regulating angels seem to be what is meant in Eph. 6.12 by the word κοσμοκράτορας – a word that itself demonstrates the ambiguity surrounding these angelic 'cosmic rulers'. On the one hand, they can be said to 'hold' (κρατέω) the world (κόσμος), administering order and justice on behalf of God; on the other hand, their holding might easily become a 'grasp' (again, κρατέω) in which they seek to detract attention from the true creator God and establish themselves as the ultimate in divine power and authority. For the author of Ephesians (whether Paul or a disciple), these angelic beings (ἀρχάς) are the 'spiritual forces of evil in the heavenly places' (τὰ πνευματικὰ τῆς πονηρίας ἐν τοῖς ἐπουρανίοις). We have seen something similar in Jub. 15.31, where the angelic overseers are portrayed as spiritual forces that turn the nations away from the true God.

In Galatians, Paul portrays the law in less dramatic but somewhat similar terms, now that Christ has come. The law had previously regulated Jewish lifestyle in ways comparable to the angelic beings who oversaw the pagan nations. But since the coming of Christ that function of the law has come to be wholly negative, detracting people from the ways of God in Christ.[36] For Paul, nomistic observance would not lead the Galatian Christians into the realms of distinctiveness before God, as in Jewish tradition (cf. Deut. 4.6–8). Instead, it would lead them back into the realms from which they have come, the realms of undifferentiated enslavement to cosmic forces other than God.[37] In short, on this side of the eschatological divide, if nomistic practice is paraded as essential to Christian lifestyle, it simply becomes another form of paganism.

Paul's discussion of the 'elements' in 4.1–11, where the law appears in exclusive relationship with a single nation, is foreshadowed earlier in Galatians. Galatians 3.20 reads: 'a mediator is not of one, but God is one.' Had Paul written this sentence as part of an essay for his theological training, his instructor might well have asked for a few sentences of clarification and explanation. But Paul does not elaborate his meaning, and so we need to reconstruct what he has in mind from other clues.

The best way to do this is to start at the end of 3.20, where Paul affirms that God is one. It is important to note that Paul is here recalling the opening words of the *Shema*, the prayer recited morning and evening by pious Jews. This prayer took its

[36] Gaston writes: 'The *stoicheia* seem to have exercised a certain positive function in the administration of order in creation, but in a world come of age their rule has come to be confining and oppressive' (1987: 42).

[37] Martyn writes: 'the cosmic landscape is now shown to be a battlefield, and the need of human beings proves to be not so much forgiveness of their sins as deliverance from malignant powers that hold them in bondage' (1993a: 144 = 1997: 153).

name from the first Hebrew word ('Hear') of Deut. 6.4: 'Hear, Israel, the Lord, our God, the Lord is one.' Not only is this God identified as Israel's own God ('the Lord, our God'), but there follows immediately in Deuteronomy the command to obey God's commandments in order that Israel might live pleasingly before God, in distinction from the other nations (Deut. 6.5ff.). Monotheism (the God whom Israel worships is 'one') and covenant election (God is our God, we are God's people) are strongly associated in the piety of the Judaism of Paul's day.

In Paul's citations of the *Shema*, however, this connection between monotheism and ethnic primacy is broken apart. This is clear from 1 Cor. 8.6, where Paul locates Jesus Christ right in the heart of this traditional confession concerning the oneness of God.[38] It is also clear in Rom. 3.29–30, where Paul writes:

> Is God the God of the Jews only? Is he not also the God of the gentiles? Yes, of the gentiles also, since 'God is one', and he will make right the circumcised on the basis of faith and the uncircumcised through [this same (τῆς)] faith.

Paul consistently seems to think of the theme of the oneness of God with reference not to the distinctiveness of Israel but to the universality of salvation. If the one who alone is worthy of worship is the God who is one, that God cannot be the God of a single nation, but must be the God of all people.

This same conviction informs Paul's thoughts in Gal. 3.20b: 'but God is one.' But this scenario, in which God relates to a collectivity of people drawn from all nations, stands in contrast to 3.20a, which describes a situation where that universal collectivity is not in sight. If the mediator of 3.19 is Moses, as seems clear, so too the mediator of 3.20a must also be Moses, the one who delivered the law exclusively to the people of Israel.[39]

---

[38] See especially Wright, 1991a: 120–36; 1991b: 45–58; B. W. Longenecker, 1997: 126–28.

[39] The article ὁ in 3.20a is anaphoric ('the mediator referred to above'), as Wright notes (1991a: 169).

Paul's meaning in 3.20a, then, is recoverable, even if it is not obviously clear. Moses, the mediator of the law, has no relation to the universal people of God, the people collected from all nations; this is because the law was given by Moses (from God, through angels) to one nation only, Israel. That fact alone suggests that the law is to have nothing to do with God's worldwide people. If God is one, then God's people are to be drawn from universal ranks; if the law was given only to Israel, then it is not (directly) relevant to the eschatological people of the one God.[40]

From what we have seen, then, both Gal. 3.20 and 4.1–11 envisage the law to have an exclusive relationship to Israel. In 3.20a the law is given to a single national entity (Israel), while in 4.1–11 it is identified as being analogous to the angelic beings who were thought to have oversight of particular nations. The contrast to this situation of national demarcation appears in 3.20b, where the one God is shown to oversee a collective people drawn from the entirety of nations. To go back to the stipulations given through the mediator Moses, to return to the influence of the weak and beggarly 'elements', is to turn away from the intention of the one, sovereign, universal God, who is creating a catholic people in Christ.

Accordingly, in Paul's thought, God's 'oneness' – that is, God's sovereignty, supremacy over competing deities, and worthiness as the one who alone is to be worshipped – is advertised in the social constituency of God's people. God's eschatological triumph results in, consists of, and is exhibited by, the establishment of a community of catholic membership. The formation of such a group is itself the placard, the display, and the disclosure of the power of the ultimate divinity.[41] This fundamental tenet of Paul's vision for Christian corporate identity is articulated succinctly in Gal. 3.28: in the eschatological community of God's people 'there is neither Jew nor Greek, neither slave nor free, neither male nor female, for you are all one in Christ Jesus'. As will be shown below, social unity

[40] On this, see especially Wright, 1991a: 157–74.
[41] See Wright, 1994: 235.

of this sort has as its counterpart a relationship of unprecedented intimacy with the triumphant God.

3. The Intimacy of Sonship in Relation to the Sovereign God

One of the distinctives traditionally attributed to Israel as a
consequence of her oversight by God, rather than by a
regulating angelic being, is a relationship of intimacy with the
sovereign God. As we have seen, Deut. 4.7 articulates this
clearly: 'For what other great nation has a god so near to it as
the Lord our God is whenever we call to him?' For Paul,
however, when nomistic observance is perceived as a necessity
of Christian lifestyle, those who would observe the law place
themselves not within a relationship of intimacy with God but
within a realm ruled by suprahuman beings who are not worthy
of worship. Paul defines intimacy in ways that bypass observance
of the law altogether.

In Gal. 3.19c, Paul states that the law was 'ordained through
angels by the hand of a mediator' (διαταγεὶς δι' ἀγγέλων ἐν χειρὶ
μεσίτου). Paul's mention of angels here does not refer to the
national deities, the 'elements' of 4.3 and 4.9;[42] instead, Paul is
tapping into a different tradition altogether, one evident from
various Jewish texts. In this tradition, a great angelic presence
accompanied the giving of the law to Israel. The Hebrew of
Deut. 33.2 speaks of God coming from Sinai 'from myriads of
holiness' or 'with myriads of holy ones'; the Greek Septuagint
clarifies the passage, rendering it 'with him were myriads of
holy ones; with him were angels (ἄγγελοι) at his right hand'.
Other Jewish texts elaborate this tradition further (Jub.
1.27–29; Philo, *Somn.* 1.140–44; Josephus, *Ant.* 15.136), as do
two early Jewish-Christian texts (Acts 7.38, 53; Heb. 2.2).[43] This

---

[42] The identification of the angels of 3.19 with the 'elements' of 4.3 and 4.9 has
been suggested by Reicke, 1951; Percy, 1964; Bornkamm, 1974. See critiques
of this view in Bandstra, 1964: 58–59; Arnold, 1996: 61–63.

[43] On this tradition, see esp. Callan, 1980. Nonetheless, the presence of this
tradition in Acts, Hebrews and Galatians might have led scholars to give it a
higher profile in Jewish tradition than the scattering of references in Jewish
sources would otherwise suggest.

tradition concerning the angelic escort of the law served to amplify the glory of the Sinaitic law given to God's own chosen people.

It is possible that the agitators in Galatia were making use of this tradition in their efforts to entice the gentile Christians towards observing the glorious law. But if so, Paul is using it to other ends, in his attempt to derail gentile interest in nomistic practice.[44] He does this, however, not (as some have thought) by depicting the law as having originated from devilish angels who sought with evil intention to lead humanity into sin.[45] His statement that the law was given 'through angels' (δι' ἀγγέλων) implies that the angels were the instrument of the giving, not the source of the giving; the implied source of the giving is God.[46] Nonetheless, this tradition of the law's angelic escort takes on a negative emphasis in Paul's handling of it, where angelic escort implies mediation and mediation implies inferior revelation. The chain of mediation (God, angels, Moses)

[44] So R. N. Longenecker, 1990: 140.

[45] So Hübner, 1984: 26–33; Drane, 1975: 34, 113; and Lüdemann, 1989: 184; cf. somewhat similarly Hamerton-Kelly (1990: 60 n. 17). Others advocate a similar position, but do not speak of the evil intentions of the instigating angels; e.g., Räisänen, 1986: 130–31; Martyn, 1993b: 143 n. 17 (= 1997: 167 n. 15); 1995: 35; Barrett, 1994: 31; Sanders, 1996: 118 (contrast his 1983: 93); Stanton, 1996: 112–13. Stanton writes: 'Gal 3:18 refers to God's gracious gift to Abraham through a promise; God's role is emphasised by the placement of ὁ θεός at the end of the sentence. In the very next verse the giving of the law is referred to, but "God" is not mentioned explicitly; the silence is telling' (113). On the other hand, it may be that the subject of the first διά clause was expected to be carried over as the implicit subject of the second. Gal. 3.19, rather than stating God's non-involvement in the giving of the law, assumes God's involvement, while at the same time assuming that the law is not God's final and definitive involvement. This is in full accord with Paul's claim in 3.21 that the law is not 'against' (κατά) God's promises, evidently since it is still God's law, although not God's ultimate revelation.

[46] See especially Westerholm, 1988: 176–79; so too Dunn, 1993a: 190–91; Dahl, 1977: 173. In his thorough study of Anatolia, in which Galatia was located, Mitchell points out that 'Belief in angels as divine messengers had a long history in central Anatolia ... Angels, who linked men with the gods in all three religious systems, helped to bind together the diverse strands of pagan, Jewish and Christian belief in later Roman Anatolia' (1993: 2.46). That the Galatian Christians would have heard δι' ἀγγέλων to mean 'by angels' (as opposed to 'through angelic mediation') goes against this evidence.

disallows a relationship of intimacy with God by means of the law.[47]

But if this is what he has in mind in relation to the law in 3.19, something different emerges when Paul considers in 4.4–7 God's self-revelation in Christ. Once again, the context is wholly eschatological, as we have already seen from our consideration of the 'elements' in 4.1–11. In the 'fullness of time' (4.4), as the world lay enslaved to the 'elements' of the world, God took the initiative to act in a definitive fashion. For Paul, the importance of this divine initiative cannot be over-emphasised, lying as it does at the very heart of his gospel of grace. That divine initiative becomes embodied in the sending of God's 'son'. The phrase 'fullness of time' is significant in the context of Paul's discussion, since in 4.1–3 he has already contrasted the situation of under-aged minors with that of 'coming of age'. Previously, all people were as under-aged minors awaiting the time of their majority; as such, they were 'not any better off' than slaves. The coming of God's son has allowed those who were formerly no better than slaves to become sons themselves: 'God sent his son . . . in order that we [slaves] might receive adoption as sons.'[48] We will consider below Paul's understanding of the mechanics whereby slaves become 'sons' (see §3.4 below); for now, the theme of intimacy deserves highlighting.

The shift in focus from what God has done in Christ (4.4–5) to Christian sonship (4.6–7) pivots on the figure of the Spirit; just as God has sent the son (4.4), so God has sent the Spirit (4.6). The Greek wording of these two sentences shows the relationship clearly: ἐξαπέστειλεν ὁ θεὸς τὸν υἱὸν αὐτοῦ is parallel

---

[47] Although Wright argues against this interpretation as exhaustive of Paul's thought in 3.19–20, he nonetheless admits that it does justice to Paul's meaning at 3.19b, although not 3.20: 'there is perhaps a hint of the law's indirectness, being given to the people at two removes; the mention of angels in v. 19 makes its own point, and does not need to spill over into v. 20' (1991a: 172).

[48] Attempts at translating the Bible with inclusive language, while laudable in general terms, do not assist in making clear the way that Paul crafted his case in Gal. 4.4–7. There, the identity of Jesus as the son of God determines the identity of Christians as 'sons' of God, who have the Spirit of his son in their hearts; to identify Christians as 'children' (as in the NRSV, for example) threatens to unravel the close interconnections of Paul's imagery.

to ἐξαπέστειλεν ὁ θεὸς τὸ πνεῦμα. Although it would be anachronistic to read Paul in the light of later 'Trinitarian' formulations and creeds of the Early Church, it is nonetheless true that Paul envisages the sovereign divinity who is one in terms of three interrelated figures: God, Jesus, and the Spirit. The first is identified in this passage as 'father' (4.6), the second as 'his son' (4.4, 6), and the third as 'the Spirit of his son' (4.6). This depiction of the Spirit plays a crucial role in linking Christians with Christ, for the Spirit has been 'sent into our hearts' and, as the Spirit of the son, brings Christians into the realm of Christ's sonship.

This is further evidenced by the heartfelt 'cry' to God that the Spirit brings about in Christians: 'Abba, father'. Two things should be said about these two words. First, it is the Spirit that 'cries' them, not the Christian. This is clear from the Greek participle 'crying' (κρᾶζον), which is neuter, as is 'the Spirit' (τὸ πνεῦμα). The transformation from the state of childhood/slavery to that of sonship is not something that can be self-performed, subjectively conjured up by changing one's own personal demeanour or perspective. Instead, this transformation is something that catches people up within itself, arising from outside of them. So it is the Spirit's 'voice' that cries out to God on behalf of Christians.

Second, the cry that the Spirit offers on behalf of others is a cry of intimacy – 'Abba, father', a cry that echoes Jesus' own address to God. From gospel portraits of Jesus, we know that, in his prayers to God, Jesus frequently referred to God as 'father', the one to whom he was obedient.[49] While Jesus' use of this term when addressing God in prayer was not unique to the Judaism of his day,[50] it was nonetheless a notable feature. The

[49] Cf. Mk. 14.36; Mt. 6.9/Lk. 11.2; Mt. 1.25–26/Lk. 10.21; Mt. 26.42; Lk. 23.34; Jn. 11.41; 12.27–28; 17.1, 5, 11, 21, 24–25.

[50] 'Father' appears as a form of address in prayers to God in Wis. Sol. 14.3; Sir. 23.1, 4; 51.10; and 3 Macc. 6.3, 8. Jeremias argued that there is no precedent in extant Palestinian literature to Jesus' prayerful address to God as 'father' (1967: esp. 29), since the references in Wisdom of Solomon and 3 Maccabees are from the diaspora, and since (Jeremias surmises) the references in Sirach should read 'God of my father' rather than 'Lord, my father' and 'God, my father'. His reconstruction of Sirach, however, is not compelling, and his point about Jesus' exclusive use of 'father' claims too much. See, for example, Charlesworth, 1988: 133.

term was not a common form of prayer-address precisely (it seems) since it connoted familial intimacy, as opposed to the usual form of addressing God as 'King/Lord of the Universe', or some such title.[51] It is, of course, significant that the Aramaic form 'Abba' has been retained in the memory of the earliest Christians and seems to have some currency even among recently-converted gentiles in the Pauline communities (as here, 4.6; cf. Rom. 8.15). This may suggest that Paul's Christian instruction to gentile converts included some synopsis of Jesus' own life of obedient sonship to God, a synopsis complete with Aramaic soundbites. If his presentation in Galatians is anything to go by, the story of Jesus' life was not simply of historical interest for Paul, but was put to use in affirming the identity of his converts as those specially related to God. They had been brought into the sphere of Jesus' own intimate and obedient relationship to God, and in them the 'Spirit of his son' articulates the son's address to God: 'Abba, father'.

The theme of intimacy with God in 4.4–7, being focused exclusively on Jesus and the Spirit, contrasts with the image of the law's mediation in 3.19; the law cannot provide direct relationship with God, since the law has been doubly mediated by means of angels and Moses. In this way, Paul has subtly turned the tradition about the angelic mediation of the law on its head. Rather than demonstrating the glory of the law, the involvement of angels and of Moses in the giving of the law implies that the law can grant only indirect relationship with God at best. The agitators seem to have paraded the law as the means of ensuring intimacy with God. Paul, however, portrays the law as an instrument that disrupts the direct and intimate relationship with God that is found in Christ; the law thwarts God's intention to establish in Christ a people collected from all the nations of the world. After the coming of Christ, the law is comparable to an enslaving cosmic power that turns people away from direct, unmediated experience of the sovereign God. The latter experience is enjoyed only as one

---

[51] Cf. Dunn, 1975: 21–26; 1980: 26–28; Charlesworth, 1988: 132–34. Charlesworth states: 'Many early Jews tended to conceive of God as distant, visiting humanity only through intermediaries such as angels' (134).

enters the boundaries of obedient sonship that Jesus incarnated.

4. Participation in the Eschatological Order of Unity

We have seen that Paul sets his Galatian letter within an eschatological context, wherein the old world has been crucified to the believer and a new world established. The latter is a world of intimacy with God (4.4–7), in contrast to a divergent, opposing world that is dominated by evil (1.4), a world under the over-lordship of divine beings other than the true sovereign God (4.1–11). It is important now to consider how it is that Paul envisages the Christian benefiting from Christ's work and living within the parameters of this new world where divine victory is manifest.

Closely associated with the evocative concept of 'new creation' is another important term that Paul uses frequently throughout his letters: the term, 'in Christ'. The association of this term with 'new creation' is evident from a comparison of Gal. 6.15 and 5.6:

6.15: For neither circumcision nor uncircumcision matter at all, but new creation.

(οὔτε γὰρ περιτομή τί ἐστιν οὔτε ἀκροβυστία, ἀλλὰ καινὴ κτίσις.)

5.6: For in Christ Jesus neither circumcision nor uncircumcision has significance.

(ἐν γὰρ Χριστῷ Ἰησοῦ οὔτε περιτομή τι ἰσχύτε οὔτε ἀκροβυστία.)

In these two passages, Paul strikes the same eschatological tone by means of different terms. Whether Paul expresses himself by the term 'new creation' or 'in Christ', the end result is the same: circumcision has no function in defining the identity of God's eschatological people. The point to note is simply that 'in Christ' and 'new creation' are used by Paul virtually synonymously in these instances.

Paul's talk of being 'in Christ' assumes a rich complex of theological notions that go right to the heart of his theology. Behind it lies the motif of union with Christ – that is, the identification of the Christian with Christ in such an all-encompassing way that the Christian's own identity becomes intricately bound to, and intertwined with, that of Christ, to the exclusion of all others (e.g., 1 Cor. 6.13b–18a; 10.14–22).

Paul explores this relationship of union from two angles. On the one hand, he speaks of the Christian being incorporated into the events of Christ's death and resurrection: 'I have been crucified with Christ' (2.19). Passages of this sort run throughout the Pauline corpus, of which Romans 6 is the most extended analogy. To cite only one verse from there, Paul writes: 'For if we have been united with him in a death like his, we will certainly be united with him in resurrection' (6.5). Paul includes a participatory note in Gal. 6.17, mentioning the 'marks of Jesus' that are imprinted on his own body – referring to the physical scars and wounds that he accumulated throughout his ministry (cf. 2 Cor. 11.23–27) and recalling his emphasis on union with Christ in his suffering and death (2 Cor. 1.4; 4.8–10; Rom. 8.17; Phil. 3.10; Col. 1.24). On the other hand, as well as imagining the Christian to be participating in the events of Christ's life, Paul can speak of Christ being alive within the lives of Christians: 'it is no longer I who live but Christ lives in me' (Gal. 2.20; cf. Rom. 8.9–10; 2 Cor. 13.5). (This aspect of Paul's thought will be considered further in the chapters 4 and 7 below.)

These are two sides of the same coin: the Christian becomes incorporated into Christ and the experiences of his ministry, while at the same time the life of the Christian becomes the vehicle through which the living Christ is 'embodied' or 'enfleshed'. This notion of union with Christ is thoroughly christological in its focus, but includes other important dimensions as well: the soteriological, in that salvation is operative in the 'in Christ' sphere (cf. 2 Cor. 5.19a; Rom. 8.1); the ecclesiastical, in that it includes a corporate focus, comparable to Paul's talk of the 'body of Christ' (cf. 1 Cor. 12.12–13); the ethical, in that those 'in Christ' have been radically transformed and Christ now lives in them (cf. Rom. 8.9–10; 2 Cor. 13.5).

It is this theological matrix concerning the union between Christ and his people that Paul often has in view when he speaks of being 'in Christ'. While the phrase 'in Christ' can have various meanings in different contexts, the locative sense of being 'in Christ' is particularly significant, signalling the 'location' in which Christians exist, the sphere in which they are now 'located'.[52] So, for instance, in Rom. 8.1 Paul writes: 'Therefore, there is now no condemnation for those who are in Christ Jesus.' If the clause 'those who are in Christ Jesus' is thought simply to be synonymous with the adjective 'Christian', the rich texture of Paul's thought is missed at this point, since he has in mind an elaborate network of ideas that cohere around the image of union with, participation in, and incorporation into, Christ. All of this is thoroughly eschatological, as is clear from 2 Cor. 5.17, where Paul links the theme of 'new creation' with that of being 'in Christ' in a way similar to Gal. 5.6 and 6.15: 'Therefore, if any one is in Christ, new creation [literally]; the old has passed away, behold the new has come.'

In Galatians, this incorporative aspect of Paul's participationistic theology is implied in 6.14: through the cross of Christ 'the world has been crucified to me, and I to the world' (cf. 5.24: 'those who belong to Christ Jesus have crucified the flesh'). It appears explicitly in 2.19: 'I have been crucified with Christ.' But its corporate implications are developed fully in 3.26–28:

> For you are all sons of God in Christ Jesus, through faith. For as many of you as were baptised into Christ have clothed yourselves with Christ. There is neither Jew nor Greek, neither slave nor free, neither male nor female; for all of you are one in Christ Jesus.

Here we see three uses of the locative 'in Christ' motif (elsewhere in Galatians, see 2.4; 5.6), a motif that presupposes the notion of union with Christ. This motif of incorporative location in Christ explains how Paul can claim in 4.4–7 that the Christian has a share in Jesus' own intimate, obedient sonship. In fact, these two passages (3.26–28 and 4.4–7) explain and reinforce

---

[52] See, for instance, Sanders, 1977: 453–61. The phrase 'in Christ' is clearly used with flexibility by Paul (Bultmann, 1952: 328–29; R. N. Longenecker, 1990: 153). Seifrid rightly brings out its variety of nuances (1993), but in so doing he does not do full justice to the participationistic dynamic (1993). Much preferable is Witherington's analysis, where the 'core usage' of this motif involves 'being in Christ and spiritually united to him', identified as a 'crucial' element in Paul's thought (1994: 278).

each other: Paul can assume in 3.26 that to be 'in Christ Jesus' is to be a son of God since Paul knows Jesus to be the son of God (4.4, 6; cf. 1.16; 2.20); so too Paul can assume in 4.5–7 that redemption involves being adopted as sons into Jesus' sonship since he imagines Christians being united with and incorporated into Christ (3.26–28). Union with Christ, then, is the mechanism whereby believers are incorporated into the sphere of the new creation, the process whereby those enslaved to suprahuman powers become sons of the sovereign God.

This union with Christ is said to come 'through faith' in 3.26, and is expanded further in 3.27 by the image of baptism; being baptised *into* Christ (εἰς Χριστόν) facilitates the union between Christ and the Christian. For Paul, baptism represents the believer's transfer from the domination of the power of Sin to the realm of Christ's lordship.[53] Moreover, as we will see, the theme of incorporation into Christ provides Paul with a means of arguing against the necessity of nomistic observance, since to be in Christ is to be in Abraham (3.29) without the need to observe the law (see below, §6.4).

But Paul takes the theme of union with Christ in another direction as well. Not only is the Christian united with Christ, and thereby a son of God and an offspring of Abraham; the Christian is also united to other Christians. This is clear from 3.28, where some of the most fundamental social distinctions of Paul's day are listed and said to be of no significance 'in Christ' (cf. 5.6; 6.14): Jew/Greek, slave/free, male/female. Paul does not mean to suggest that Christians no longer have ethnic, social or sexual identity and differentiation; being 'in Christ' does not render Christians androgynous, for instance (although this was the way some in Corinth might have understood Paul).[54] Paul does not envisage the identity of Christians to be

---

[53] See Carlson, 1993; Meeks, 1983: 150–57.

[54] The issue of androgyny seems to lie behind Paul's statements in 1 Cor. 11.1–16. Some women were understanding God's salvation to involve the obliteration of sexual differentiation by androgynous transformation. Whatever else Paul might say in this passage, he is ultimately concerned to reinstate sex as an important aspect of one's personal identity, an identity that is not obliterated even if it is transformed. On this, see Scroggs, 1972; 1974; Meeks, 1974; Talbert, 1987: 67–71; Jervis, 1993: 235–38.

monolithically identical in matters of this sort. Unity for him does not mean uniformity. Paul perceives Christian unity to involve the coming together of diverse members who are joined despite (or better, because of) their diversity.

This social dynamic lies at the forefront of Paul's understanding of the new world in which God's eschatological power is at work. The corporate body of those 'in Christ' becomes unified not by a process of 'like attracts like', for the God who is one is the God of the plurality of peoples, and the testimony to God's transforming power is evident in a corporate body where the plurality becomes unified. In that collective of human diversity, Paul perceives God's eschatological power to be at work. The interconnectedness of diversity is unrealisable within the sphere of the present evil age from which Christ has delivered his people. Outside the sphere of God's power, plurality fragments into negative disassociation; within the sphere of God's power, plurality is brought within the positive context of interconnectedness and wholeness.

It is important to recognise that ecclesiastical unity for Paul is not an end in itself nor an anthropological maxim of some sort, as if he thought simply that being associated with others is an obvious good. Instead, the unity of diverse humanity in Christ is a theocentric symbol. It testifies to God's sovereignty in overcoming the forces of chaos that threaten his handiwork. It advertises God's transforming power and overlordship in Christ. Christian unity evidences that the high God, who is one and who alone is worthy of worship, is at work in the corporate body of those in Christ.

Paul is well aware, however, that ecclesiastical unity does not simply transpire out of nothing. Instead, it is the result of a transformation within the moral identity of those in Christ. The corporate unity that follows from God's triumph is itself the product of a pattern of social life animated wholly by the eschatological Spirit. It is to these matters that we now turn.

4

Eschatological Moral Identity

We have seen how Paul envisages a new sphere of existence to have been established in Christ, a sphere overseen by God rather than any lesser suprahuman forces, and one in which diversity is channelled into a balanced unity. But Paul has more to say about the way in which the machinery of this new sphere of existence is oiled, how healthy relations among the diversity of members are maintained in good order in order to testify to the triumph of God. Fundamental in this matter is the moral identity of the Christian and the Christian community. And, as will be shown, even on this score Paul retains a wholly eschatological point of reference.

This chapter highlights the way in which, for Paul, Christian self-giving love is itself a testimony to God's transforming power since, by necessity of its distinctiveness, love of this sort has its origin in no other source (§4.1). Conversely, any behaviour or attitude that does not spring from this kind of love is ruinous to God's new world order and detrimental to God's reputation as the world-sovereign. Paul's presentation in Galatians suggests that the latter applies to those who promote circumcision and nomistic practice as salvifically necessary (§4.2). Paul expects Christian moral identity to be exhibited in patterns of life that evidence the working of the Spirit. The embodiment of the Spirit within Christians results in the promotion of wellbeing both within and beyond the boundaries of the Christian community (§4.3). Moreover, the law finds its proper fulfilment in Christian self-giving, an eschatological trait enabled exclusively by the power of God (§4.4). In short, Paul envisages divine triumph to have as its corollary a transformation in the moral identity of God's people, a transformation at odds with the patterns that characterise life beyond the boundaries of the new creation.

1. Eschatological Conflict in Moral Orders

Even when he gives consideration to the practicalities of everyday lifestyle, Paul slips into an eschatological framework of thought. So, for instance, in Gal. 5.16–18 he incorporates the imagery of warfare to describe the moral situation of Christians in contrast to that of others:

> Walk by the Spirit, I say, and you will not perform the desire of the flesh. For the flesh desires in a way contrary to the Spirit, and the Spirit desires in a way contrary to the flesh; for these are at war with each other, in order that[1] you might not do the things that you would want to do. But if you are led by the Spirit, you are not under law.

Paul imagines a battle being waged between two powerful forces: that of the 'flesh' and that of the eschatological Spirit. Whereas here flesh can be spoken of as the operating principle of the present evil age, the Spirit is the operating principle of the new sphere of existence, the world that exists in contradistinction to the world to which Paul has died. The fundamental opposition between these two worlds comes to expression in Paul's imagery of conflict and warfare (5.17), a conflict that is being played out within the context of morality.[2] The two worlds that Paul envisages make themselves evident

---

[1] As this translation indicates, I take the ἵνα here to signal purpose rather than result.

[2] In this regard, we need to be clear about Paul's meaning when he writes in 5.17: 'in order that you might not do the things that you would want to do.' This is frequently read against the background of Romans 7, where the 'I' who speaks finds himself unable to do the good that he wants to do. But in Gal. 5.17 the phrase 'things that you would want to do' does not refer to 'good' things, as in Romans 7, but to the things that the flesh promotes (thereby relating closely to 5.13: 'Do not allow your freedom to be an opportunity for the flesh'). The warfare between the Spirit and the flesh means that enlistment with one or the other is required, and if one's enlistment is with the Spirit, then it cannot be with the flesh, thereby preventing the things that the 'flesh' would otherwise produce. On this, see especially Barclay, 1988: 112–15; Hansen, 1994a: 169–71; Fee, 1994b: 434–47 (cf. 428–29).

and are displayed in two distinct kinds of moral lifestyle: that determined by the flesh and that determined by the Spirit.

Paul does not leave his audience guessing as to what these contrasting forms of morality look like in concrete terms, but gives two lists of the kind of thing he has in mind, each of which helps to define the other by way of contrast. The second introduces what Paul calls the 'fruit of the Spirit' (5.22–23), which is said to consist of: love (ἀγάπη), joy, peace, patience, kindness, goodness, faithfulness (πίστις), gentleness, and self-control. These are qualities that enhance corporate life. Moreover, it may not be coincidental that love appears first in the list, giving it pride of place. Paul has emphasised love on three occasions thus far in his letter, and all of them in important contexts. Not only is love (as opposed to circumcision) the characteristic of those 'in Christ' (5.6; cf. 5.13), it is so precisely because Christians are joined in union with the one who himself demonstrated love (2.20). The love that Christ exhibited is defined further in 2.20 as his self-giving, the same quality that Paul highlights at the start of his letter (1.4). This quality of self-giving love seems, to Paul's mind, to be a wholly eschatological phenomenon, an eschatological quality reproduced in the lives of those united with Christ by means of the Spirit of Christ.[3] It is little wonder, then, that it appears first in the list, since Paul considered it to be the fundamental characteristic of Christ's own life and imagined it to be the context out of which all other Spirit-generated characteristics arise.[4]

In §3.4 above, we noted the important place in Paul's

---

[3] Paul also knows, however, that self-giving does not automatically come under the category of love, for there are other kinds of self-giving. So, in 1 Cor. 13.3 he writes: 'If I give away all my possessions, and if I hand over (παραδῶ) my body so that I may boast [or 'to be burned'], but do not have love, I gain nothing.' Paul is aware that extreme acts of charity and goodness may be motivated by interests other than love. A self-giving action may even be self-centred if, by performing such an action, one seeks to capture the attention of others or enhance one's own reputation. Paul knows that Christians may attempt to imitate Christ's own self-giving (cf. δίδωμι in Gal. 1.4; 1 Tim. 2.6) without replicating his attitude of love. Such people have missed the point, and 'gain nothing'.

[4] See Barrett, 1994: 45; Witherington, 1994: 297.

thought of the notion of union with Christ. As we saw, this includes both the Christian's having died with Christ as well as Christ's living within the Christian. The same idea is evident in 4.19 where Paul writes of Christ himself taking form within the corporate life of the Galatians: 'My children, for whom I am again in the pain of childbirth until Christ is formed in/among you (μέχρις οὗ μορφωθῇ Χριστὸς ἐν ὑμῖν).' The same is evident in another metaphor in 3.27 where, having been baptised in union with Christ, Christians are depicted as having been 'clothed with Christ' (Χριστὸν ἐνεδύσασθε). Being reclothed was commonly used in antiquity as a metaphor for spiritual transformation, but to be reclothed with Christ also carries other connotations of meaning, especially thespian imagery of an actor who dresses in a costume and assumes another person's character. In this way, the whole of life might be compared to a theatre in which Christians 'perform' Christ by means of their Christ-like character. For Paul, the corporate life of the Christian community is to be the social embodiment of the self-giving and loving Christ. This same conviction is evident also in 5.22–23, where the fruit of the Spirit can be thought of as dynamic extensions of Christ's own character and lifestyle, the means whereby Christ is embodied and performed.[5]

In essence, then, Paul perceives the issue in Galatia to be about the character and ethos of the eschatological community of the sovereign God, about the 'spirituality' of that community. Paul perceived social character to be demonstrative of a fundamental spiritual condition of a community's constituency, as the re-formation of an inner condition results in a re-formed community. Paul's case throughout Galatians is, then, primarily a charter and blueprint for social relationships within the eschatological community in which the sovereign creator is transforming people in conformity with the character of the loving and self-giving son.[6]

---

[5] Malina and Neyrey demonstrate how the metaphor of being clothed in certain apparel identifies one as belonging to a social group with certain characteristics and common traits: 'in antiquity and up to rather recent times, ethnic groups each had common, characteristic clothing, so persons were known by the clothes they wore' (1996: 133).

[6] On this as a general Pauline theme, see Hays, 1996b: 16–46.

This feature of self-giving love stands in stark contrast to the list of things that the flesh produces (5.19–21):

> sexual transgressions, impurity, debauchery, idolatry, sorcery, enmity, discord, jealousy, anger, self-promotion, dissensions, factions, envy, drunkenness, perverted revelry, and similar things.

Many of these entries appear in the plural in the Greek, suggesting that they refer not simply to internal attitudes, but also to concrete practices: attitudes and practices of enmity (ἔχθραι), of anger (θυμοί), of self-promotion (ἐριθεῖαι), and of envy (φθόνοι). Almost every entry of the list, then, has at least some tangible aspect to it. Paul does not think much about emotional disposition apart from its practical expression and outworking. The same applies, of course, to entries of Paul's fruit of the Spirit, so that when he speaks of 'love', for instance, the emotional connotations of this word are far overshadowed by the practical, concrete aspect whereby 'love' becomes realised in action. The same is true when Paul speaks in 5.6 of 'faith *working practically* (ἐνεργουμένη) through love'.

Paul's catalogue of 'works of the flesh' includes characteristics common to ancient vice-lists, whether those of Judaism or of hellenistic philosophers and Stoics. It does not take Christian insight to see the detrimental effect that many of the entries would have upon corporate life. But Paul's catalogue does more than parrot conventional vice-lists, and is not simply a list of corporate cancers. It serves as a collage of items that are expressions of, and are reducible to, a more fundamental demeanour: self-centredness, self-interestedness, self-indulgence, self-aggrandisement – in short, a demeanour of unhealthy self-referentiality. Such a disposition stands in complete disparity with the self-giving love of Christ and those united with him. This is especially clear in the middle of the list. After beginning the catalogue with items drawn from Jewish sensitivities concerning idolatry and immoral sexuality, Paul highlights attitudes and behaviour which are fundamentally self-referential. This point is also clearly made in 5.26, as Paul urges his readers not to become self-conceited, nor to provoke and compete with one another, nor to be envious of one another. It is as if Paul imagines a causal relationship in these aspects, indicating how a prior attitude of self-referentiality (self-conceited, or literally 'empty glory') becomes manifest in social situations marked out by discord and one-upmanship.

Paul's catalogue of 'works of the flesh' instils little hope for the health, stamina and durability of a 'fleshly' community, as its fabric will be torn apart by chaotic internal forces. He makes this point suggestively in 5.15: 'But if you continue to bite and devour one another, watch out lest you are consumed by one another' (cf. 5.26). These kinds of exploitative, destructive behaviours and attitudes have nothing to do with the cosmic power of the God who brings all things alive in a new creation. In fact, they run directly counter to Paul's view of the corporate character of God's people in Christ. The eschatological people of God are even in their diversity to be marked out by unity and solidarity, 'for you are all one in Christ Jesus' (3.28). This union of diverse people is enabled only by the eschatological character exhibited by Jesus Christ and brought to life within his people by the Spirit of Christ: that is, by means of love, defined not in terms of emotion or sentiment, but in terms of committed self-giving on behalf of others. Corporate unity within a diversity of unlimited proportions is both the demonstration and the microcosm of God's eschatological power. It is the mark and the result of God's invading sovereignty. Anything that undermines the cohesion of this eschatological product of God's powerful creativity obviously does not derive from God; undermining God's reputation as the cosmocrator, it belongs instead to the sphere of the 'flesh'.

2. The Moral World of the Agitators

Having mapped out two opposing spheres of morality, it is important to note where Paul locates those who are promoting nomistic observances as a necessary part of Christian lifestyle.

On this score, the picture is wholly clear. At every point, those who solicit others to observe the law are characterised in derogatory moral terms. On occasion they are depicted as manipulators and exploiters of others. So in 2.4 we hear of 'false brothers' who were secretly spying out those who found their 'freedom' in Christ, with the hopes of 'enslaving' them. In this regard, even the pre-Christian Paul plays a negative role, being portrayed as one who 'excessively was persecuting the church of God and trying to destroy it' (1.13). Just as 'works of the flesh' can destroy God's people from within their corporate body, Paul's 'earlier life in Judaism' resulted in the attempt to destroy God's people from outside their corporate body.

Elsewhere, those who promulgate nomistic practice are depicted in terms of self-promotion and the enhancing of one's own reputation. So in 4.17 Paul says that the Galatian agitators 'are zealous for you with improper motives', meaning that they seek the allegiance of the Galatians with the hopes of enlisting them as inferior dependants upon the agitators. Similarly in 6.12–13 the agitators want to 'make a good showing in the flesh' in order that 'they might boast about your flesh' – that is, they seek to heighten their influence, prestige and stature by bringing others under their control.

It is little wonder, then, that Paul considers the way of nomistic practice to end in fierce competitiveness and ambitious, cut-throat rivalry (5.15, 26).[7] So too, it is hardly surprising that, on three occasions, Paul couples together the destructive workings of 'the flesh' and nomistic practice: (1) to consider 'works of law' as salvifically necessary is to be controlled 'by the flesh' (σαρκί) rather than 'by the Spirit' (πνεύματι, 3.3); (2) to define Abrahamic heritage in terms of ethnic identity is to inherit identity that is 'according to the flesh' (κατὰ σάρκα) rather than 'according to the Spirit' (κατὰ πνεῦμα, 4.29); (3) those who are led by the Spirit are not 'under law' (ὑπὸ νόμον, 5.18), just as those who have been crucified with Christ have 'crucified the flesh' (τὴν σάρκα ἐσταύρωσαν, 5.24; cf. 2.19).

In passages of this sort, Paul links nomistic practice and the flesh together in a way that flies in the face of the whole of the Jewish tradition, where the law was thought to counter and be the corrective to what Paul calls 'the flesh'. No doubt the pre-Christian Paul would have maintained the same traditional view, as would those who were stirring up interest in nomistic

---

[7] Esler comments on 5.26: 'What we have here is virtually a summary of Mediterranean man, always seeking to provoke others who were not kin to social contests of challenge and response in order to win honour and to be able to boast accordingly' (1996: 236).

obedience at Galatia. But here the Christian Paul associates law and flesh in a context that opposes the Spirit. So, claiming that to be led by the Spirit results in not being under law, Paul immediately gives a catalogue of 'the works of the flesh' (5.19–21), as if his reference to the law paved the way for this 'fleshly' list. This list reinforces the point, depicting qualities which, to many a Jewish mind, mark out the decadence of the pagan world, in contrast to the obedience of God's covenant people. So, Paul unmasks the value-system of those who would observe the law and shows it to be nothing but a web of corruption and perversity.[8]

From this, the following observations need to be noted. In current study of 'Paul and the law', one might be forgiven for thinking that what Paul thought was wrong with the law and nomistic practice was either one of two things. On the one hand, some argue that the fundamental problem with observing the law was, for Paul, 'ethnocentrism', in which God's grace was thought to be restricted to a single national entity that observed the law – that is, ethnic Israel. On the other hand, others argue that the law was inadequate for Paul due to its failure to correct an inner, deeply-seated spiritual problem at the very core of human identity, and that Paul was addressing something far more radical than ethnocentric covenantalism. These two interpretative options have become deeply entrenched within scholarly camps that frequently have had little time for each other and that see the matter in an 'either-or' fashion.

This debate is unfortunate, precisely because it makes a dichotomy of two things that Paul holds together as one, introducing a distinction where Paul sees none. It is certainly true that the issue of nomistic observance focuses on matters of social boundary markers and group identity which pertain to ethnic Israel. But it is also the case that Paul finds the 'ethnocentric covenantalism' of the agitators to be a full-blown example of something fundamentally wrong within the human condition: that is, the tendency toward egocentrism and self-interestedness.

---

[8] Esler: The notion of 'flesh' stereotypes 'the whole social order which beckons beyond the boundaries of the group' of those in Christ (1996: 232).

To promote 'works of law' is to incorporate matters of the flesh into the gospel, thereby stripping it of the power of the sovereign God who brings into existence a united community transformed into the image of the self-giving Christ; instead, the gospel becomes a tool testifying to the power of those who would perpetuate their own self-interests by transforming others into their own image (4.17; 6.13). The ethnocentrism frequently induced by nomistic practice was itself, at least in Paul's analysis, a national advertisement of the egocentrism and narcissistic self-referentiality that is fundamental to the human constituency apart from the regenerative and recreative power of the sovereign God. Ethnocentrism and egocentrism are not different matters in Paul, but are one and the same phenomenon carried out on two different levels of existence; the contours of covenant ethnocentrism are themselves perceived to be demonstrations of the fundamental human condition.

Of course, Paul himself could be accused of promulgating a new form of 'centrism' – an 'ecclesiocentrism', or something of that sort. Paul's theological reasonings have social effect and, from one perspective, might be said simply to prioritise one social group by marginalising another. Moreover, such efforts might be thought of as themselves an exercise in self-promotion and advancement. But Paul did not find his ecclesiocentrism to be problematic or think of it in these terms, precisely because he perceived the social group of those in Christ to have a radically different type of identity to that of all other social groups. That is, the social cohesion of those in Christ did not derive from anything of their own doing. Their solidarity could not be attributed simply to a mutual interest, a common trait or a joint preoccupation. In Paul's mind, the social cohesion of those in Christ derives wholly from divine power, in contrast to all other forms of collective grouping. This is precisely why Paul finds the agitators' efforts to be so alarming, and why he envisages them to be introducing matters of the flesh into Christian community. As soon as Christian identity is founded on anything other than the invading grace and power of God, it takes on the character of any other social group. And as Paul seems to know, ordinary social groups cannot contain unlimited diversity without self-destructing (cf. 5.15, 26). For Paul, there is only one social group that can manage to sustain that delicate balance, and that group is not an ordinary one; it consists of those in Christ, whose corporate life is animated exclusively by divine power, thereby marking it out from all other social groups.

3. Christian Moral Identity

If, as we have seen, Paul understands the Spirit to be the driving force behind Christian moral identity, precisely this point drew sharp criticism from many of his contemporaries due to the dangers inherent in it. Some early Christians considered Paul's gospel, with its emphasis on freedom from the law, to result in and promote ethical antinomianism or libertinism – that is, self-indulgent lifestyle without moral restriction of any kind. In Rom. 3.8, Paul indicates that he has been credited with saying, 'Let us do evil in order that good might result', the point being that the worse one's behaviour, the greater God's grace is shown to be. The same perspective lies behind Paul's comments in Rom. 6.1 and 6.15: 'Are we to continue in sin that grace may abound? ... Are we to sin because we are not under law but under grace?' On each occasion, Paul rebuffs such a view of his gospel emphatically (μὴ γένοιτο, 6.2, 15; cf. 3.8).

Despite denials of this sort, in some quarters Paul seems to have acquired a reputation as an ethical antinomian. Some found this to be a theological deficiency lying at the very heart of Paul's gospel and were concerned with its dangers.[9] Others, however, seem to have been attracted to what they considered to be an ethical loophole in Paul's gospel. So, for instance, even

---

[9] Contemporary scholars often hold similar views. Schweitzer argued that Paul's ethical thinking had no recourse to the 'doctrine' of justification by faith (1931: 221). More recently, Lüdemann writes approvingly: 'Paul's opponents had ... noticed a real difficulty of Paul's doctrine of justification through faith, namely, that it did not necessarily lead to ethics' (1989: 186). While Gal. 5.6 shows their claims to be overstatements, it is true that Paul's ethics generally flow from a theology of union with Christ. But, as is demonstrated in chapter 5 below (esp. §5.5), Paul's 'faith' language is itself a language of participatory union in relation to the faithfulness of Christ, which serves as one platform for Paul's considerations of Christian moral identity.

prior to writing his letter to the Roman Christians, Paul knew of Christians in Corinth who had misapplied his gospel with disastrous ethical results. This is clear from 1 Cor. 6.12–20, for instance, where we learn that some Corinthian Christians were (for whatever reason) seeking the services of prostitutes. Significantly, they seem to have found Paul's own gospel to promote this perspective and behaviour, as in the slogan, 'All things are lawful for me' (cited twice in 6.12, and twice in 10.23). Paul's gospel of freedom from the law had reinforced their view of the body and the material world as fairly irrelevant to one's 'spiritual' constituency and inner being. To say that Christians are free from the law was taken to be equivalent to saying that Christians are free from moral concerns and ethical behaviour.[10] But Paul hopes to instil within the Corinthians an understanding of the ethical dimension of the physical body and the material world. The concrete situations of this world are the arena in which God's power is to be displayed in the everyday lives of transformed people. Since they have been united with Christ (6.15–17) and their bodies are the temple of the holy Spirit (6.19), he urges them to 'glorify God in your body' (6.20).

A similar problem seems to be evident in 1 Cor. 5.1–13, where a man is living immorally with his stepmother (5.1). What seems even worse to Paul is the fact that many of the Corinthian Christians were proud of this fact and boasted about it (5.2, 6). Presumably their boast lay in the assumption that this somehow proved that they were the 'spiritual' people whose salvation could not be affected one way or another by mere ethical concerns of this earthly world.[11] Here again Paul expects them to recognise that concrete behaviour is part and parcel of the

[10] Views of this sort had currency in various gnostic perceptions of the world, becoming full-blown systems in later centuries. On this perception of ethics in gnostic circles, see Rudolph, 1984: 252–57. On the Galatians' concerns about this view, see Mussner, 1974: 364.

[11] A similar dichotomy between salvation and the things of this concrete world seems to lie behind other issues in Corinthian Christianity, especially the view that salvation involved the transcendence of sexual differentiation (1 Cor. 11.1–16) and that salvation involved the soul shedding the mortal coil of the body (1 Corinthians 15).

salvation that God has effected on their behalf, and that moral identity falls within the orbit of salvation, rather than being irrelevant to it.

We have evidence that, even prior to these episodes within the Corinthian church, Paul's gospel was thought to lack ethical consequences and import. So, in his Galatian letter (probably written before 1 Corinthians), Paul seems cognisant of the charge that his gospel makes Christ to be 'an agent of the power of Sin' (ἁμαρτίας διάκονος, 2.17), a charge that he vehemently refutes. Christ is not a puppet through which the cosmic power of Sin is operative. Christians in Galatia were concerned to obey the law not simply in order to be included among the heirs of Abraham but also because it was the divinely-given standard by which behaviour is managed and regulated.[12] To say that the law is no longer relevant invites moral and social chaos – a form of chaos that runs contrary to the ways of the creator and covenant God of Israel, who overcame chaos in the ordering of creation (Genesis 1).

If Paul's case concerning Christian freedom from the law is ultimately to have force with these Galatian Christians, it must address this matter of practical lifestyle. Without a demonstration of how his gospel provides a framework out of which moral and social responsibility emerges, the concerns of the Galatians would not have been fully addressed.[13] It is no coincidence, then, that the main body of Paul's letter to the Galatians moves in its latter stages to consider the matter of Christian moral

---

[12] Philo argued that circumcision was a means of keeping libertinistic impulses in check, finding it to be symbolic of 'the excision of excessive and superfluous pleasure, not only of one pleasure but of all the other pleasures signified by one, and that the most imperious' (*Spec. Leg.* 1.9).

[13] Some have postulated that Paul's paraenesis in Galatians owes to the fact that after their conversion to Christianity the Galatians were in a state of 'moral confusion' (Barclay, 1988: 218) and needed ethical directives to restrain 'the lures of libertinism' (Jewett, 1971: 209) and '[f]lagrant misconduct' (Betz, 1979: 273; cf. 8–9). Such was possibly the case, although it is more likely that Paul's discussion of Christian moral identity arose as a consequence of his own theological presentation; as Drane writes, 'If Paul was to abolish the Torah for Christians, he had to show that this would not have disastrous ethical consequences' (1975: 8).

identity (5.13–6.10).[14] Galatians 5.13–6.10 has all too often been treated as if it were a mere footnote or appendix to the primary theological concerns of the letter. But in fact, this section is part and parcel of the singular matter that Paul has been addressing all along: the transformed identity of the Christian community. Before taking pen in hand and writing his own concluding paragraph in 6.11–18, Paul closes his dictated reflections in 6.10 with the strong double particle 'Therefore, then' (ἄρα οὖν). This draws the readers' attention to the point that is being made, as if to signal that the flow of Paul's thought is coming to a culminating point. And that point is shown to be about moral identity:[15] 'Therefore, then, as often as God gives the opportunity, let us work the good (ἐργαζώμεθα τὸ ἀγαθόν) for all people, especially for those of the household of faith.' In the previous verse Paul said something similar: 'Let us not grow weary in doing good' (τὸ καλὸν ποιοῦντες, 6.9).

It would not be surprising if Paul intentionally chose to emphasise, at the conclusion of this ethical section, these two notions of 'doing' and 'working'. If the Galatians imagined salvation to involve 'works' of law (2.16; 3.2, 5) and 'doing' the things of the law (3.10, 12; cf. 5.3), even Paul's message of freedom from the law includes an aspect of 'working' and 'doing' (cf. 6.4). Paul is insisting that his gospel, rather than being ethically deficient, includes the social dimension within its remit.[16] If

[14] On the paraenetic section of Galatians (Gal. 5.13–6.10) as essential to the theological dispute concerning the law, see especially Barclay, 1988; Matera, 1988; Fee, 1994a. Matera points out that 5.1–12 and 6.11–18 are closely related sections that argue against circumcision and bracket the paraenetic material of 5.13–6.10; in this way, 5.13–6.10 is drawn into the argument against circumcision, and is neither extraneous to the theological programme nor simply an explanation of the implications that arise from it. See also the interesting article by Esler, 1996, despite his excessive polemic.

[15] Cf. Rom. 5.18; 7.3, 25; 8.12; 9.16, 18; 14.12; 1 Thess. 5.6; 2 Thess. 2.15; Eph. 2.19. R. N. Longenecker suggests that 6.10 is the concluding point not simply of 6.1–10 but of 5.13–6.10, so that 5.13 and 6.10 form an *inclusio* of sorts (1990: 282).

[16] Contra Dibelius, who found Gal. 5.13–6.10, along with the rest of Paul's ethical exhortatory passages, to 'lack an immediate relation with the circumstances of the letter' (1934: 238); rather, Paul's ethical instruction is simply borrowed from hellenistic culture. Cf. too Betz, 1979: 292. Much preferable are the views of Barclay, Matera, Fee and Esler (see n. 14 above).

Christian transformation annuls the requirement to observe the law, it does not degenerate into ethical irrelevance. So Paul states at the beginning of 5.13–6.10: 'For you were called to freedom; but do not allow your freedom to be an opportunity for the flesh' (5.13).

In Paul's mind, transformation by the Spirit results in a dramatic inversion of lifestyle. So, as Paul expresses it in 5.6 (again cleverly reworking the notion of working), what matters is 'neither circumcision nor uncircumcision but faith working practically (ἐνεργουμένη) through love' – the love which itself is fostered by the Spirit. In this regard, it is important to notice the way that the list of the fruit of the Spirit in 5.22–23 becomes further amplified in 6.1–10. The character of 'gentleness' (πραΰτης) listed in 5.23 becomes the basis for Christian discipline and accountability in 6.1, wherein transgressors are to be dealt with 'in a spirit of gentleness' (πραΰτητος) rather than in an attitude of haughty contempt (cf. 5.15, 26). Similarly, the charge to 'bear one another's burdens' in 6.2 looks to be an amplification of the character of 'love' (ἀγάπη) listed in 5.22, since already in 5.13 Paul has identified service towards one another as being the product of love (διὰ τῆς ἀγάπης δουλεύετε ἀλλήλοις). Moreover, the exhortation to work for 'the good' (τὸ ἀγαθόν) in 6.10 has its antecedent in the list of the fruit of the Spirit which includes the character of 'goodness' (ἀγαθωσύνη, 5.22).

It seems, then, that Paul's admonitions in 6.1–10 are practical (but generalised) examples that demonstrate what a community is to look like when the Spirit of God is at work within its members. While it does not involve the abandonment of ethical living, as some wrongly suspected, neither does it result in the kind of haughty 'watchdog' morality that marked out the agitators who promoted observance of the law (§4.2 above).[17] Instead, it involves the considered enactment of personal and corporate responsibilities under the auspices of God. If the substance of Paul's exhortations in 6.1–10 are not distinctive from the moral codes of Paul's day, his

---

[17] Garlington (1991) contrasts the attitude of 'gentleness' in 6.1–2 with the portrait of Paul's zealous persecutions in 1.13–14.

understanding of the source from which ethical lifestyle springs is altogether different. For Paul, Christian ethical behaviour emerges from the Spirit who produces manifestations of eschatological character. As we have already seen, this eschatological character is itself an amplification of the character of the one who loved and who gave himself. And as we will see, Paul claims that the same character is the fulfilment of the law, a claim to which we now turn.

4. Christian Fulfilment of the Law

After the letter introduction of Gal. 1.1–5, Paul curses those who 'pervert the gospel of Christ' (1.6–9), thinking of the agitators who were encouraging Galatian Christians to become circumcised and observe the law. About these people he has nothing good to say, even suggesting that they castrate themselves (5.12) if they are so interested in cutting. Moreover, his description of the law includes a rather negative aspect. Despite having been given by God, it has no power to bring life or righteousness (3.21) and, since the time of Christ's coming, it acts like an enslaving tribal deity that detracts people from knowledge of the true sovereign God (4.8–9). To do the law is to be children of slavery rather than children of freedom (4.21–5.1), and results in being severed from Christ (5.4).

With all this in view, it is of great significance that Paul found a place for Christian fulfilment of the law within his gospel.[18] If, as we have seen, Paul considered the character of Christ-like self-giving love to be the manifestation of God's eschatological in-breaking, in 5.13–14 he goes further to say that this same eschatological character is also the means whereby the law is fulfilled.[19] Having established that Christian freedom is not to become an opportunity for the flesh in 5.13a, Paul continues in 5.13b–14 to draw out the converse side of Christian freedom – that is, Christian responsibility: 'through love, live lives of

---

[18] Cf. Lüdemann: 'Freedom from the law only inadequately describes Paul's attitude to the law' (1989: 186). Cf. Davies: 1984: 96.

[19] Cf. Mussner: '[D]as Gesetz ist immer dan erfüllt, wenn das Liebesgebot erfüllt wird' (1974: 370 n. 26).

service to one another. For the whole law is fulfilled in one word: "you shall love your neighbour as yourself".'

To summarise the law in terms of love is not without precedent in the Judaism of Paul's day,[20] but the effect of Paul's statement runs directly contrary to Jewish expectations. To the majority of his Jewish contemporaries, if the law can be said to be fulfilled in love, it would have been illegitimate to say further that loving behaviour replaces the need to obey the law. But that is precisely what Paul has in mind. For Paul, all that the law was intended to bring to fruition materialises and is fulfilled in manifestations of Christian love. Although Paul does not use this conviction to argue explicitly against the need to observe the law at this point, this is the effect of his statement. It is as if Paul is saying to the Galatian Christians: 'You want the law? Fine with me, but in fact the law is fulfilled not by observing its commands, as you have been led to believe, but by living cruciform lives of self-giving service.'

Here we can contrast what Paul says in 5.3: 'Again I testify that everyone who becomes circumcised is bound to do the whole law.' The difference between 'doing the law' in 5.3 and 'fulfilling the law' in 5.14 lies primarily in the verbs 'to do' (ποιεῖν) and 'to fulfil' (πληροῦν). Those who consider circumcision and other 'works of law' to be required for membership in the covenant people of God must recognise that adherence to the law demands doing all the prescriptions of the law. By contrast, those who walk by the Spirit in loving service to others meet the standard upheld in the law by means of that service, even though they do not observe the prescriptions of the law (cf. Rom. 8.4; 13.8–10).[21] Although the period of law

[20] E.g., Mk. 12.32–33; Lk. 10.26–28; b. *Šabb.* 31a; *Gen. Rab.* xxiv.7; *Sifra* on Lev. 19.18.

[21] See especially Westerholm, 1988: 201–205; Barclay, 1988: 135–41. Hübner locates the difference between 5.3 and 5.14 in the Greek construction of ὅλος ὁ νόμος (5.3) and ὁ πᾶς νόμος (5.14); the substantival construction of the former allows for a reference to the Mosaic law, while the attributive construction of the latter demonstrates that something else is in view, an ironic reference to a generalised sense of law that applies to the Christian (1975). Hübner is followed by Hamerton-Kelly (1990: 67), but the criticisms of this view are compelling; see, for instance, Barclay, 1988: 136–37.

One passage needs further consideration in defence of the interpretation

observance has come to an end, the Mosaic law nonetheless comes to its fullest and proper expression in the loving service of those who are being transformed by the Spirit of Christ into conformity with the self-giving character of Christ.[22] In this way, whereas law and Christ seem to have been at odds with each other in Paul's mind throughout the letter thus far, in 5.13–14 he brings them together in terms of a Christ-like attitude of service and love.

A similar phenomenon is evident in Gal. 6.2, where fulfilment of the law (πληροῦν again) is seen in the relationships of those who live by the Spirit as they 'bear one other's burdens'. Says Paul, this fulfils 'the law of Christ' (ὁ νόμος τοῦ Χριστοῦ). It is often claimed that Paul does not mean ὁ νόμος here to refer to the Mosaic law;[23] instead, it must refer to the social teaching of Jesus as a form of Christian halakah,[24] or in a more general way to a 'norm' or 'principle' of Christian living patterned on

---

given here. In Rom. 2.14, Paul speaks of non-Christian gentiles 'doing' (ποιεῖν) the law; there, however, the context of Paul's case is quite different, his intent is enormously polemical, and his train of thought itself is problematic (see B. W. Longenecker, 1991: 186–89, 194–95), to the extent that the occurrence of ποιεῖν there should not be used to interpret its meaning in Gal. 5.3. Cf. Westerholm, 1988: 203 n. 18. Barclay calls Rom. 2.14 'an erratic block on the Pauline landscape' (1995: 108).

[22] Paul's view diverges from some Christian ecclesiastical traditions, as well as the view of a few Pauline scholars. Lüdemann, for instance, claims that for Paul 'Christians fulfill it [the law] in practicing the love-command and the decalogue' (1989: 185). This seems to me to be precisely the opposite of what Paul intended, at least in Galatians. The law is fulfilled by Christians, true, but in Paul's view Christians do not practise anything except walking by the Spirit (Gal. 5.16–18, 25) and putting their faith in practice through love (Gal. 5.6); in these things, the law is indirectly fulfilled. To seek to fulfil the law or any part of it, however, even 'the love-command and the decalogue', opens the door to fleshly competitiveness and its disastrous consequences. This point is not qualified or controverted by Paul's talk of Christians doing the 'commandments of God' in 1 Cor. 7.19, which does *not* refer to prescriptions of the law, some of which are relevant to gentile Christians (contra Tompson, 1990; 1996); such a view over-interprets this expression, which should be pressed no further than referring 'to the ethical imperatives of the Christian faith' (Fee, 1987: 313).

[23] So Lührmann, 1978: 97; van Dülmen, 1968: 66–68.

[24] Dodd, 1968; Davies, 1980: 142–45.

Christ's own model.[25] There is some cause to think that Paul is redefining things here somewhat, but it seems unwise to evaporate all reference to the Mosaic law in this phrase; the links between 5.13–14 and 6.2 are too strong to suggest otherwise. Both passages speak of (1) relationships of Christian mutuality and service in connection with (2) the verb 'fulfil' (πληροῦν) and (3) the noun 'law' (νόμος). That 'law' in 6.2 includes some reference to the Mosaic law finds further support from the possibility, suggested by some, that the term 'the law of Christ' had first been introduced to the Galatian situation by the agitators who claimed that the Mosaic law has been affirmed and rightly interpreted by God's Messiah.[26] If Paul is countering the agitators' understanding of such a phrase, he does so by claiming Christian relationships of loving service to be the sole fulfilment of that law.

In 5.13–14 and 6.2, then, the concept of law has undergone such a drastic redefinition with reference to the Spirit of Christ and the community of Christ that Paul can go so far as to identify it as the 'law of Christ' – that is, the Mosaic law that comes to its fullest and proper expression in the relationships of mutual service within the community of those whose lives are being transformed by the Spirit in conformity to the character of Christ.[27]

Accordingly, Paul's comments in these passages depict a dramatic shift in his tone about, and characterisation of, the law. Whenever he has the matter of nomistic observance in view, Paul attacks the law as a threat to the singularity of the gospel. In Gal. 5.14 and 6.2, however, the context has shifted, allowing Paul to claim that the singular gospel facilitates, in an indirect

---

[25] Räisänen, 1983: 79–80; Hays, 1987: 276. Räisänen finds νόμος in Rom. 3.27 and 8.2 also to mean 'principle', two passages where I suspect Paul still has the Mosaic law in view (B. W. Longenecker, 1991: 207–10, 241–45). See also P. W. Meyer, 1990; Hays, 1996a: 153–54; Dunn, 1996b.

[26] See Martyn, 1985b: 314–17 (cf. 1997: 17–18); Hong, 1993: 114.

[27] For similar views, see Sanders, 1983: 97–98; Barclay, 1988: 125–35; Kertelge, 1984: 389–91; 1989: 333; Dunn, 1993a: 322–24; Hong, 1993: 170–83; Stanton, 1996: 15–16. Martyn asks whether it is 'better to see in 6:2 a referent to a different Law or to a principle? By no means! All thirty-two instances of the term νόμος in Galatians refer to the Law of Moses' (1995: 38; cf. 39 n. 60).

fashion, the fulfilment of the law.[28] If Paul's context of thought has shifted, the constant throughout it all is the singularity of the gospel, whereby observance of the law is excluded and whereby the law is indirectly fulfilled by means of Christian character. Despite all that Paul has said against living in accordance with the prescriptions of the law, in the end he wants to demonstrate that his gospel not only excludes the charge of antinomianism but also provides the only possible avenue for 'fulfilling' the Mosaic law (as distinct from 'doing' it) within the community of those in Christ. It is perhaps here in Gal. 5.14 and 6.2, more than anywhere in the Pauline corpus, that we can observe most clearly Paul's deeply-ingrained impulse to maintain a place for the law within his understanding of the gospel. In a letter where such a concern is least likely to appear, even there Paul finds a way to situate the law within the context of the gospel in a fashion (albeit highly polemical) that is not antagonistic to the gospel.

We do well here to compare Paul with Jewish covenantal theologians of his day. For them, two things usually defined each other mutually: the law and the people of God. That is, the way that the law was defined impacted upon the definition of the identity of the covenant people, just as one's understanding of the latter determined how one understood the former. These two notions, the law and the people of God, were to cohere with one another, dovetailing and blending with each other.[29] In this, Paul's claims at 5.14 and 6.2 seem little different. Even for Paul, the people of God are those who, by definition, fulfil the law (although this has been defined so as to exclude any notion of 'doing' or 'performing' the law).

Along with this, it is important to note that Paul seems to apply the term 'the Israel of God' (τὸν Ἰσραὴλ τοῦ θεοῦ) to the Christian community whose constituents are of various ethnic origins and identities (6.16). If this is the correct interpretation

---

[28] Lull: 'The law finds its fulfillment in the fulfillment of the Abrahamic covenant' (1991: 261 n. 42).

[29] Sandmel: 'the people Israel and the Torah constituted a blended entity; without Israel the Torah had no significance, and without the Torah Israel had no uniqueness' (1978: 182).

of the phrase,[30] then Paul has eroded the ethnic reference of this term in order to apply it not simply to believing Jews but to Christians whose ethnic heritage may have nothing to do with Jewish parentage.[31] So, after having charged that what matters is 'neither circumcision nor uncircumcision but a new creation' (6.15), Paul pronounces a blessing of peace and mercy 'upon those who walk in line with this precept – that is, upon the Israel of God'. Having identified those in Christ as the offspring of Abraham (3.29; 4.21–31) and the sons of God (4.5–7), it is a short step to identify them, as he does at the close of his letter, as 'the Israel of God'. In the end, Paul demonstrates that his gospel is the only means whereby the law is fulfilled by those in Christ who, consequently, can be identified as the Israel of God. No covenant theologian of Paul's day could have hoped to demonstrate more by way of a convergence in the notions of nomistic fulfilment by the people of God.[32]

Having seen how Paul reformulates notions of the law and 'the Israel of God', it now is pertinent to determine whether there is any sense in which, after such a drastic redefinition of terms, Paul continues to retain a significant place for the ethnic people of Israel. Moreover, does he envisage God's eschatological ways to relate in any way to the ethnic people of Israel, whom Paul elsewhere identifies as 'beloved for the sake of their forefathers' (Rom. 11.28)? Issues of this sort will be discussed in the next chapter.

---

[30] For a defence of this reading of τὸν Ἰσραὴλ τοῦ θεοῦ, see Becker, 1989: 492–94; Kraus, 1996: 251–52. This reading is simply asserted without defence of any sort by Harvey, 1996: 225–26. An opposing view is held by, among others, Dunn, 1993a: 345–46.

[31] He does something similar in Phil. 3.3 where he identifies Christians as 'the [true] circumcision'; cf. Rom. 2.25–29. It is important to note, however, that Paul uses the term 'Israel' in Romans 9–11 with a wholly ethnic reference, even in 9.6 where he narrows it briefly to refer to ethnic Jews who believe in Christ.

[32] Compare Sanders' observation of the 'two pillars to all forms of Judaism: the election of Israel and faithfulness to the Mosaic law' (1983: 208). Paul's presentation in Galatians seems to involve the redefinition of these two pillars in the light of his christology and pneumatology, but not the abandonment of them.

5

Christ, Israel, and Covenant
Theology

We have already seen (in chapter 4, above) that, despite his criticism of 'doing' the law, Paul orchestrates a way in which he can claim that the law is fulfilled by the Christian community whose members act in ways of self-giving love and service. For Paul, this is the only way that the law can be 'fulfilled' in any sense of the word. Moreover, we saw that Paul applies the title 'the Israel of God' to the Christian community of Jewish and gentile believers. Further still, as we have yet to see (in chapter 6, below), Paul suggests that the law was intended to have influence over the people of Israel only within a certain period of time. These aspects of Paul's case converge on questions of salvation history: What views did Paul hold in Galatians concerning the history and people of Israel, in relation to God's eschatological activity in Christ?

These matters will be addressed in this chapter. In the first section (§5.1), we consider the view that salvation history is absent in Galatians, and highlight the few but significant passages which suggest that a more nuanced view does better justice to the matter. Then, we discuss the controversial Greek phrase πίστις Χριστοῦ (§§5.2 and 5.3), and consider its role as a key theological centre of Paul's presentation in Galatians, especially in articulating a Christian form of covenant theology (§5.4). These features affirm that the situation of the covenant people of Israel plays an important role in Paul's understanding of God's eschatological activity in Christ, and demonstrate Paul's ability to engage on occasion in certain forms of covenant theology.

1. Christ and the Situation of Israel

In chapter 1, we considered the views of J. C. Beker and J. L. Martyn concerning the vacuity of a salvation historical perspective in Galatians. For Beker, this theological vacuum represents a shattering of Paul's overarching worldview, caused by the way in which a theology of salvation history was being exploited by those who promoted nomistic observances. In effect, to use Beker's own terminology, the 'coherence' of Paul's gospel was undermined in his letter to the Galatians by the pressures of situational 'contingency'. In Galatians Paul does not depict Abraham as the father of the Jewish people, as he does in Romans 4, nor as one of the Jewish patriarchs from whose ethnic lineage the Messiah comes, as in Rom. 9.5. Instead, in Galatians the dispensation of circumcision and law is irrelevant to the promises given to Abraham and fulfilled in Christ. The law, according to Beker, was not given in order to create a covenant people of God; instead, it served merely a negative function, demonstrating the plight of sinful humanity in order to augment the solution of God's activity in Christ. While this might be said to have salvation-historical significance of sorts, it nonetheless has nothing to do with a salvation-historical view whereby God's activity in relation to his people culminates in Christ as the apex of it all.

On this point, Martyn is in complete agreement, ardently expressing the view that the people of the law in the period before Christ is not perceived by Paul in Galatians as a covenant people, and that, moreover, Christ in Galatians has no positive relationship to the history of a covenant people. According to Martyn, there is no salvation history prior to Christ, at least as Paul argues in Galatians; instead, salvation history begins with the coming of Christ.

Beker and Martyn rightly find that the situation in Galatia seems to have caused Paul to emphasise the discontinuous aspects of his gospel at the expense of a fully-articulated view of salvation history. If one hopes to find a developed Pauline view of eschatology that is simultaneously favourable to the notion of salvation history, one would do well to begin with texts other than Galatians. Nonetheless, the view of Beker and Martyn is in need of some adjustment. And even if this is a small adjustment, it is a significant one nonetheless, and one that puts the matter of Israel's history solidly on the agenda in the study of Galatians. This important revision to the view of Beker and Martyn focuses on the way that Paul locates the coming of God's son within Israel's own historical context.

This conviction is evident in passages outside of Galatians, as is especially clear from Rom. 15.8–9: 'Christ has become a servant of the circumcised to reveal the covenant truthfulness of God (ὑπὲρ ἀληθείας θεοῦ), in order to confirm the promises given to the patriarchs, and in order that the gentiles might glorify God for his mercy.' That is, Christ has entered into the history of Israel's own situation, demonstrating in the process how God is faithful to the promises made to the patriarchs of the Jewish people; and moreover, this confirmation and culmination of God's covenant relationship with Israel (focused on the person of Christ) results in salvation even for the gentiles.[1] (Paul says something similar in 2 Cor. 1.20, where he simply affirms that God's promises 'find their "Yes" in him [Christ]'.) For our purposes, what a text like Rom. 15.8–9 makes clear is that the extension of God's covenant 'truthfulness' to include even the gentiles has passed through the terrain of Israel, whose 'servant' Jesus became. Here Paul has assumed much about a theology of salvation history and God's covenant with Israel in relation to eschatological salvation in Christ.

But if such can be said for a text like Romans, Beker and Martyn think the same cannot be said of Galatians, where a salvation-historical perspective of Israel's past is undetectable. But is it really? Two passages seem to suggest otherwise. In Gal. 3.13–14 Paul writes: 'Christ redeemed us from the curse of the law, having become a curse for us ... that the blessing of Abraham might come upon the gentiles in Christ Jesus, that we might receive the promise of the Spirit through faith.' It is important to determine the referent of 'us' in 3.13: 'Christ redeemed *us* from the curse of the law ... by having become a curse for *us*.' Does 'us' refer to Christians generally, or to Jews, specifically Jews who have put their faith in Jesus? While a case

---

[1] For an interesting, if speculative, study of Rom. 15.7–13, see Keck, 1990.

can be made for either reading, the latter seems preferable, especially in view of the lexical and structural similarities between 3.13–14 and 4.4–5. The verb 'redeem' (ἐξαγοράζειν) alone is enough to turn our attention to 4.5, since that verse is the only other place in the Pauline corpus where 'redeem' carries the same meaning as it does in 3.13.[2] An analysis of 4.4–5 will lend clarity to Paul's case in 3.13.

Galatians 4.4–5 is theologically suggestive even in its structure, since it appears to have been constructed along the lines of a carefully balanced *chiasmus* in which the structural centrepiece and focus is Israel, her situation and her redemption (B and B[1]):

A   God sent his *son*, born of a woman
  B   born under the *law*
  B[1]   in order that he might redeem those under the *law*
A[1]   in order that we might receive adoption as *sons*.

The theological import of this passage is highlighted by the careful structuring evidenced in the pattern noted above. As the centre-point of the *chiasmus* indicates, God's eschatological activity operates through Christ who 'was born under law in order to redeem those under law'. God's universal redemption required that the messiah come 'under law', where Israel herself had been (3.23; cf. 4.21; 5.18), rectifying that situation (e.g., 'to redeem those under law') in order that Jesus' intimate sonship to God might be made available to others beyond that situation. In this way, Gal. 4.4–5 reveals the following chronological series of events: (1) the situation of Israel is the context into which God's son was 'sent', in order that (2) that same situation might be redeemed, with the result that (3) salvation might be offered on a universal scale, beyond the exclusive boundaries of the people of Israel.[3] The means of salvation

---

[2] ἐξαγοράζειν appears elsewhere only in Eph. 5.16 // Col. 4.5, where it has a different sense.

[3] Martyn argues against this interpretation of Gal. 4.4–5 (1991: 178 n. 41). He claims that Christ's identity 'under the law' refers to his identity as a human being, since Paul viewed the human condition as one of enslavement (as the preposition 'under' might suggest). But this is certainly a forced reading of the passage, devised perhaps to salvage his arguments about the absence of

for the Jewish people has been effected by the entry of Christ Jesus into their own situation; this results in the opportunity of salvation extending to the gentiles by this same Christ Jesus.

This pattern sheds light on 3.13–14, and in particular on the double reference to 'us' in 3.13. Just as the redemption of those 'under law' in 4.4–5 refers to a redemption of Jews (evidently Jewish Christians, the 'remnant' spoken of in Rom. 11.5), so too the 'us' in 3.13 is not inclusive of Jews and gentiles but has a decidedly ethnic referent: 'Christ redeemed us Jews' – that is, Jewish Christians. Accordingly, these verses envisage a scenario in which Christ (1) takes upon himself the Jewish condition of being cursed by the law (3.13b), and (2) redeems that condition (3.13a), in order that (3) a new age might be established in which salvation is available to all in Christ (3.14).[4]

Along with Rom. 15.8–9, then, these two passages in Galatians depict a process in which the historical situation of the people of Israel needed to be redeemed before a new eschatological sphere of existence could arise. It is not wholly legitimate, therefore, to suggest a dramatic contrast between Romans and Galatians in relation to a salvation-historical perspective and the people of Israel. In both cases, the redemption of Israel's covenant context is assumed to be the prerequisite for the subsequent expansion of salvation to an unlimited, universal extent. While the passages in Galatians do not explicitly outline a progressive development in salvation history leading up to a final eschatological conclusion in Christ

---

any form of salvation history in Paul's thought in Galatians. While Paul may well have viewed the human situation as conditioned by enslavement, as Martyn suggests (e.g., Gal. 4.1–9), the point is that the form of enslavement taken by Christ was precisely that of Israel, 'under the law'.

[4] On this, see especially Hays, 1983: 116–17; Donaldson, 1986. Donaldson writes: 'the redemptive road passes through the territory of the law (and its people) ... It was not possible to make an end run around the law and those in its domain. Rather, the way forward for both Jew and Gentile required the redemption of Israel from its plight ... For Paul the law was not a dead end side trail but rather something lying squarely on the path of redemptive history' (102–103; cf. 106). The same point is made in relation to a proposed 'extended exile' theology by Wright, 1991a: 137–56, and by Scott, 1993. A quite idiosyncratic, and unconvincing, view is proposed by Dalton, 1990.

(and on this we are in agreement with Martyn and Beker), they do depict a scenario in which Israel's situation has been, and needed to be, addressed and remedied before salvation could be extended without restriction.

It is also significant that, although this view appears in only two passages in Galatians and does not receive extensive elaboration, the two passages play an important role in the development of Paul's argument and are centres of weighty theological reflection. Moreover, both passages are frequently thought to have been traditional material or formulae, something especially likely to be the case for Gal. 4.4–5, which probably circulated within the Christian circles of Paul's day. Accordingly, Paul seems to be tapping into well-known material that centres attention on Israel as the locale of redemption in relation to universal redemption. Even in Galatians, Paul does not feel the need to expound upon or explain the traditional material, but assumes that his audience is familiar with it, even developing his own case on the basis of that assumption.

So we see two significant passages in Galatians that are suggestive of an underlying theology of salvation history in relation to ethnic Israel. In effecting salvation in Christ, God has not avoided, neglected, trivialised or rendered irrelevant Israel's situation. Instead, the situation of Israel is the arena wherein God's transforming power has initially been operative before extending to universal proportions. The rectification of Israel's predicament, rather than its abandonment, stands as the prerequisite for the inauguration of the new world. Israel's own situation has been the place where God had already been at work (e.g., giving the law), and it has become the inaugural locus of God's eschatological initiative (e.g., sending his son) in order to transform Israel's situation and consequently to inaugurate a new age. Eschatological deliverance required the initial transformation of Israel's situation. Instead of an aversion to a theology of salvation history in relation to the covenant people Israel, Paul's case in Galatians positively requires it, even if that theological dynamic is neither developed extensively nor worked out in terms that place the Christian community within the unfolding story of ethnic Israel.

For Paul, then, even in Galatians the redemption of Israel's predicament is the necessary pre-condition for the establishment of the new age. From what we know of Jewish covenant expectations of the day,[5] it is likely that, in his pre-Christian career, Paul would have maintained the same inseparable connection between the restoration of Israel and the emergence of the eschatological age. And even after his encounter with the risen Lord, Paul's expectations in relation to these two intertwined phenomena remained intact. They simply became associated with Jesus Christ who had effected the means for Israel's redemption and, thereby, inaugurated a new age of salvation that included not only Jews but gentiles as well.

As we will see in chapter 6 (§6.6 below), the redemption of Israel from the curse of the law (3.13) has as its theological presupposition the notion of the 'faithfulness of Christ' – an important feature in Galatians from which Paul gets much theological mileage in articulating his own version of covenant theology, as the rest of this chapter demonstrates.

2. The 'Faithfulness of Christ' Tradition

On two occasions in Galatians Paul uses a phrase that has been the subject of occasional controversy. Recent decades have seen a growing dispute regarding the meaning of the phrase πίστις ['Ιησοῦ] Χριστοῦ, and it might be fair to say that neither side of the debate can claim to have settled the matter. On the one hand, it is possible to read the phrase to mean that Christ is the object of πίστις ('faith'), in which case Χριστοῦ is (usually identified as) an objective genitive ('in Christ'), rendering the phrase to mean 'faith in Christ'. On this reading, the πίστις is that of human believers who acknowledge and commit themselves to Christ. On the other hand, it is possible to read the phrase to mean that Christ exemplified πίστις ('faithfulness') within his own life, in which case Χριστοῦ is (usually identified as) a subjective genitive ('of Christ'). On this reading, the πίστις

[5] See, for example, Wright, 1992a: 268–79, 331–34. The 'we' of 3.14 is ethnically inclusive (= 4.5b), unlike the 'us' of 3.13 (= 4.4–5a).

is that of Christ himself who demonstrated within his own life a quality of 'faithfulness' before God.[6]

A decision on this matter is determined by a mixture of intricate considerations, and there is plenty of room for interpretative artistry to enter the decision-making process one way or another, as one interpreter will give more weight to one consideration while the next will give more weight to another. This is the kind of issue on which a consensus view is unlikely to emerge.

Having said this, however, it appears to me that, of the two options, reading the genitive as subjective ('faithfulness of Christ') is preferable. In the 1980s, both sides of the debate presented grammatical, stylistic and exegetical arguments to support their positions.[7] The superior arguments were shown to favour the subjective genitive reading.[8] More recently, a syntactical grammar of the New Testament has shown that the objective genitive reading ('faith in Christ') has little force, concluding that on balance the subjective genitive reading has better evidence in its favour.[9]

A further factor supporting the subjective genitive reading comes from Rom. 3.25. There, Paul incorporates into his presentation what is likely to be an established Christian

[6] Some who hold to this interpretation translate πίστις as 'faith', the 'faith of Christ'. I prefer to render it 'faithfulness' for two reasons. First, because it seems the broader of the two terms, in that it includes the other within its own meaning, whereas the opposite is not immediately obvious. Second, because it seems more appropriate to the theological issue of covenant fidelity that is evident in most places where the phrase appears in Paul, thereby doing better justice to the dynamics of Paul's case.

[7] Especially Hultgren, 1980, and Williams, 1987: 431–37.

[8] We await a serious response to Williams' consideration of relevant syntactical matters that demonstrate the strength of the subjective genitive reading (1987). Dunn tried to offer this (1991), but relied heavily on Hultgren's argument (1980) concerning the anarthrous formulation of πίστις Χριστοῦ as his primary argument in favour of the objective genitive reading, without taking into account Williams' compelling counter-arguments. Moreover, Dunn seems to accept a subjective genitive reading of διὰ τῆς πίστεως αὐτοῦ in Eph. 3.12 (733), a significant concession on his part! So too he finds Jas. 2.1 'to speak of Christ's faith, that is, Christ's faithfulness' (1991: 212).

[9] Wallace, 1996: 114–16. Wallace notes that Dunn's grammatical arguments in favour of the 'faith in Christ' reading (1991) contains some miscalculations.

confession. Within this traditional material we find the Greek phrase διὰ [τῆς] πίστεως: 'God set him forth to be an atoning sacrifice, διὰ [τῆς] πίστεως, by means of his blood.' This Greek phrase is commonly thought to be a Pauline insertion into the formula – an insertion that makes the formula more 'Pauline', since it now includes a reference to Christian faith. That it is an insertion is further indicated by its awkward placement between two notions that focus on Christ rather than the believer: Christ was put forward as an 'atoning sacrifice' by means of his 'blood'.[10]

But this argument fails to be convincing. It is not at all obvious that Paul has awkwardly inserted πίστις into the otherwise natural phrase 'atoning sacrifice by means of his blood' (ἱλαστήριον ἐν τῷ αὐτοῦ αἵματι). If that had truly been the traditional phrase, and if Paul had wanted to include a reference to Christian faith within it, surely he could have done so in a manner that avoided clumsy, second-rate measures without interrupting the flow of the imagery describing Christ's death. Ultimately the insertion theory adds mistake to mistake. In doing so, it unfortunately draws attention away from a crucial aspect of early Christian thought: the faithfulness of Christ. The far better view of the phrase διὰ [τῆς] πίστεως finds it to be original to the traditional material in 3.25, rat ιer than a Pauline insertion. Moreover, the πίστις phrase is most naturally under-stood to be an attribute of Jesus' life.[11] Accordingly, all three terms of Rom. 3.25a (ἱλαστήριον, πίστις, αἷμα) are descriptive of Jesus in his obedient death on the cross: 'whom God put

[10] E.g., Käsemann, 1980: 98; Wilckens, 1978: 1.194; Martyn, 1993a: 133 n. 2, 138 n. 2 (=1997: 143 n. 6, 147 n. 14). Martyn, however, thinks that, as a close second, it may be original, in which case it refers to the faithfulness of God (cf. Pluta, 1969). Either way, Martyn thinks the 'faithfulness of Christ' motif (πίστις Χριστοῦ) to be Paul's own invention (141). As will be shown below (§5.4), however, in Gal. 2.15–16 Paul seems to think of the faithfulness of Christ as something that all Christian parties have in common.

[11] As noted above (n. 10), some have taken διὰ [τῆς] πίστεως to be a reference to God's covenantal faithfulness. This would make good theological sense, but the notion of God's covenant fidelity is spoken of later in the tradition by the term δικαιοσύνη rather than πίστις (3.25b–26). Moreover, a reference to divine fidelity would interrupt the obvious descriptions of Christ's death (ἱλαστήριον, αἷμα).

forward as an atoning sacrifice (ἱλαστήριον), through (Jesus') faithfulness (πίστις), by means of his blood (αἷμα).'[12]

Romans 3.25 seems, then, to include an established confessional statement within earliest Jewish Christianity that speaks of the faithfulness of Christ as a central feature in the process of salvation. This then provides the necessary control for understanding the πίστις Ἰησοῦ Χριστοῦ formulations that occur in Rom. 3.22 and 3.26 (one on either side of πίστις in 3.25), both of which expect the subjective sense, as would all other occurrences of the phrase throughout the Pauline corpus.[13]

The importance of this traditional feature of early Christian theology for Paul's letter to the Galatians will be considered specifically below (§5.4). First, however, it will be instructive to consider how this traditional feature was put to use by Paul in letters other than Galatians.

3. Paul's Use of the 'Faithfulness of Christ' Theme outside of Galatians

Outside of Galatians, Paul uses the phrase 'the faithfulness of Christ' in Phil. 3.9 and Rom. 3.21–26 (cf. also Eph. 3.12). In the former case, having listed the features for boasting in his Jewish identity and fervour for the law, Paul cites these features of his past life to be now as 'loss' (ζημίαν) and 'excrement' (σκύβαλα) to him, in order that he might be found in Christ (ἐν αὐτῷ). And so he states: 'Not having my righteousness on the basis of

---

[12] See B. W. Longenecker, 1993. Cf. van Henten, 1993, who finds πίστις to be one feature of a traditional martyriological triad (πίστις, ἱλαστήριον, αἷμα), in which 'πίστις probably refers to the faithfulness of the martyr until death'. For an earlier articulation of this view, see Williams, 1975. D. A. Campbell finds πίστις to refer to the faithfulness of Christ, but does not think this passage to be a pre-existing tradition of the church (1992), while Kraus takes πίστις to refer to Christian faith and thinks the passage to consist of an earlier Christian formula (1991: 187).

[13] I take almost all occurrences of πίστις which are not modified by a genitive in reference to Jesus (as in Gal. 2.16, 20; 3.22; Rom. 3.22, 26; Phil. 3.9; Eph. 3.12) to be references to the faith of the Christian, except for (1) ἐπὶ τῇ πίστει in Phil. 3.9 which refers back to the just mentioned πίστις Χριστοῦ, (2) the τὴν πίστιν formulations of Gal. 3.23 and 3.25, which primarily (but not exclusively) refer to the just mentioned πίστις Ἰησοῦ Χριστοῦ of 3.22 (the τὴν is anaphoric), and (3) the πίστις of Rom. 3.25.

law but on the basis of the faithfulness of Christ' (μή ἔχων ἐμὴν δικαιοσύνην τὴν ἐκ νόμου ἀλλὰ τήν διὰ πίστεως Χριστοῦ), a righteousness described further as being 'from God based on that [τῇ] faithfulness' of Christ (τὴν ἐκ θεοῦ δικαιοσύνην ἐπὶ τῇ πίστει).

This is a dramatic redefinition of right relationship with God centred on Christ and his faithfulness, in contrast to Paul's own nomistic observance. The most poignant note here is the contrast between, on the one hand, Paul's own 'blamelessness' with regard to righteousness 'in [the sphere of] law' (κατὰ δικαιοσύνην τὴν ἐν νόμῳ γενόμενος ἄμεμπτος, 3.6) and, on the other hand, the righteousness that comes through the faithfulness of Christ (τὴν διὰ πίστεως Χριστοῦ, 3.9). A new order of 'power-existence' (3.10) has come into being through Christ which can be said to arise out of a faithfulness (Christ's own) that qualitatively surpasses all other expressions of faithfulness. In fact, with Christ's faithfulness in view, Paul looks back with hindsight upon his own blamelessness in the law and sees it to be as worthwhile as excrement. To be in Christ is to have his (and only his) faithfulness as the mark of one's own identity before God.[14]

The same notion is evident in Rom. 3.21–26. Positing a contrast between 'works of law' (ἔργα νόμου, 3.20) and the 'faithfulness of Jesus Christ' (πίστις Ἰησοῦ Χριστοῦ, 3.22, 25), Paul writes in 3.21–22:

> The righteousness of God (δικαιοσύνη θεοῦ) has now been manifest apart from law ... through the faithfulness of Jesus Christ (διὰ πίστεως Ἰησοῦ Χριστοῦ) to all who believe (εἰς πάντας τοὺς πιστεύοντας).

Here Paul envisages God's faithfulness to the covenant promises (δικαιοσύνη) being fulfilled in, and operating through, Christ's own faithful life, for the benefit of those who have faith.

---

[14] The participationistic note of ἐν αὐτῷ in 3.9 needs to be highlighted, lest an unnecessary criticism be thrown at the 'faithfulness of Christ' interpretation at this point in the manner of Dunn's charge: 'the vital means by which the righteousness actually comes to the individual is left unexplained' (1991: 744).

The same is true of 3.26, where Paul claims that God 'brings into right relationship' (δικαιοῦν) the one who lives on the basis of the faithfulness of Jesus (τὸν ἐκ πίστεως Ἰησοῦ), and that such even proves God's covenant faithfulness to Israel (δίκαιον). This appears to mean that the faithfulness of Christ, through which God's eschatological righteousness has broken into this world,[15] is being replicated within the lives of those who believe, and only on that basis is a right relationship with God established.[16] The believer is one in whom the faithfulness of Christ is operating, as opposed to one whose identity is marked out by faithful nomistic observance.

In all of this, there is an implicit contrast between the fidelity of Jesus and that of Israel. In Rom. 2.17–3.20, one of Paul's concerns is to demonstrate that Israel's corporate life was marked out by 'faithlessness' (ἀπιστία, 3.3) due to her position 'under the power of Sin' (3.9), along with the gentiles (cf. 1.18–32). The result of Israel's election (2.17–20) has not been, as it should have been, the affirmation of the sovereignty of God throughout the world, but the dishonouring of God (2.23) and the consequent mockery of Israel's God by the gentiles: 'For, as it is written, "The name of God is blasphemed among the Gentiles because of you"' (2.24). This disastrous result is the outcome of Israel's disobedience (2.21–24), her lack of covenant fidelity. In contrast, Jesus' faithfulness serves as the embodiment of fidelity through which God's covenant righteousness can now flow to the whole world. Rather than gentiles blaspheming the name of the covenant God of Israel due to Israel's own disobedient faithlessness, gentiles can now enter into the salvation offered by God by means of their faith, due to the obedient faithfulness of Jesus Christ.

This is not much different from Paul's claim in Rom. 15.8–9,

---

[15] The eschatological note of all this is significant (νυνὶ δὲ πεφανέρωται ... διὰ πίστεως Ἰησοῦ Χριστοῦ, 3.21–22; πρὸς τὴν ἔνδειξιν τῆς δικαιοσύνης αὐτοῦ ἐν τῷ νῦν καιρῷ, 3.26), being reminiscent of ἀποκαλύπτεται in 1.17.

[16] Accordingly, Dunn's estimate is wrong on two accounts when he claims: 'To understand πίστις Χριστοῦ as referring to *Christ's* faithfulness would not only weaken the emphasis on human faith (like that of Abraham) but also confuse and even divert attention from the emphasis on *God's* faithfulness' (1991: 742).

as we have seen above (§5.1). In that passage, Jesus' life of service to 'the circumcised' was the means of demonstrating God's covenant truthfulness to Israel, 'in order that the gentiles might glorify God for his mercy'. Following on from this, Paul immediately cites four scriptural passages which demonstrate further that the purpose and result of this process has always been the praise of the God of Israel by the nations of the world (15.9–12).

In this way, in both Romans 2–3 and Romans 15 Paul seems to be tapping into a long-established (but not unanimously held) scriptural view that Israel was to be the locus of divine splendour throughout the world (Isa. 49.3), a light to the gentiles concerning the sovereign God of Israel (Isa. 42.6–7; 43.10–21; 44.8; 49.6), and the channel through which the peoples of the earth will process to worship God in obedience (Isa. 2.1–4; Mic. 4.1–3; Zech. 2.11; 8.20–23).[17] In the faithful ministry of Jesus, Israel's commission has been fulfilled, as salvation is now available to all through the one who embodies faithfulness acceptable to God. So, an expansive, paraphrastic rendering of Rom. 3.25–26 is as follows:

> God has put Jesus forward as a means of atonement through (Jesus') faithfulness by his blood … in order to demonstrate his own (God's) covenant righteousness (δικαιοσύνης) in the present time of eschatological dawning (ἐν τῷ νῦν καιρῷ), thereby proving that he is faithful to his covenant promises (δίκαιον) and brings into right relationship (δικαιοῦντα) those who live on the basis of the faithfulness of Jesus (τὸν ἐκ πίστεως Ἰησοῦ).

Informing this significant passage is a view of covenant relationship that is evident in much of the literature of Early Judaism – a view in which the authentic fulfilment of the covenant between Israel and her God was expected to result in the eschatological dawning of a rightly-ordered world under the sovereignty of Israel's God.[18] With this expectation in view,

---

[17] Only biblical passages have been cited here, although many extra-biblical Jewish sources depict the same conviction; see further, B. W. Longenecker, 1989: 107–11.

[18] See, for instance, Wright, 1992a: 268–79.

Rom. 3.25–26 suggests that a new-world order of divine sovereignty is emerging from the context of Jesus' faithfulness.

The above quotation from Rom. 3.25–26 has omitted a clause which needs to be considered here in relation to this theme of the fulfilment of the covenant relationship between Israel and her God. After stating that God put Jesus forward to be a means of atonement, we hear that this was 'to demonstrate God's covenant righteousness (δικαιοσύνης) due to his forbearance by not dealing harshly with sins formerly committed'. Mindful that this is probably part of an early formula that originated in Christian circles predominantly Jewish, this reference to previously committed sins would seem to refer (at least primarily) to sins committed by Jews prior to the time of Christ.[19] Within this early Christian confession, there lies an implicit contrast between the way that Israel's sin was dealt with before Christ and the way it has been dealt with by God in handing Jesus over as a means of atonement.

Many questions could be asked on the basis of this formula as to how the early Jewish Christians envisaged the relationship between what occurred in Christ and what went on previously in the Jewish sacrificial system. For our purposes, however, it is enough to note how the theological perspective of this formulaic material coheres with the conviction that the salvation of Israel's situation results in the emergence of a new eschatological situation. In Rom. 3.25, the forgiveness of Israel's sins, which previously had not been fully dealt with, has now been accomplished in the death of Christ, with the result that the eschatological age has dawned not simply on behalf of the people of Israel, but on behalf of those who, by faith, are caught up within the arena of Jesus' own faithfulness. This is much the same as the theological convictions evident in Gal. 3.13–14, 4.4–5 (itself a strong candidate for being an early Christian tradition) and Rom. 15.8–9. In Rom. 3.25–26, the death of Jesus is the means whereby the redemption of Israel can take effect. This is the consequence of God's initiating activity

[19] See Stuhlmacher, 1994: 61; Dunn, 1988: 173; Martyn, 1993a: 133–34 n. 4. Contrast Williams, who thinks it to refer to the sins of gentiles prior the time when they became Christians (1975: 26–34).

(3.25a) and the demonstration of God's covenant faithfulness (3.25b–26a), in order that right relationship with God might be extended in the eschatological age to all those who are identified with Jesus' own faithfulness (3.26b).

We have seen various places and ways in which Paul, often using formulaic material of the early church, affirms that God's action in Christ had to do in the first instance with the righting of Israel's situation. But this redemption of Israel had immediate consequences, both temporally and logically, resulting in the extension of God's offer of salvation on a universal scale without regard for ethnicity. Moreover, the motif of the 'faithfulness of Christ' plays an important role in this theological perspective. Paul borrows this motif and elaborates it in his own discourse on the purposes of God in relation to Israel and the world. It now remains to consider how he applies the same motif within his letter to the Galatians.

4. The Faithfulness of Christ as a Theological Centre in Galatians

In his letter to the Galatians, Paul uses the motif of Christ's faithfulness at three places: 2.16, 2.20 and 3.22–23. Our primary focus will be on the former two occurrences and their place within 2.15–21. Initially, however, consideration will be given to Gal. 3.22–23, which may indicate something about the relationship between the believer's faith and Christ's faithfulness.

Paul's reference to the 'faithfulness of Jesus Christ' in 3.22 continues to have some effect in 3.23, where he speaks of πίστις having 'come' (ἐλθεῖν, cf. 3.25) and having been 'revealed' (ἀποκαλυφθῆναι). Although the faith of believers may be included within Paul's sights at 3.23, he likely has Jesus' own faithfulness primarily in view,[20] as his use of articles and verbs suggests. The article τήν appears before each occurrence of πίστις in 3.23 and in each case is anaphoric, thereby signalling that what is being spoken about is the πίστις previously mentioned in 3.22, where πίστις is that of Jesus Christ. This is further confirmed by Paul's choice of verbs in this verse, since it would

---

[20] Cf. Hays, 1985: 230–32; Martyn, 1997: 122.

be strange to speak of generic human faith having 'come' and 'been revealed' (note also the aorist tense of each verb). Moreover, the latter verb is used in Galatians only in relation to God's own 'apocalyptic', revelatory initiative (1.16; cf. 2.2). It is possible, however, that Christian faith is also included in the πίστις of 3.23, since he speaks in 3.24 of Christians being justified 'by faith'. In this case, at least as Paul envisages the matter here, Christian faith cannot be separated from the faithfulness of Christ. Whereas πίστις Ἰησοῦ Χριστοῦ includes a subjective genitive in 3.22, it seems to take on the character of a genitive of origin or authorship or source when it is anaphorically referred to by πίστις in 3.23. So, Paul envisages Christ's πίστις leading to the enlivenment of πίστις in the lives of others.

With that relationship in mind, the rest of this chapter gives consideration to Gal. 2.15–21, one of the most important passages in Galatians where Paul engages in a theological discourse concerning Christian identity – a discourse informed by covenantal categories of thought.

That 2.15–21 includes an exploration of covenant theology is signalled early on by Paul's comments in 2.15, where 'Jews by nature' (φύσει Ἰουδαῖοι) and 'gentile sinners' (ἐξ ἐθνῶν ἁμαρτωλοί) function as stereotypical depictions of insiders and outsiders to the covenant – stereotypes common in much of Jewish literature of the time but soon to be disqualified by Paul. If the stereotypes are shown to be defective, however, the context of covenant theology is not. This is clear from the five occurrences of the δικαι- root in 2.15–21 (2.16 [three times], 17, 21). 'Righteousness' terminology is firmly rooted in the deep soils of Jewish covenant theology. To be marked out by righteousness, or to be justified, is primarily about having membership within the covenant people of the just and sovereign God whose own covenant righteousness will be established once and for all in the eschatological in-breaking of divine sovereignty.[21] Our purpose here will be to see how the motif of the faithfulness of Christ informs the theology of Gal. 2.15–21.

---

[21] 'Righteousness' terminology is flexible enough to connote various nuances, but they generally cohere within the broader context of the covenant relationship between the creator God and God's elect people. See, for instance, Onesti and Brauch, 1993; Williams, 1980: 260–63; Hays, 1992.

In section §5.2 above, we saw that the motif of the faithfulness of Jesus Christ was not a Pauline invention but was already a central component of early Christian understanding about God's covenant righteousness processing triumphantly in eschatological splendour (Rom. 3.25–26). In view of this, it comes as no surprise to find Paul assuming in Gal. 2.15–16a that some level of agreement exists among Christians over the fact that covenant righteousness is through the faithfulness of Jesus Christ. While there may have been disagreement as to the implications of this, nonetheless Paul expected all those cognisant of this articulated form of Christian covenant theology to affirm (εἰδότες) that the basics of Christian identity have first and foremost to do with the fidelity of Jesus Christ (διὰ πίστεως Ἰησοῦ Χριστοῦ) rather than with the performance of covenant 'works of law' (ἐξ ἔργων νόμου). As in Rom. 3.25, so too here Paul goes back to the basics of Christian covenant theology upon which all are agreed: the πίστις (Ἰησοῦ) Χριστοῦ, which, as in Rom. 3.25, refers to the faithfulness of (Jesus) Christ.

In Gal. 2.16b, Paul suggests that Christians participate in Jesus' own fidelity simply by their faith and not by their works of the law. At this point, it seems, he has taken a common Christian conviction in a direction that many found to be unacceptable. It is one thing to locate the centre of fidelity in the faithfulness of Christ, as in the covenant tradition of early Christianity; it was quite another thing to allow that centre to invalidate 'works of law', rendering them to be salvifically irrelevant and unnecessary for Christian lifestyle. While others had no difficulty in thinking that Christ's faithfulness should be wed to the covenant faithfulness of his people in their observance of the law (ἔργα νόμου), Paul found these two points irreconcilable, stressing instead that the appropriation of Jesus' faithfulness (πίστις) comes only through faith (πίστις). So, says Paul, 'we believed in Christ Jesus'[22] in order that his faithfulness

---

[22] Williams argues for a strong participationistic sense of εἰς Χριστόν Ἰησοῦν ἐπιστεύσαμεν, 'we believed *into* Christ', in parallel with εἰς Χριστόν ἐβαπτίσθητε of Gal. 3.27 (1987: 442–43). Cf. Dunn, 1993: 56; and somewhat differently Lull, 1991: 264 n. 52. Hays gives a different interpretation of the verbal clause in Gal. 2.16, translating it as 'we have placed our trust in Christ Jesus' (1991b: 725).

might be effective for us. The same thought appears in Gal. 3.22, where God's promise to bless the nations through Abraham (3.15–22) is earthed in the assurance that this promise 'has been given through the faithfulness of Jesus to those who have faith' (ἐκ πίστεως Ἰησοῦ Χριστοῦ δοθῇ τοῖς πιστεύουσιν). By their faith, and not by their covenant 'works of law', others enter into the sphere of covenant relationship with God that is centred in, and emerges from, Jesus' own faithfulness.

Paul's language of 'faith' in these verses, then, is fundamentally a language of 'participation', a language that presupposes Paul's theology of union with Christ whereby Christians are incorporated into Christ (see above, §3.4). Whereas Paul can speak of being crucified with the crucified one, of dying with the one who died in order to live with the one who lives, and of Christian 'sonship' arising out of participation in the 'sonship' of Jesus, so he can talk of Christian participation in the faithfulness (πίστις) of Jesus through their own faith (πίστις) – a faith occasioned and inspired by the coming of Christ's faithfulness. If God's in-breaking into the world has emerged from the faithfulness of Christ and resulted in the establishment of a new world, so Christian faith in the faithful one is the means of participation in that eschatological event, in anticipation of its future culmination.

The issue being debated in Galatia was not the question of more modern, individualistic forms of Christian theology: 'How can I, a sinner, be saved by a just God? Is it by my works or by my faith?' Instead, the issue is one of covenant theology. Although the faithfulness of Christ was recognised by all as the locus wherein covenant relationship between God and his people is securely instituted, the dispute concerned the means whereby others were caught up in that eschatological phenomenon. In Paul's view, the in-breaking of faithfulness (Christ's own) elicits Christian faith as the sole means of inclusion within that eschatological event and the blessings that flow from it.

As a consequence of this conviction, throughout the rest of this passage Paul continues to dissociate law from covenant identity, with which it had for so long been associated. For him, to attach salvific significance to anything other than the

faithfulness of Christ is an affront to the covenant grace of God
(2.21) and makes one a transgressor of the will of God (2.18).[23]
Paul is redefining a theology of covenant relationship in a way
that severs it from the 'givens' of covenant theology typical of
most forms of Early Judaism, where the will and grace of God
are inseparable from the law that leads to righteousness. For
Paul, living to God does not involve living in observance of the
law but, instead, dying to law observance (2.19) since, as Paul
maintains throughout 2.15–21, law observance has nothing to
do with righteousness – that is, with living in covenant
relationship to God.

But Paul has three more things to say in 2.15–21 concerning
his version of Christian covenant theology, all of which follow
on from, or have to do with, the motif of Christ's faithfulness.
These three include: (1) a redefinition of the notion 'sinner',
(2) a consideration of the law's pronouncement upon sinners,
and (3) a description of how Christ's faithfulness envelops the
moral life of the Christian.

REDEFINING THE NOTION 'SINNER'

In Gal. 2.17, Paul writes: 'If, seeking covenant relationship "in
Christ", we ourselves were found to be sinners . . .'. This verse is
one of those where Paul is saying something significant, but he
does so in such a condensed fashion that it is not wholly clear
what he is saying. Most of the interpretations of this verse
currently on offer have weaknesses of one sort or another,[24] and

---

[23] Reading παραβάτην of Gal. 2.18 in the manner urged by Lambrecht, 1991. Cf.
Duncan, 1934: 69.

[24] Soards points out some weaknesses of the traditional interpretations of this
verse, and proposes his own reading of the passage. He suggests taking
ζητοῦντες not as a circumstantial participle but as a supplementary participle
completing the verb εὑρέθημεν. That is, the problem in Paul's mind is the
attempt to be justified ('we were found seeking'), despite being in Christ
(1989). Three weaknesses make his case unconvincing: (1) the syntactical
construction makes it unlikely, a weakness he admits (244); (2) ζητοῦντες is
understood negatively, in the light of an unnecessarily negative reading of the
ζητέω in Rom. 10.3; neither occurrence in itself conveys the sense of living
antithetically to God; (3) the relationship between the first three parts of 2.17
are strained; Paul should at least have included an οὖν or ἄρα as part of
Soards' self-contained clause καὶ αὐτοὶ ἁμαρτωλοί.

there may be scope for proposing another solution, one
understood in the light of what has been seen already in
relation to Paul's redefined covenant theology laid out in
2.15–16. In order to do this, it is helpful to understand how the
term 'sinner' functioned in traditional Jewish covenant theology.

In Early Judaism, if the term 'the righteous' served to identify
those who were members of God's covenant people, the term
'sinners' frequently signified 'those outside the boundaries of
the covenant', and who thereby were thought to be in some
form of opposition to the ways of God. Notions concerning who
was to be numbered among the 'righteous' and who among the
'sinners' varied from situation to situation, according to the
needs of self-definition within particular groups. For some (e.g.,
Pseudo-Philo), the category of those within the covenant was
quite large and encompassed most of the Jewish people, the
'righteous'. They were distinguished from the 'sinners' –
gentiles as well as those Jews who had sinned 'with a heavy
hand', intentionally disregarding or scorning covenant obligations and thereby breaking out of the boundaries of the
covenant people. For others (e.g., the sectarian covenanters at
Qumran), the category of the 'righteous' was far more
restricted, encompassing a much smaller number of Jews who
alone were thought to have been faithful before God; the large
majority of the Jewish people were thought to have abandoned
their covenant status, thereby joining the ranks of the 'sinners'
along with the gentiles.

In this way, 'righteous' and 'sinner' operated in Early
Judaism almost as technical terms in relation to prior convictions about the boundaries of covenant fidelity.[25] The term
'righteous' denoted those who please God, who live according
to God's ways and maintain the responsibilities of their

---

[25] See Dunn, 1990. Opponents of this view suggest that 'sinner' is primarily a
theological rather than social marker, depicting one who intentionally goes
against the will of God and lives beyond the realms of God's salvation, as for
instance in Rom. 5.19 (cf. Soards, 1989: 240–41). But the 'either-or' of this
way of looking at the issue is unnecessary and unhelpful, for in many instances
of Early Jewish covenant theology the two go hand in hand. Interpretative
problems increase when either aspect goes unaccompanied by the other.

covenant life; the term 'sinner' denoted those who do not please God, who live contrary to God's will and fall outside the boundaries of God's covenant people.

The same understanding of these technical terms can be framed within Paul's thinking in Galatians. His case in Gal. 2.15–17 seems to follow the same simple rules of covenant definition and demarcation, although in his view the embodiment of covenant faithfulness is not an ethnic people (Israel), nor a sub-group within that people (e.g., Qumran), but a single individual – Jesus Christ; his faithfulness alone is the catchment of covenant relationship with God and the vehicle through which God is creating a new sphere of existence. For Paul, the consequence of restricting the boundaries of faithfulness to a single individual is that all others find themselves to be 'sinners', outsiders to covenant relationship.

An initial glimpse of Paul's redefinition of the term appears in Gal. 2.15, where he sarcastically ridicules the traditional distinction between Jews and 'gentile sinners'. Further, we read in Gal. 2.17: 'If, seeking covenant relationship "in Christ", we ourselves were also found to be sinners . . .'. Paul is not referring here to some pre-conversion consciousness of sin that led him to seek out Christ, as some have thought. Nor, as others have thought, is he referring to the post-conversion situation of being free from the law in Christ, therefore being a so-called 'sinner' ('sinner' at least as far as the law was concerned, although not actually perceived as such in the eyes of God).[26] Rather than anything of this sort, what this verse highlights is the theological process of the marking out of covenantal boundaries. Christ's faithfulness so fills the category of covenant righteousness that, consequently, Paul expects all others to find themselves within the category of sinners.[27]

[26] E.g., Bruce, 1982: 140–41; Dunn, 1993a: 141; Betz, 1979: 120; Watson, 1986: 68.

[27] Notice that Paul does not say here what he is often thought to mean, which is: 'After having been justified "in Christ", we found that we too are sinners' – that is, so-called "sinners" due to our relaxation of nomistic observance.' If he had intended that meaning, he would not have used the present participle ζητοῦντες in conjunction with the infinitive δικαιωθῆναι. The aorist participle δικαιωθέντες alone would have conveyed that sense, the aorist tense clearly indicating that this action occurred prior to the time of the main verb of the

This seems to have been a repugnant notion to some of the Jewish Christians of Paul's day, who considered their nomistic observance to prove that the term 'sinner' was not appropriate for them, even if Christ's faithfulness was the primary arena of covenant fidelity. But Paul applies the term especially in their case (the 'we ourselves' [αὐτοί] of 2.17 corresponds primarily to the 'we who are Jews by birth' of 2.15). For him, 'sinner' remained the primary category of self-identity for 'all flesh' (πᾶσα σάρξ) apart from Christ (2.16), a condition that does not find its remedy in ethnic identity (φύσις, 2.15) or nomistic practice (ἔργα νόμου, 2.16) – such things only build up that which has been torn down, thereby making one a transgressor of the will of God (2.18). The implication of all this is clear: all those who would supplement the efficacy of the faithfulness of Christ with their nomistic practice are not furthering righteousness but are themselves aiding the cause of the power of Sin.

Here, Paul has turned the tables on those who belittled his understanding of the gospel. They found it to implicate Christ as a 'servant of the power of Sin' (2.17)[28] because of its potential ethical deficiencies. In their view, by side-lining the law from the equation of covenantal definition, Paul has removed the guide for, and standard of, moral behaviour. For them, the faithfulness of Christ as the centre of covenant relationship has nothing to do with excluding the law from covenant relationship; such a move simply invites antinomian practices, making Christ little

---

sentence, εὑρέθημεν. Had Paul constructed his sentence in this fashion, then he would have meant what he is usually taken to mean – that the finding of one's self to be a sinner occurred as a consequence of, or in sequential relation to, being 'justified' in Christ. But instead of this construction, Paul uses a present participle (ζητοῦντες), thereby denoting simultaneous occurrence. In this way, the finding of one's self to be a 'sinner' occurred in the same process as the seeking of δικαιοσύνη in Christ. Moreover, Paul's use of ζητέω seems intended to highlight that he is not talking of an already-enjoyed experience of δικαιοσύνη, as the parallel use of ζητέω and δικαιοσύνη in Rom. 10.3 clearly shows. Instead, ζητέω signals a disposition whereby some end is envisaged, something one is looking towards that at present is not realised (e.g., Rom. 2.7; 1 Cor. 7.27; 2 Cor. 13.3) – the goal in this case being 'righteousness in Christ'. Accordingly, both Paul's lexical choice and tense signifier within this verse support the interpretation given here.
[28] On ἁμαρτία as a 'spiritual power' in Gal. 2.17, see Soards, 1989: 246.

more than a puppet through which the power of Sin promotes itself.

But Paul has argued the opposite, finding that those who seek to observe the law in relation to the faithfulness of Christ make themselves transgressors of God's will (2.18). It is little wonder, then, that elsewhere Paul evaluated his 'blamelessness in the law' (Phil. 3.8) to be of no worth, or that in Galatians he fiercely chastised those who would supplement the efficacy of the faithfulness of Christ with their own nomistic practice. Christ's faithfulness is appropriated solely on the basis of faith, the exclusive means whereby one is transferred out of the ranks of the 'sinners', resulting in inclusion among the people of God in covenant relationship, or 'righteousness'.

THE LAW'S PRONOUNCEMENT UPON SINNERS

Having placed nomistic observance in opposition to the true will of God (2.18), Paul goes on to make a rather enigmatic claim in 2.19: 'For I died to the law, through the law' (ἐγὼ γὰρ διὰ νόμου νόμῳ ἀπέθανον). It is not wholly clear what Paul means by dying 'through the law'. Perhaps he is referring to his own experiences of observing the law, a lifestyle that led to his persecution of the church and ultimately to his own encounter with the risen Christ. If so, then 'through the law' might signal the events of his own life that he recounts in 1.13–16.[29] Or perhaps he means that, since he has been crucified with Christ, the Christ whom the law cursed (3.13), so too the curse of the law has also fallen upon him. In a sense, then both Christ and the Christian have died 'through the law'.[30]

Each of these views has received support from professional students of Paul, but each is marred by weaknesses of one sort or another. The first takes the 'I' too autobiographically, applying it exclusively to Paul's own experiences; as in 2.18, the 'I' of 2.19 is probably intended in a more general sense of being universally the case for all Christians. Although the second interpretation is feasible, it suffers from having to explain an earlier verse by a later verse – in this case, 2.19 is understood in

[29] So, e.g., Dunn, 1993a: 143.
[30] So, e.g., Bruce, 1982: 143.

the light of 3.13. While occasionally necessary, this method has an obvious weakness: such a method was not available to the original hearers of the letter on its first reading.[31] Accordingly, another interpretation is advocated here that avoids the weaknesses of other interpretations while following precisely the lines of covenant theology that we have come to expect from Paul in this section of his letter.

Within the Jewish scriptures and literature, the law is consistently depicted as a means to life for the covenant people, offering them the blessing of abundance (Deut. 28.1–14), 'prosperity and life' (Deut. 30.15). According to Pseudo-Philo, for example, God made this pronouncement concerning the people of Israel: 'I gave them my Law and enlightened them in order that by doing these things they would live and have many years and not die' (*Bib. Ant.* 23.10).[32] This function of the law with regard to covenant insiders contrasts sharply with the function of the law with regard to covenant outsiders, against whom it pronounced a curse (Deut. 28.15–68; 29.19–28) that resulted in 'death and destruction' (Deut. 30.15).[33] A near-contemporary of Paul's even talks of the Messiah destroying covenant outsiders 'by the law' (4 Ezra 13.38),[34] by which the author probably means 'in accordance with the pronouncement of the law'.

When Paul speaks of having died *through* the law, his point seems much the same: If the boundaries of the covenant have been drawn in such a way that 'all flesh' (πᾶσα σάρξ) stands outside the boundaries of righteousness, then the pronouncement of the law upon all is 'death'.[35] Ironically, this death is 'to

[31] Although Paul probably expected his letter to be heard several times over (see above, chapter 3 n. 1), this should not imply that he had no concerns to be understood sensibly on the first hearing. Further hearings were expected to enhance initial understanding, not simply to begin the process of understanding.

[32] Cf. also Psalm 1; Lev. 18.5; Pss. Sol. 14.2–3; 4 Ezra 7.127–31; 14.22, 29, 34.

[33] Cf. also 4 Ezra 7.20–24, 46–48, 62–75; 9.32–37.

[34] In the Syriac version; other versions are corrupt.

[35] In Romans 7, Paul gives from a Christian point of view an elaborate description of the experience of 'the Jew' who is outside the boundaries of those in Christ and for whom the law is *not* unto life; see B. W. Longenecker, 1991: 225–45.

the law' (νόμῳ) – that is, death that severs all relationship with the law. The construction of 2.19a is important, where Paul literally writes: 'For I, through the law, to the law died.' The phrase 'to the law' appears before the verb for the sake of emphasis – Paul's own clever spin in which he reworks the motif of the law's pronouncement of death to include the severing of the dead person's obligation to the law itself (cf. Rom. 7.1–6). In 2.19b Paul elaborates further the significance of the law's pronouncement of death, stating that it results in life – that is, the life promised to those within the boundaries of the covenant, expanded in 2.19c to include those who, like Paul, have been crucified with Christ. The law's pronouncement of death carries no 'sting' for those who are united with Christ in his death.

The whole of Gal. 2.19, then, might be paraphrased in this manner: 'For through the pronouncement of the law upon covenant outsiders, I died to the obligation to observe the law, in order that I might enjoy covenant life by being crucified with Christ'.

CHRIST'S FAITHFULNESS ENVELOPS THE CHRISTIAN'S MORAL IDENTITY

In Gal. 2.19c–21 Paul lays the foundation for his rebuttal of the charge of antinomianism that seems to have been laid against his gospel. Behind 2.17 we hear the charge that Paul's Christ is a servant of the power of Sin. But Paul does not accept this accusation, and here constructs another line of defence against it.

Having been crucified with Christ, Paul claims that he no longer lives but that Christ now lives continually (ζῇ) in him. As we have seen (§4.3 above), it is this aspect of Paul's christology, 'Christ living in me', that later is developed into a full-scale rebuttal of the charge of antinomianism (5.13–6.10). In the final verses of Galatians 2, Paul expands the 'Christ living in me' motif by drawing once again upon the traditional 'faithfulness of Christ' motif. Even in the mortal body,[36] he says, the believer

---

[36] Paul speaks here of σάρξ, rather than σῶμα, perhaps, as Betz suggests, in order to counter 'widespread enthusiastic notions, which may have already found a home in Christianity, according to which "divine life" and "flesh" are mutually exclusive' (1979: 125).

is marked out by faithfulness to God precisely because the life of the faithful Son of God is being lived out within the believer: 'I live continually by the faithfulness of the Son of God' (ἐν πίστει ζῶ τῇ τοῦ υἱοῦ τοῦ θεοῦ).[37] In Paul's covenant theology, the believer's life is marked out neither by nomistic observance nor by ethical antinomianism, but by the faithfulness of the Son of God.[38] Paul expands the traditional motif of the faithfulness of Christ in the rest of the verse,[39] where faithfulness in the life of Jesus is defined concretely in terms of love and the giving of himself for the benefit of others – a quality of Jesus' life highlighted right at the start of the letter: 'the one who gave himself' (1.4).[40]

In this way, the traditional motif of the faithfulness of Christ has been put into the service of Paul's ethical defence, by means of his theology of Christian union with Christ. The dispute in Galatia concerning the law was not simply about ethnic identifying marks (e.g., circumcision), but about how life is to be regulated on a daily basis. On that score, the agitators upheld the law as the means whereby Christian behaviour is governed and managed; without the law, Paul's gospel was seen to promote antinomianism and libertinism. Accordingly, as we have seen, without his presentation in Galatians 5–6, Paul's explanation of the gospel within the Galatian crisis would have been incomplete. Conversely, the ethical section of Galatians 5–6 is itself little more than an elaboration of the rudimentary

[37] Cf. Hays, 1983: 167–69. Elsewhere Hays writes: 'If Paul intended to designate "the Son of God" as the object of the verbal idea in the noun πίστει, he certainly chose a very odd way to do it' (1991b: 726). See too the interesting views of Samuel Taylor Coleridge on πίστις Χριστοῦ, in Janzen, 1996.

[38] Precisely at this point the subjective genitive reading of πίστις ['Ιησοῦ] Χριστοῦ allows Paul's case a force that it does not otherwise have. If Paul is pressed to show how faith apart from 'works of law' does not deteriorate into antinomianism (an issue apparently introduced in Gal. 2.17), the claim that 'I live by faith in the Son of God' would be simply a feeble restatement of the problematic point, whereas 'I live by the faithfulness of the Son of God' addresses the point directly.

[39] The three δέ connectives in 2.20 all serve to unpack the Χριστῷ συνεσταύρωμαι of 2.19c.

[40] Furnish: If 2.20 makes reference 'to the Son's own faith, then this is specifically identified with Christ's love and voluntary death for others' (1993: 115).

ethic spelt out in Gal. 2.20, where the Son of God, whose own faithfulness was expressed in terms of love and the giving of himself, lives continuously in the very existence of Paul. Thus, Paul's use of the faithfulness of Christ motif in Gal. 2.20 opens the floodgates to his discussion of Christian ethics in Galatians 5–6. Consequently, the faithfulness of Christ has shown itself to be an important theological centre of Paul's presentation in Galatians.[41]

From what we have seen, we can conclude the following. First, when Paul composed Galatians, he remained cognisant of a covenant relationship between God and Israel (§5.1); second, he drew on a traditional form of Christian covenant theology that frequently made use of the motif of Christ's faithfulness (§§5.2 and 5.3); and third, he developed that tradition in Galatians in ways that reinforced his own emphasis on freedom from nomistic observance and his rejection of antinomianism. Such observations need not imply that Paul is everywhere and in every way a covenant theologian. But here at least, perhaps even due simply to the requirements of the Galatian situation, Paul's presentation seems remarkably at home with the *structures* of covenant theology typical of many forms of Judaism in his own day, even though the *content* that he gives to those structures proved to be enormously untypical.

The motif of the faithfulness of Christ, mentioned explicitly in Gal. 2.16, 2.20 and 3.22–23, has provided the occasion for analysing Gal. 2.15–21 in some detail. As we will see below (§6.6), however, it also serves as a theological presupposition to Paul's claim in 3.13 that Christ took upon himself the curse of the law that fell upon the people of Israel. But that verse is densely packed and, in order to be fully appreciated, requires some reconstruction of Paul's view of the problems associated with nomistic observance. Accordingly, it is to such issues that we now turn.

---

[41] Hays seems to hit the mark directly when he writes: 'Gal 2:20–21, with its emphasis on union with Christ's grace-giving death, looks more and more like the hermeneutical centre of the letter' (1991a: 242).

6

The Law, Abraham, and Christ

The preceding chapters have traced Paul's convictions that eschatological salvation (1) has nothing whatsoever to do with works of the law, (2) has everything to do with the initial redemption of the people to whom the law had been given, and (3) results in the law finding its proper fulfilment in lifestyle that enhances the lives of others. Clearly, then, in Galatians Paul enunciates a theology of divine triumph in ways that frequently converge on the matter of the law. In fact, in Galatians Paul gives his most extended arguments concerning the nature and purposes of the law.

This chapter canvasses the way Paul depicts the law in Galatians, noting initially the various roles and functions that Paul assigns to it (§§6.1 to 6.3). Attention is then given to the way Paul finds scripture itself to disqualify the performance of the law as a salvific necessity for those whose identity is aligned with Abraham and Christ by faith (§§6.4 to 6.6). Almost every point in the following analysis reveals something of the distinctiveness of Paul's understanding of the law within the context of his day.

1. The Temporality of the Law

One of the central tenets of Paul's view of the law in Galatians has to do with the marking of time. Paul restricts the law's purpose to the 'Mosaic dispensation', the period that fell 430 years after Abraham (supposedly) and up to the coming of Christ. That period has nothing to do with the promises that God made to Abraham, promises that were authenticated with the coming of Christ. This temporal argument is best seen at 3.15–19, 23–25, and 4.1–4, where temporal indicators abound: 'added ... until' (3.19); 'before faith came' (3.23); 'until faith should be revealed' (3.23); 'until (εἰς) Christ came' (3.24);[1] 'now that faith has come we are no longer ...' (3.25); 'as long as' (4.1); 'until' (4.2); 'when' (4.3); 'when the fullness of time came' (4.4).

In Galatians, Paul's case against the need for nomistic observance in the eschatological age relies heavily on this temporal case. While it may fall easily upon the ears of Christians whose faith has been nurtured by his letters, in the Judaism of Paul's day such a temporal restriction would have been preposterous. In Early Judaism, it would have been inconceivable to restrict the law within temporal boundaries, since the law was known to be eternal in its glory and function.[2] If God's 'wisdom' or immanence was thought to be the instrument of God's creating activity (e.g., Prov. 8.30), permeating and sustaining the whole of creation,[3] and declaring the glory of God,[4] so too that same divine 'wisdom', the immanent power of God, was said to have resided with Israel and been embodied within the Torah.[5] In this way, the created order and the stipulations of the law cohere, since both are embodied by God's wisdom. In a sense, Torah requirements are built into the very structure of the world and the heavenly realms; Jubilees 15, for instance, demonstrates how circumcision is 'an eternal ordinance ordained and written in the heavenly tablets' (15.25; cf. 15.9, 11, 13, 28), since the law itself is 'for all the eternal generations' (15.25). Were the Torah to be annulled, God's wisdom would be compromised or revoked, and the whole of creation would tumble into chaotic upheaval and anarchy. In this view of things, if Paul's temporal claim about the law were true, it would result in nothing else than the complete collapse of the created order.

---

[1] The εἰς of 3.24 is best interpreted temporally ('until Christ came'; cf. the εἰς of 3.23) rather than teleologically ('pointing to Christ').

[2] On this, see Moore, 1927: 1.263–80.

[3] Cf. Sir. 24.3–6; Wis. Sol. 7.24; 8.1.

[4] Cf. Ps. 19.1–4; Wis. Sol. 13.1–5; cf. 1 En. 41.8; 2 En. 66.4; 2 Bar. 54.5, 17.

[5] Cf. Sir. 24.8, 23; Bar. 3.9–4.4; 2 Bar. 38.2, 4; 48.22–23.

Paul seems almost to admit as much when he speaks metaphorically of the cosmos having been 'crucified to me, and I to the world' (6.14), or when he claims: 'For neither circumcision counts for anything, nor uncircumcision, but a new creation' (6.15). Paul's metaphorical image here suggests that he was cognisant of the intimate connection between creation and Torah that was central to most forms of the Judaism of his day. No doubt Paul did not worry about creation literally tumbling back into chaos since, as we see elsewhere in his letters, he came to view Jesus Christ as the embodiment of wisdom (e.g., 1 Cor. 1.24; Col. 1.15–20), and found in him all the attributes of wisdom previously associated with Torah. Paul confesses Jesus Christ to be the one through whom the world was created (1 Cor. 8.6; Col. 1.16), continues to be sustained (Col. 1.17), and will one day be redeemed (Rom. 8.19–23; Col. 1.20). According to Paul, Christ crucified is the embodiment of God's wisdom – the divine creative, sustaining and redemptive power. Claims of this sort fly in the face of the traditional view that the Torah and its stipulations were built into the very structures of the world. Instead of being eternal ordinances, Paul depicts Torah stipulations to be of a different order, being limited to the time between the giving of the law at Sinai and the coming of Christ.

Another point at which Paul breaks company with the traditions of Early Judaism is his claim that the law is not a means to life, to which we now turn.

2. The Law Is not a Means to Life

Whereas in Early Judaism the law was thought to hold a central place in God's plan of salvation, Paul maintains that it has no direct relevance for godly behaviour in the new era that has dawned. Naturally arising might be the question, 'Is the law in opposition to God's ways in Christ?' – a question Paul asks on behalf of his audience in 3.21. We might expect his answer to be 'Yes', for certainly the agitators would have answered such a question with a definite 'No'. There is no opposition between law and Christ, they would have said, since both have their origin in God.

But Paul's answer, too, is an emphatic 'Impossible' (μὴ γένοιτο). Although the agitators would have heartily agreed with this negation, they would nonetheless have rigorously disputed the rationale that Paul gives in support of it. The law and Christ (or, 'God's promises' to Abraham) are not in conflict, he says, because the two were never intended for the same purpose; there is no rivalry where functions diverge.

The function that Paul highlights initially is the ability to give life, asserting that 'if a law had been given which could bring life, then righteousness would indeed be by the law' (3.21; cf. 2.21). This would have been an incredulous claim to the agitators, since one of law's primary purposes lay in providing the means to life for Israel, being identified as 'the law of life' (Sir. 17.11). Text after text in the Jewish tradition demonstrates this conviction, articulated clearly in Lev. 18.5, which Paul cites in Gal. 3.12 (cf. Rom. 10.5): 'The one who does them [the commands of God] shall live by them.' Similarly, according to Pseudo-Philo, God states concerning the people of Israel: 'I gave them my law and enlightened them in order that by doing these things they would live and have many years and not die' (*Bib. Ant.* 23.10; cf. Pss. Sol. 14.2–3; Bar. 3.9). The doing of the law is equated with life throughout the Jewish scriptures and literature.[6]

In Paul's view, however, this relationship between law and life, which one would expect to be fruitful, has in fact been fruitless. Although the law may in principle set out a means to life, as passages like Lev. 18.5 suggest, in practice something seems to have gone wrong. Here, Paul evidently assumes a fundamental problem not with the law itself but with the condition of humanity; the law sets out a path to life, but those who seek to live by it inevitably fail to do so.[7] Paul gives a long analysis of this same situation in Romans 7. There he paints a desperate portrait from his Christian perspective of the condition of one who seeks in every way to please God by conforming to the law, but who finds his situation to be exploited by the

---

[6] Cf. Deut. 4.1; 5.32–33; 6.24–25; 8.1; 30.15–20; Ezek. 18.9, 21; 20.11, 13, 21; 33.10; Prov. 3.1–2; 6.23; Neh. 9.29. On the understanding of the Torah as being unto life in the Judaism of Paul's day, see Lichtenberger, 1996.

[7] See Barrett, 1985: 34.

power of Sin, rendering him unable to do what pleases God. This passage is Paul's Christian case study of the Jewish predicament, whereby unregenerate human nature meets the 'spiritual' law.[8] Something similar must lie in Paul's mind when he speaks of the law's inability to bring life, just as he has already said, 'if righteousness could be gained through the law, Christ died for nothing' (2.21). In each case, Paul's convictions are far from those expressed repeatedly in the Jewish literature of his time.

Paul is far more pessimistic about human ability to do the law than most Jews of his day.[9] While there is a tendency, especially in the context of prayer, to emphasise one's own failings, inadequacy and utter dependency upon God for salvation, there is another sense in which doing the law was not beyond the capability of well-meaning Jews, especially when supported by God's gracious assistance. Paul's conviction regarding an entrenched human sinfulness that undermines one's ability to do the law might have been countered by a passage like Deut. 30.11–14, where God says to Israel: 'Surely, this commandment that I am commanding you today is not too hard for you, nor is it too far away' (30.11). It is not surprising to find Paul, in Romans, having to engage with Deut. 30.11–14, reinterpreting the passage in a christological fashion, finding it to mean that the *gospel* itself is not too far away, but is on the lips and hearts of those of faith (10.6–9).

But this reinterpretation aside, there remains a fundamental difference in perspective between Paul and most of his Jewish contemporaries on this matter of doing the law. For Paul, it seems that human infractions of the law's stipulations indicate human inability to keep the law. In Judaism and its scriptures, however, human infractions of the law are sins, indeed, but keeping the law includes repenting and making atonement for those sins. Keeping the law was generally not thought to involve perfect obedience to each and every stipulation without error or

---

[8] For fuller defence and explanation, see B. W. Longenecker, 1991: 225–45.

[9] Coming a close second to Paul in this is the author of the late first-century apocalypse, 4 Ezra, whose work now forms most of 2 Esdras. See B. W. Longenecker, 1995.

remainder, but was thought to involve the serious intent to live as God has commanded, and reliance on the grace of God to forgive the unfortunate but inevitable offences of those who were repentant.[10] Elsewhere in his letters Paul shows cognisance of this traditional Jewish perspective, claiming in Philippians that, in his pre-Christian days, he was 'blameless with regard to righteousness under the law' (Phil. 3.6). He does not mean here that he had never committed an infraction of the law, but that, as one who was faultless in his motivation to live by the pronouncements of the law, his faults in practice were dealt with by means of personal repentance, the making of atonement and divine forgiveness.[11]

This kind of thinking is a world away from the Paul of Galatians, however, where 'doing the law' is thought to involve the complete observance of the law's commands without error. And it is this assumption that allows him in 3.21 to break the traditional association of 'law' and 'life'; the law did not lead to life due to a fundamental flaw in the human constituency, resulting in human inability to do the law. This same conviction regarding human inability also allows him to make other claims about the law that would have appeared illegitimate to most of his Jewish contemporaries, as demonstrated below.

3. The Purposes of the Law

If the law is unable to transform the sinful condition of humanity and lead to life, then what purpose did it serve? Paul gives several answers to this in Galatians. Unfortunately, each

---

[10] See especially, Sanders, 1976; 1977; 1992: 241–78. Although Sanders' portrait of Early Judaism as 'covenantal nomism' seems to do justice to the majority of Jewish traditions in Paul's day, some qualifications may be in order. See, e.g., Stanton, 1996: 104–105; Quarles, 1996. Sanders himself identifies the Jewish text Testament of Abraham (first century C.E.) in a quite different fashion (1983: 877–78). I remain convinced, however, that the problems in Galatia have arisen as a consequence of a form of Christianity informed by something approaching Sanders' 'covenantal nomism', or 'ethnocentric covenantalism', as I have sought to call it (1991: 34).

[11] See, e.g., Seifrid, 1992: 174.

passage where Paul discusses this matter has been the subject of a fair amount of interpretative debate.

Paul first addresses the matter in 3.19, where he says, 'It was added because of transgression'. Clearly, the verb 'added' (προσετέθη) accentuates the temporal aspect of the law. What is less clear is how the rest of Paul's statement should be understood. 'Because of transgressions' (τῶν παραβάσεων χάριν) is frequently compared with what Paul says in Rom. 5.20, where the law is said to increase transgressions, causing sins to multiply, provoking them, bringing them into existence.[12] While this 'causative' interpretation is not without its problems, it cannot be ruled out, especially in the light of Rom. 5.20. Moreover, it may strike chords with what Paul says in Gal. 3.22, as we shall see.

In another interpretation, this verse is compared with several others in Romans where Paul speaks of the law revealing sin (3.20; 4.15; 5.13; 7.7), bringing about an acute awareness of human sinfulness that would otherwise be obscure in human discernment. In this 'cognitive' interpretation, the law does not cause or create wrongdoing (as in Rom. 5.20), but is simply the means whereby wrongdoing is made recognisable to human perception.[13]

A third interpretation finds Paul to have in mind here a 'corrective' function of the law. In this view, the law served to restrain sinful desires and to protect Israel from excessive sinful indulgence.[14] (Paul may even have had in mind the law's role in providing an interim means of atonement for the sins of God's

---

[12] According to Betz, this phrase 'is to be taken in a wholly negative way' (1979: 165). Cf. Barrett, 1985: 33; 1994: 81; Westerholm, 1988: 178. But see the criticisms of this view offered by Lull, 1986: 483–85.

[13] Hansen, who advocates this interpretation, gives this analogy. Imagine a country 'in which there are many traffic accidents but no traffic laws. Although people are driving in dangerous, harmful ways, it is difficult to designate which acts are harmful until the legislature issues a book of traffic laws. Then it is possible for the police to cite drivers for transgressions of the traffic laws. The laws define harmful ways of driving as violations of standards set by the legislature. The function of the traffic laws is to allow bad drivers to be identified and prosecuted' (1994: 101).

[14] See Lull, 1986: 482–86; Dunn, 1991a: 135–37.

covenant people.)[15] This interpretation, highlighting the preventative function of the law, has strong ties with Paul's depiction of the law as a pedagogue in 3.24–25, and with his analogy of a child being under guardians and trustees prior to his coming of age. It also has less difficulty than the causative and cognitive interpretations when explaining the manner in which Paul continues in the remainder of the verse: 'until the offspring [Christ] should come.' The law's corrective (i.e., preventative and/or atoning) function was valid only until the coming of the new age. The law may not have been able to transform people or set them free from the power of Sin, but it could at least prevent the pollutants from multiplying and overshadowing goodness.

It is extremely difficult to decide between these three readings, called here the 'causative', the 'cognitive' and the 'corrective'. Nor does understanding Paul's depiction of the law necessarily get any easier when considering his statement in 3.22 concerning the function of the law. There, Paul speaks of 'scripture' confining all things (συνέκλεισεν ... τὰ πάντα) under the control of the power of Sin.[16] The expression 'under the power of Sin' (ὑπὸ ἁμαρτίαν) appears in only two other places in the extant Pauline corpus (Rom. 3.9; 7.14), each time referring to the cosmic power of Sin, as it does here (cf. 2.17). The verb συνέκλεισεν denotes imprisonment, not in the sense of punishment, but of confinement or restriction. It suggests being enclosed by and enveloped within something – in this case, the cosmic power of Sin.

Notice how, in principle, such a statement involves an implicit threat to the sovereignty of God, since a cosmic power other than God seems to be in control of everything, without remainder. Yet two things reveal this threat to be ineffective. First, in the second half of 3.22, Paul speaks of the fulfilment of God's promise to Abraham, a fulfilment that is established 'by the faithfulness of Jesus Christ' (ἐκ πίστεως Ἰησοῦ Χριστοῦ), the

---

[15] See Dunn, 1993a: 189–90.

[16] It is not clear whether Paul had a single passage of scripture in mind (e.g., Deut. 27.26, cited in 3.10), or a series of passages (such as the scriptural catena of Rom. 3.10–18), or whether he was simply thinking about scripture as a collective whole.

benefit of which 'is given to those who believe' (δοθῇ τοῖς
πιστεύουσιν). In the faithfulness of Christ, God's promise is
established and validated, without compromise or negation.
Here again we see how important the faithfulness of Christ is to
Paul's theology, being the means whereby God's sovereignty is
assured, revealed and effective.

Second, the inclusion of all things within the grasp of the
power of Sin is itself kept within the parameters of God's will.
Ironically, scripture plays a part in demarcating and binding
everything to be held within the clutches of the power of Sin.
This does not go contrary to the intentions of God but, in fact,
in a strange fashion, is held within God's purposes and forms
part of God's own plan, through the instrument of scripture
itself. Here Paul reinforces his claim of 3.21 that the law is not a
means to life; instead, one of its purposes is to prevent and
obstruct the way for any who seek to find life anywhere other
than in Christ. Scripture confines all things under Sin's own
influence, so that salvation from the power of Sin might be seen
to be exclusively found in Christ, by his faithfulness, to all who
believe. The strangeness of God's ways in the past is, in Paul's
mind, the prerequisite for the demonstration of the glory of
God's ways in Christ.

This may help to shed light on the phrase 'because of
transgressions' in 3.19. As we saw above, that phrase might
mean that the law was added in order to induce transgressions
(the causative interpretation), a notion that might resonate
with and fill out Paul's claim in 3.22 concerning the confinement of everything to the control of Sin by means of the law.[17]
Unfortunately this is not the only interpretation of 3.19 that
could cohere with his meaning in 3.22. It might just as well be
that the law, confining all things to the power of Sin, brings
about awareness of transgressions (the cognitive interpretation)
in order to indicate this enslavement. Or it may even be that the
law, although confining all things to the power of Sin,
nonetheless provided some means of guidance, restraint or
atonement (albeit in a provisional fashion) for the people of
Israel while they were held in that condition (the corrective

---

[17] Cf. R. N. Longenecker, 1990: 144–45.

interpretation), until the coming of Christ. At this point, the process of knitting together from Galatians a coherent theology of the law's purpose looks to be a rather arbitrary exercise. And there remains one more important piece of the puzzle to consider.

A further image of the law appears in 3.23–25 and spills over in a slightly different form into the beginning of chapter 4. This is the image of the law as a 'pedagogue' (παιδαγωγός), a Greek term that has no precise English equivalent. While the law confines all things within the clutches of Sin, it also served to confine the Jewish people ('we') under its influence until the coming of Christ (3.23). Making these two statements back to back serves to highlight the twofold situation of the people of Israel prior to Christ. On the one hand, they were no different from anyone or anything else, being confined under the power of Sin and having no way out of that desperate situation other than Christ. On the other hand, they were under the supervisory restraint of the law, even during that period. In Romans Paul highlights the same twofold situation, claiming that 'both Jews and Greeks are under the power of Sin' (3.9) while also maintaining the great advantage of the Jewish people as a consequence of having been given the 'oracles of God' (3.1–2; cf. 9.4–5).

While Paul's image of the pedagogue has occasionally been thought to include negative connotations,[18] more recent consideration of the identity and role of the pedagogue in Graeco-Roman society suggests that positive connotations are included in this imagery. The pedagogue, who would have been a slave, had a supervisory role within the Graeco-Roman households, guiding, caring for and overseeing a boy until the time when he ceased to be a child and outgrew the need for pedagogical control. Just as today, so in Paul's day, children needed to be managed rather than left to their own devices, if only for their own good and protection. Although differentiated from a formal teacher and not to be confused with one, the pedagogue indirectly helped to shape the boy's identity by directing his upbringing, meting out discipline, and encouraging certain kinds

[18] E.g., Betz, 1979: 177.

of conduct, all in accordance with the mandates stipulated by the boy's father.[19]

This analogy serves Paul's purposes well, since it corresponds with several other features of his characterisation of the law. First, it advocates a positive function for the law, a supervisory role, by which the people of Israel were guided and their corporate life governed (3.23–25; 4.1–2). It is precisely this social function of the law that has been highlighted by recent work on the purpose of the law in Early Judaism's covenantal theology.[20] The second attraction of the pedagogue analogy is its in-built temporal dynamics. The pedagogue's function comes to an end with the child's 'coming of age'; after that point, it would be quite improper for the pedagogue to continue to exert supervisory influence. In Paul's view, precisely the unnaturalness of that situation marks out the Galatians' own interest in observing the law.

Within this analogy of the law as a pedagogue, Paul can talk about the people of Israel having been 'under law' (ὑπὸ νόμον). This is important since Paul frequently uses the preposition 'under' to signal the influence of a spiritual power, just as he has spoken of scripture consigning all things 'under' the power of Sin in 3.22. As we have seen already (§3.2), in Galatians Paul depicts the law as a spiritual power charged with oversight of a particular nation, like the other angelic national overlords or 'elements of the world' (στοιχεῖα τοῦ κόσμου, 4.3). While this function of the law is a positive one prior to the coming of Christ, with the changing of the ages it has become a negative one; the helpful supervisory influence of an angelic overlord has become a negative force that diverts people's energies away from knowing God and being known by God (4.8–9). After the

---

[19] Matera: 'the law established a pattern for the moral and ethical conduct of those under its power' (1996: 168). On this, see esp. R. N. Longenecker, 1982; 1990: 146–48; Lull, 1986: 489–94; Young, 1987: 151–69; Gordon, 1989. Young writes: 'there seems to be no thought of the law as some brutal and tyrannical disciplinarian in his metaphorical use of παιδαγωγός in Gal. 3' (1987: 171). Meeks likens God in Paul's analogy to 'a proper, well-to-do *paterfamilias*' (1993: 170).

[20] As in Sanders' 1977 study. On the image of the law as pedagogue within the context of Jewish covenantal convictions, cf. Young, 1987: 170–76.

inauguration of the new age, the supervisory angel can all too easily become the primary point of religious reference, detracting attention away from God who seeks to transform 'minors' into those come of age in Christ.

We have seen how Paul suggests three purposes for the giving of the law, two of which are relatively clear: (1) the law was given in order to envelop everything within the control of Sin in order that Christ's significance as the exclusive means of salvation might be highlighted (3.22); (2) the law was given to regulate the life of the people of Israel during their infancy prior to the time of Christ (3.23–25; 4.1–2). The second of these sits well with the understanding of the law promulgated within most traditions of Early Judaism, although the first does not. It is not clear, however, what Paul intended by the law having been added 'because of transgressions' (3.19). This may suggest that the law brought Israel's sinfulness to life and produced sins, or that the law made Israel's state of sinfulness recognisable, or that it played a corrective role in relation to Israel. In my judgement, the third is most likely, although certainty on this matter will always be elusive.

Throughout Galatians 3–4, then, Paul gives various explanations of the law's function, although he seems never to work them out within an explicit, overarching theological package. The one constant in Paul's pronouncements on the purpose of the law is this: the law is not to have regulatory force in determining the identity of those in Christ. For Paul, all roads lead to this conclusion. The connection between Abraham and Christ is devoid of any nomistic performance, a claim ensured by Paul's novel refiguring of the nature and purposes of the law. And Paul finds a proper reading of the law to testify to this same claim, a point illustrated in the following sections of this chapter.

4. Abraham's Offspring in Christ

Paul's discussion of the temporality and functions of the law in Galatians 3–4 appears within a larger consideration of the identity of Abraham's offspring. So in Gal. 3.7 Paul gives his definition of what it means to be 'sons [υἱοί] of Abraham', while in 3.29 the same concept is spoken of in terms of the 'offspring [σπέρμα] of Abraham'. Evidently the promotion of circumcision and works of the law was being carried out in Galatia with reference to this notion of the identity of Abraham's descendants. Notice, for instance, the way that Paul cites Gen. 15.6 in Gal. 3.6, drawing from it a conclusion about the identity of Abraham's 'sons':

> Abraham 'had faith in God, and this was recognised as being for him righteousness'; therefore, you know that those who have faith are sons of Abraham.

Many things might have been said about Gen. 15.6, but Paul takes it to say something about Abrahamic descent, a topic that has not been mentioned previously in Galatians or even in the citation of Gen. 15.6. Moreover, it is a topic that seems to need no explanation or introduction. Evidently, the agitators' advocacy of circumcision and nomistic observance was taking place in connection with Abraham and his descendants. The same is implied by Paul's allegory of Hagar and Sarah in 4.21–31, which considers the identity of Abraham's two sons (δύο υἱούς, 4.22). Paul found it pressing to give an interpretation of their respective identities in harmony with his own gospel, evidently because Abrahamic descent was the issue that gave rise to the promotion of circumcision and other practices of the law (see chapter 2 above).

This is not surprising, especially in view of the high regard in which Abraham was held in Early Judaism. Not least, Abraham was regarded as having turned from paganism to the worship of the God who is one, the God of the covenant (e.g., Jub. 11.15–17; Apoc. Abr. 1–8). The Galatians themselves are portrayed in a similar light by Paul in Gal. 4.8–9, and it is possible that agitators were doing the same – comparing the Galatians to Abraham, who like them had turned away from pagan idolatry to serve the God of the 'everlasting' covenant (e.g., Gen. 17.7). The covenant between God and Abraham with his descendants includes a promise that Abraham's offspring would be numerous (Gen. 12.2; 13.16; 15.5; 17.4–5; 18.18; 22.17). But the scriptures restrict true Abrahamic lineage to the descendants of Abraham's son Isaac rather than his son Ishmael

(Gen. 17.19–21; 21.12; cf. Jub. 16.16–18). As Gen. 17.19 makes clear, through Isaac God will establish 'an everlasting covenant for his offspring after him'. As participants in God's covenant with Abraham, Abraham's rightful offspring were required to be circumcised, a rite that symbolised the 'sign of the covenant'. Without it, any male would be cut off from God's covenant blessings, as Gen. 17.10–14 makes as plain and explicit as possible.

A view of this sort must represent the basics of the agitators' point of view in their advocacy of circumcision as an essential requirement for those who would be included in the people of God. In all likelihood, they would have gone further, linking the Abrahamic covenant with the giving of the Mosaic law on Mount Sinai, not least since Abraham was frequently depicted as having observed the requirements of the (eternal) law long before it was given.[21] As in most forms of Judaism, the agitators probably perceived the Mosaic law to ratify the covenant with Abraham and his descendants; keeping the law results in covenant blessing and life (e.g., Lev. 18.5), while breaking it results in a curse and death (e.g., Deut. 27–30). In this way, God's covenant blessing of Abraham (e.g., Gen. 12.2–3) falls to those who obey the law, just as the curse against the enemies of Abraham (Gen. 12.2–3) falls upon those who disobey the law. The clarity of these scriptural guides is hard to dispute, and the agitators need only have referred the Galatians to the Abraham cycle in Genesis to make most of their points.

If Abraham and the Mosaic law were intricately associated in the minds of the agitators, Paul insists that the giving of the law was completely unrelated to the Abrahamic promises (3.17–18). If the Sinai Torah was being associated with Abrahamic descent through Isaac, Paul's Hagar–Sarah allegory rearranges the association, linking Ishmael's mother Hagar with Sinai (and the earthly Jerusalem) and Isaac's mother Sarah (unnamed in the allegory) with freedom – that is, freedom in Christ (4.25–31).

There is good reason to think that some of the scriptural

---

[21] Cf. Jub. 16.28; Sir. 44.20; 2 Bar. 57.2; Philo, *Abr.* 5–6, 60–61, 275; b. *Yom.* 286; m. *Kid.* 4.14; cf. Gen. 25.6.

passages that Paul cites explicitly in Galatians might already have been put to good use by the agitators in support of their case. In 3.8, for instance, Paul cites Gen. 12.3 (cf. 18.18; 22.18), where God promises to bless all the nations 'in Abraham'. It might well be that the agitators found this passage to mean that gentiles would share in the blessings to Abraham by becoming 'in him' through circumcision and the practice of the law.

Moreover, in 3.6, Paul cites Gen. 15.6 in a fashion that goes against the grain of typical interpretations of that verse. The 'reckoning' of righteousness to Abraham spoken of in that verse is clearly due to his πίστις (although the verbal form is used: ἐπίστευσεν), but theological debate appears to have surrounded the interpretation of that Greek word. The agitators probably had interpreted it in accord with the Jewish interpretative norm, in which Abraham's 'faithfulness' in times of great testing was thought to be exemplary of Jewish faithfulness to the covenant obligations and observance of the law.

Jub. 17.17–18 makes this point repeatedly, finishing with these words: 'In everything in which he [God] tested him, he was found faithful. ... And he was not slow to act because he was faithful.' The same is clear from Sir. 44.20, which reads:

> He [Abraham] kept the law of the Most High, and entered into a covenant with him; he certified the covenant in his flesh, and when he was tested he proved faithful (πιστός).

The ultimate test of his faithfulness to God is recorded in Genesis 22, the (so-called) 'sacrifice' of Isaac. After recounting this event, Jubilees draws this conclusion concerning Abraham:

> All of the nations of the earth will bless themselves by your seed because you obeyed my word. And I have made known to all that you are faithful to me in everything (18.16).

Three features merge in this single verse: (1) the blessing of the nations; (2) the mention of Abraham's seed; and (3) the highlighting of Abraham's faithfulness as expressed in his obedient behaviour. Similarly, 1 Macc. 2.52 shows how natural it was to associate the πίστις of Abraham spoken of in Genesis 15 with the record of his faithful actions in Genesis 22: 'Was not

Abraham found to be faithful (πιστός) when tested, and "it was reckoned to him as righteousness"?' For the author of 1 Maccabees, Abraham provides a model of how faithful Jews should 'be zealous for the law' and, in times of persecution, 'give your lives for the covenant of your fathers' (2.50).

In both Rom. 4.3 and Gal. 3.6, Paul finds it necessary to address this deeply-entrenched understanding of Abraham as the faithful example of covenant zeal for the law in obedience to God. In Galatians, he does this by severing two phenomenon which most Jews would have thought to be closely related: works of law and faith.[22] Paul dissociates these two, first in his theological argument of 2.16–21, and next in his recollection of the experiences of the Galatians in 3.1–5, recalling that their reception of the Spirit resulted from their faith rather than any 'works of law'. (The same contrast of faith and 'works' appears in 3.11–12.) With this 'either-or' having already been established, Paul can use it as the interpretative lens through which Gen. 15.6 is read. Consequently, the verb πιστεύειν has nothing to do with Abraham's 'faithfulness' as exemplary of Jewish covenant faithfulness. Instead, it speaks simply of his 'faith' in God as the occasion for righteousness being reckoned to him. Having already set out in 2.16–3.5 the interpretative context in which to read scripture, Paul cites Gen. 15.6 in 3.6 and simply draws his exegetical conclusion in 3.7: it is 'those of faith' (οἱ ἐκ πίστεως) who are 'sons of Abraham' (υἱοί 'Αβραάμ),[23] the obvious implication being that the practice of the law has nothing to do with Abrahamic descent.

This provides Paul with his first definition of what it means to be descendants of Abraham: it means to be marked out by the same phenomenon of faith that Abraham himself demonstrated. This also provides Paul with the occasion to give an explanation of what it means for the nations to be blessed 'in' (ἐν) him (Gen. 12.3 and 18.18; cited in 3.8): it means that their faith, like his, leads to their blessing 'with' or 'alongside' (σύν) him (3.9).

---

[22] Cf. Schoeps, 1961: 202–204; Stanley, 1990: 504.
[23] Hansen rightly notes the implied premise between 3.6 and 3.7: 'as God dealt with Abraham, so he will deal with all' (1989: 112).

But in Galatians Paul gives yet another explanation of Abrahamic descent, an explanation focused on Christ rather than on the believer (as in 3.6–7). Paul is aware that the promise was made to Abraham and his 'seed' (σπέρμα, as in Gen. 13.15 or 17.8 and cited by Paul in 3.16). Interpreting this word, Paul contends that, since it is not in a plural form, it cannot refer to plurality of people ('seeds') but must instead refer to a single person, and that single seed is Christ.

This is quite a claim, especially since Paul is well aware that the singular 'seed' is a collective noun (cf. 'crowd' in English) which contains plural significance not in its grammatical form but in its lexical meaning.[24] Paul employs this same term with its normal collective sense in Romans 4, where a different exegetical argument allows him to sound almost like one of the agitators. The Abrahamic promise, he claims there, is guaranteed 'to all his descendants' (παντὶ τῷ σπέρματι, 4.16). Coupling Genesis 15 and Genesis 17, Paul states that, since God had promised to make him 'the father of many nations' (citing Gen. 17.5 at 4.17), 'so shall your [Abraham's] descendants (τὸ σπέρμα) be' (citing Gen. 15.5 at 4.18). Unlike his case in Romans, however, in Galatians Paul insists that the word has a single referent first and foremost, simply asserting that referent to be Christ.

But even in Galatians Paul allows the word a collective meaning when, in 3.29, he states that those who belong to Christ (the single 'seed') are themselves the 'seed' or descendants of Abraham (τοῦ Ἀβραάμ σπέρμα). By means of their union with Christ (cf. 3.26–28), Christians are joined to the single seed of Abraham and thereby find themselves to be the collective 'descendants of Abraham'. The mechanism in this christological argument is not simply one of similarity of characteristic (i.e., 'faith'), as in 3.6–7, but of incorporation into true Abrahamic descent by means of participation with Christ.

It seems that Paul's interpretations of scriptural passages

---

[24] It may be that there is precedent for this messianic interpretation of the singular 'seed' in Jewish interpretations of 2 Sam. 7.12–14; see Hays, 1989: 85, and those he cites on 203 n. 3.

throughout Galatians 3–4 have been occasioned by the agitators' use of similar passages and themes to argue for the necessity of circumcision and the observance of the law. There is one further scriptural passage on which both the agitators and Paul focus their attention, as part of their respective theological arguments: that is, Deut. 27.26, which Paul cites in Gal. 3.10. The importance of this passage for Paul's presentation in Galatians is considered in the next section.

5. The Curse upon 'those of Works of the Law'

If a survey were taken among professional students of Paul asking them to identify and rank the most difficult passages in the Pauline corpus, one might well expect Gal. 3.10–14 to appear among the most frequently and highly ranked passages.[25] Paul's thoughts are densely packed here, and unravelling them can be complicated business. Accordingly the passage is being analysed in this book in three different chapters: 3.13–14 was considered in the previous chapter (§5.1); 3.11–12 will be considered in the next chapter (§7.4); in this chapter, the connection between Paul's statements on the curse in 3.10 and 3.13 will be considered (both here and in §6.6 below).

Galatians 3.10–14 is closely related to Paul's comments on Abraham in the preceding verses, since it introduces the notion of a 'curse', the expected contrast to the notion of a 'blessing' mentioned in 3.8–9. Galatians 3.10–14 itself is a relatively self-contained piece, incorporating a complex interweaving of closely related scriptural texts and their interpretation. The construction of this passage is indebted to the Jewish interpretative practice of linking words that are common to various passages and constructing an interpretation from the resulting interplay of texts. One such link is the word 'cursed' (ἐπικατάρατος) found in both Deut. 27.26 and Deut. 21.23, cited in 3.10 and 3.13 respectively. Another is the phrase 'to do them'

---

[25] Cf. Hooker: These are 'some of the most obscure verses in the whole New Testament' (1994: 32); Dunn: this passage 'is one of the most difficult to follow that Paul ever dictated' (1993b: 83).

(ποιεῖν αὐτά) found in both Deut. 27.26 and Lev. 18.5, cited in
3.10 and 3.12 respectively. A third link is 'will live' (ζήσεται)
found in both Hab. 2.4 and Lev. 18.5, cited in 3.11 and 3.12
respectively.[26]

The theological connections involved in the 'curse' linkage
are made difficult primarily because Paul's statements in
relation to Deut. 27.26 are difficult to understand in and of
themselves. In 3.10, Paul says that 'those of works of law' are
under a curse, citing Deut. 27.26 to bolster his charge. The
problem is that this scriptural passage seems to suggest the very
opposite of Paul's charge. The text would be of real benefit to
Paul if it did not contain the negative ('not'); instead, it states:
'Cursed is everyone who does *not* abide by and do everything
written in the book of the law'. According to Luther:

> These two statements, Paul's and Moses', are in complete conflict.
> Paul's is: "Whoever does the works of the Law is accursed." Moses'
> is: "Whoever does not do the works of the Law is accursed." How
> can these be reconciled? Or (what is more) how can the one be
> proved on the basis of the other?[27]

For this reason, it is frequently maintained, and seems most
likely, that Deut. 27.26 formed part of the platform for the
agitators' position.[28] In 3.10 Paul is out-smarting the agitators,
returning their serve while adding his own theological spin to
the passage. Unfortunately, it is not wholly clear what that spin
is since, peculiarly, Paul seems to have assumed an important
theological point which he does not explicitly mention.

---

[26] Stanley shows how Paul has carefully crafted his citation of the latter two
passages in order to create a close parallelism between them (1992:
244–45).

[27] 1963a: 252. Caneday claims that this problem is avoidable if ὅσοι ἐξ ἔργων νόμου
is translated 'as many as are nomists' (1989: 193–94); cf. Kruse, 1996: 81 n. 61.
In the end, however, this distinction seems unproductive. Braswell also tries to
avoid the matter by suggesting that the curse is not actively upon 'those of
works of law' but is only a potential threat (1991), a reading I find wholly
unconvincing.

[28] See, e.g., Barrett, 1985: 24–25. According to Hengel, Paul himself probably
used this verse in his pre-Christian career against the emerging hellenistic
Jewish church (1990: 195).

Various suggestions have been made as to what this implied premise might have been. A few have argued that Paul assumes that the scriptural command to 'do the law' refers in fact to Christian faith or to the fulfilment of the law in Christ; accordingly, those who are cursed are those who literally keep the stipulations of the law, since in Paul's view keeping the law refers to putting one's faith in Christ exclusively. In this reading, those who perpetuate a literal conformity to the law are themselves law-breakers, since the law is rightly about faith in Christ.[29]

This interpretation of Paul's unstated assumption suffers from the fact that the important link phrase 'to do them' is forced to mean two different things in the scriptural quotations at 3.10 and 3.12. On the one hand, the phrase 'to do them' of Deut. 27.26 in 3.10 is said to refer to putting faith in Christ; the curse falls on everyone who does not 'do them' by believing in Christ exclusively. On the other hand, the same idea of Lev. 18.5 in 3.12 is said to refer to nomistic observance; the law does not involve faith but rather the doing of the law by keeping its stipulations. This complete shift in meaning of the single phrase (ποιεῖν αὐτά) is too much to expect, especially since it undermines Paul's technique of linking associated texts by means of a shared link word or phrase. While in 3.11–12 Paul contrasts two texts that share the same link ('to live', ζήσεται), the contrast involves not the link word itself but what is said about that link word in each case; the link itself is semantically

---

[29] See Dunn, 1985. Cf. Bring, 1969: 44, 56ff.; Lull, 1980: 124ff. Wright calls Dunn's case 'tortuous and improbable', since 'none of the steps in the argument as Dunn reconstructs it corresponds with what Paul actually says' (1991a: 153 and 153 n. 51). According to Dunn, when Paul says in 3.13 that Christ redeemed us from the curse of the law, he means that the death of Christ frees believers from the *misperception* that the law is about nomistic observance rather than faith (536). This rather truncated view of the epochal significance of Christ's death has drawn strong criticism. To my knowledge, Dunn is followed only by Cranford (1994: 249, 254) and Braswell (1991: 87, without crediting Dunn). Cranford thinks he has avoided the necessity of finding an implied premise in 3.10, but in fact he, like Dunn, has simply replaced one implied premise (that obedience to the law must be perfect) with another (that obedience to the law is Christian faith, and vice versa).

consistent in the two occurrences. The same is true of the other link word in this passage, 'curse'. It is unlikely, then, that the link between 3.10 and 3.12 could sustain different meanings on each occasion.[30]

Another explanation of Paul's unstated assumption in 3.10 finds Paul to be building his case on a common Jewish theology of an extended exile of the Jewish people. This theological background involves the belief that, although Israel had long since returned from Babylonian exile, she still remained effectively in exile, since the glorious future promised to a post-exilic Israel was still pending. In this situation, rather than enjoying the blessings promised to a covenantally-faithful Israel in Deuteronomy 27–30, an Israel in extended exile remained under the curse described there. With this theological background in view, Gal. 3.10–13 claims that 'those of works of law' are cursed because they are identifying with Israel in her exilic situation instead of identifying with Christ who exhausted Israel's curse and ushered in the age of blessing and restoration.[31]

This interpretation has great attraction, and repays close consideration in its fully articulated form.[32] But despite providing a stimulating and engaging analysis, this interpretation is not without its problems. While in Paul's day the notion of exile

---

[30] Neither can the verb 'to do' (ποιεῖν) carry this christological meaning at 5.3.

[31] See Wright, 1991a: 137–56. Cf. N. Elliott: 1994: 134–38; Scott, 1993. Thielman has a similar view, although his interpretation rests fundamentally on the view that the law is impossible to keep perfectly (1989: 65–72).

[32] One attraction is that Paul's attention would be seen to retain a corporate focus throughout. He is, after all, concerned primarily with the definition of the corporate identity of the people of God, rather than engaging in a more individualistic project, wherein the mechanisms are laid out whereby a sinner can approach a just and powerful God. On the other hand, it is quite possible to define corporate identity by speaking of the situation of individuals within larger corporate groups, as Paul does, for instance, in Romans 7; the same is true, I think, of Gal. 3.10. A second advantage of this interpretation would be that Paul could not be accused of making claims excessive and preposterous within the context of the Judaism of his day, such as 'The law cannot be perfectly fulfilled'. Again, however, we only need to look to Romans 7 to find one occurrence where untypical depictions of the experience of 'the Jew' have taken hold in Paul's thinking. See further below.

could be employed as a powerful theological symbol, pregnant with emotive and evocative meaning,[33] it is not obvious from the literature of Early Judaism that an overarching theology of extended exile had been adequately established for an author simply to assume as a given. No doubt expectation concerning the restoration of Israel permeated most forms of Early Judaism, but it remains to be demonstrated that such expectations existed in the form of a theology of extended exile. Were the people of Israel thought to be under a curse, or simply in some intermediate state of anticipation for the fulfilment of God's promised blessing? And even if a theology of extended exile is evident in some parts of Jewish literature, it remains to be demonstrated that such a theology played an important role in Paul's own thinking. Presumably Gal. 3.10–14 is the place to begin since, of all the Pauline texts, it has the best potential to be read in this fashion.[34] But even this passage throws up problems for the 'extended exile' reading, since it is not clear how an interpretation of this kind does adequate justice to what Paul says in 3.11–12. None of the advocates of this interpretation has yet explained the association of these verses and the exile motif *per se*, despite the fact that 3.11 must be seen as closely related to the previous verse (ὅτι δέ).[35] This is especially true for Paul's statement in 3.11 that 'by law no one is justified before God'. If Paul were asked why this is the case, the answer 'Because Israel is in extended exile' is hardly a satisfactory explanation; rather than getting to the bottom of things, it simply raises more issues. Accordingly, a theology of extended

---

[33] Besides those mentioned in footnote 31 above, see also the stimulating article by Bolt (1994), where the book of Tobit is shown to be permeated with an 'extended exile' theology (although Bolt does not use the expression) that marked out Pharisaic (but not Sadducean) interests in the period of Paul's day.

[34] In future writings, Wright will no doubt suggest how the extended exile theology informs further passages. Beyond Gal. 3.10–13, he has thus far argued his case closely only in relation to Romans 2 (1996).

[35] Wright rightly shows how Paul's argument in 3.11–12 has force in opposition to an ethnocentric covenantalism, but he fails to show how the extended exile theology animates these verses (1991a: 137–56). Scott does not engage in discussion of these verses in any of his relevant works: 1992; 1993; 1995.

exile seems unable to explain Paul's unexplained premise of 3.10.[36]

Occasionally it is argued that Paul has no implied premise in 3.10. So, one prominent scholar has suggested that Deut. 27.26 is not intended to give a logical explanation of Paul's claim that those of works of law are cursed. Instead, it is simply the only passage in the whole of scripture were 'curse' appears alongside of 'law'. In this view, Paul cites it simply to link the two words in his readers' minds, despite what the text explicitly states.[37] To my knowledge, the number of scholars who hold this view is one, but even that would seem to be too many.

There are other views that could be entertained further, all with their own particular nuances and intricacies. The ones cited above are simply interpretations that have been proposed by prominent students of Paul in reaction to the widespread, traditional view of Paul's implied premise in 3.10. In that interpretation, Paul is thought to have assumed that no one could fulfil the law perfectly, so that all are under a curse. This interpretation works well within the context, with 3.11 explaining that no one can be justified by the law, apparently because of human inadequacy and inability to keep all of the prescriptions of the law. This is bolstered further by the contrast of scriptural passages in 3.11–12, where faith is shown to be the only means to life, rather than doing the law, again apparently because doing the law perfectly is a human impossibility. The solution is given in Christ's death (3.13), who took upon himself the problem of human inability to do the law and opened the way of faith. In this interpretation, the whole of 3.10–13 is supported by an assumption regarding the impossibility of obeying the law fully (an assumption frequently thought to lie behind 5.3 as well).

This reading, self-evident to many throughout Christian history, may make good sense of the passage, but it is highly problematic within the historical context of the Galatian

---

[36] In the New Testament, 'exile' terminology appears in 1 Peter (1.1, 17; 2.11), where it is more of a motif than a theological superstructure, and the notion of a 'curse' is never evoked as a correlation or consequence of this motif.

[37] Sanders, 1983: 21–22, whose views here represent a change from his earlier advocacy of a more traditional view, as in 1977: 137.

dispute. This is because (as we have seen) the assumption that the law could not be successfully kept goes against the fundamental convictions of Judaism, based on scriptural assurances suggesting precisely the opposite of Paul's supposed assumption.[38] The law itself made provisions for transgressions, so that 'doing the law' included the repentance of the transgressor and cultic atonement for sins, all this under the aegis of a gracious and forgiving covenant God. Accordingly, some have argued that, if Paul had assumed the impossibility of keeping the law, one would expect him to have defended such a view explicitly since this point, the very motor that supposedly would be driving his argument here, would have been quickly exposed as a theological foul, ruled out of bounds according to the parameters defined by Jewish traditions and reflections on scripture. It is too much to believe, the argument goes, that after the agitators had introduced Deut. 27.26 into the debate, Paul puts it back into the arena with a new spin, something that he can do only on the basis of an assumption that he does not state and that would not have carried much weight anyway since the agitators and Paul's own addressees would not have shared such an assumption.

While this is a significant objection, affording it too much weight can distort attempts to read Paul aright. For clearly, Paul's Christian convictions have caused him to re-evaluate his previous practices, convictions and worldview. Nowhere is this clearer than in Romans, where in 9.32 and 11.5–6 (cf. 9.11–12) Paul separates Jewish 'works' from divine 'grace'. A similar feature appears in 4.4–5, where he compares Jewish concern for 'works' with a worker who expects to be rewarded in accordance with his labours, trusting in his own works rather than in God. While the kind of Judaism that Paul seeks to undermine in Romans is ethnocentric (e.g., 2.17–20; 3.29–30) rather than legalistic, he nonetheless finds that, from a Christian perspective, Judaism's ethnocentric covenantalism reduces to nothing else than legalism. When saving grace is restricted to those 'in Christ', those beyond the boundaries of the Christian

---

[38] See, for example, Moore, 1927: 3.150–51; Räisänen, 1983: 118–27. Hong seems to miss the point completely (1994).

community are left with nothing but works to effect their salvation, despite their own convictions that their works are in response to grace. And if works are the only other avenue possible, the performance of those works would need to be perfect and without error.

Similar to this line of thought, Romans 7 demonstrates how far Paul's Christian reflections on Jewish experience apart from Christ have veered away from traditional Jewish categories. In Paul's portrait, 'the Jew' is completely incapable of doing the law, despite the best of intentions. Diverging from entrenched Jewish traditions, Paul entertains no ideas about repentant Jews being met by God's gracious forgiveness, except in Christ (8.3). In Paul's view, the non-Christian Jew does not say, as the Qumran covenanters did:

> I lean on thy grace,
>   and on the multitude of thy mercies,
> For thou wilt pardon iniquity,
>   and through thy righteousness
> [Thou wilt purify man] of his sin.[39]

Instead, Paul's Jew cries out, 'Who will deliver me from this body of death?' (7.24).

These examples depict how Paul has drastically reinterpreted the meaning of 'doing the law' in a fashion that has little semblance to the traditional Jewish view that he held in his pre-Christian days (cf. Phil. 3.6).[40] The conviction that gave rise to the statements considered above seems also to be implicit in Gal. 3.10: that the law cannot be done, despite the best of intentions by covenantally motivated Jews, and that apart from Christ the Jewish condition is desperate, along with the rest of humanity. Moreover, if such profoundly novel depictions of traditional forms of Judaism and Jewish experience have made their way into Paul's letter of self-introduction to a community

---

[39] 1QH 4.37 in Vermes, 1995: 203; in García Martínez, it appears as 1QH 12.37, and is translated: 'For you have supported me by your kindness and by your abundant compassion. Because you atone for sin and cle[anse man] of his fault through your justice' (1994: 336).

[40] See further, B. W. Longenecker, 1991: 211–14; 1997: 139–43; Westerholm, 1988: 152, 163, 220.

with a significant Jewish contingency (i.e., Rome), it is not too much to assume that the Christians in Galatia with whom Paul had lived and worked would have been well aware of precisely this aspect of his Christian worldview. The Paul who introduced himself to Christians in Rome by distinguishing circumcision from what it means to keep the law (Rom. 2.25–29) is the same Paul who writes to Christian communities in Galatia which know him well and are already acquainted with the contours of his theology. Accordingly, while some maintain that Paul could not have assumed the premise of the impossibility of doing the law at 3.10 since it is not an accurate depiction of Judaism and since his audience would not have been aware of it, such a view of the matter seems unfounded when the full picture is considered.

Having attended to some of the more acute issues pertaining to the interpretation of 3.10, we can now consider Paul's comments in 3.13, where Christ is depicted as the one who bore the curse of the law for the benefit of others.

6. The Cursed Christ

Paul believed that the people of Israel lay under a curse pronounced by the law on those whose obedience was insufficient (3.10). This curse still applied to those Jews who failed to trust in Jesus Christ, but those who put their faith in him solely have been brought out from under the curse of the law, since Christ has already come under the burden of their curse on their behalf (3.13). To prove the last point, Paul cites Deut. 21.23 (with slight adjustments): 'Cursed is everyone who hangs on a tree.' Most interpreters of Paul think that this would have been an important scriptural passage in his arsenal against the Christian movement during his pre-Christian days. He would have understood it to mean that Jesus had been cursed or rejected by God, as his curse-laden manner of death presumably had demonstrated. This Jesus could not, then, have played any part (let alone a central part) in God's redemptive activity, and consequently the Christians were introducing pollutants into Judaism. Paul has the same notion in mind when he speaks of a crucified Messiah being a 'stumbling block for Jews' (1 Cor.

1.23), or when he says in 2 Cor. 5.16 that 'even though we previously appraised Christ according to human standards, we now no longer appraise him in that fashion'.[41]

Paul's understanding of Christ's crucifixion became reconfigured after he became a Christian. In 3.13, he depicts Christ's death as the occasion when the law's curse against its offenders fell upon Christ, resulting in liberty from the curse for the people of Israel who have put their faith in him. Whether or not his pre-Christian worldview included the conviction that the law's curse had hung over the people of Israel, this conviction is evident within Paul's Christian worldview. And Paul coupled it with the conviction that that same curse has been transferred to Christ, the object and carrier of the curse, releasing those who identify with him from it without remainder. By taking their destiny in its full force upon himself, he has effected the means of their redemption.[42]

Notice what this assumes about Christ. The Deuteronomic curse has fallen upon the people of Israel due to their infidelity (3.10); the removal of that curse comes about in relation to one who belongs to a different category altogether, one whose fidelity is acceptable. The premise for all this has already been stated clearly in a passage like 2.16: 'no one is justified by works of law, but instead through the faithfulness of Jesus Christ.' The first clause is represented by Paul's comments in 3.10 ('cursed are all those of works of law'), while the second is the assumption for his claim in 3.13 ('Christ redeemed us from the curse of the law'). This contrast between faithlessness and faithfulness, like that between disobedience and obedience in Rom. 5.12–21, corresponds to the contrast in 2 Corinthians between those who had committed 'trespasses' (5.19) and the one who 'knew no sin' (5.21). The fact that Christ's life was 'materially' different from that of others is the prerequisite for

---

[41] This reconstruction of the pre-Christian Paul's understanding and use of Deut. 21.23 has been called into question by Fredricksen (1991: 550–52; cf. N. Elliott, 1994: 144–45). For her, the appearance of Deut. 21.23 at Gal. 3.13 is due simply to the contours of Paul's argument concerning blessings and curses in Galatians 3, without positing a hypothetical reconstruction of how Paul might have understood the passage in his pre-Christian days.

[42] On the substitutionary nature of the metaphor, see McLean, 1996: 126–31.

his taking their destiny upon himself; because of his faithfulness, the curse that applied to faithless others could be transferred to him, for their benefit.

In all this, the law has played an important part. Although some have interpreted the phrase the 'curse of the law' to mean that the law itself is a curse that needs to be removed,[43] this is not what Paul had in mind. The genitive 'of the law' is not epexegetical, identifying the law itself as a curse. Instead, the genitive is a subjective genitive or genitive of origin: the curse that the law pronounces, or the curse that proceeds from the law. Notice also that Paul does not suggest that the law was wrong in its pronouncement of the curse and that God overturned its incorrect pronouncement. Although Paul never argues this way, some interpreters have found the origins of Paul's rejection of the law to lie in this theological connection. The law had shown itself to be wrong, thereby invalidating itself; accordingly, it could no longer be seen as speaking for God. In this interpretation, Jesus' death on the cross is less about the law's judgement on Christ and more about God's judgement on the law.[44]

Paul's thought, however, is far more complex and nuanced than this interpretation allows. Paul imagines the law to have acted in accordance with God's will by pronouncing a curse upon Christ, not because Christ was deserving of it but because, in doing so, he established the means for the redemption of Israel from the curse, resulting in the bestowal of the Spirit on the gentiles (see above, §5.1). The law's pronouncement of a curse on Jesus was carried out within the redemptive purposes of God, performing a specific function that had salvific

---

[43] Cf. Betz, 1979: 149; Calvert, 1993: 236.

[44] Kim writes: 'God reversed or annulled the verdict of the law upon Jesus. Paul was thus compelled to recognize that it is no longer the Torah but Christ who truly represents the will of God, that Christ has superseded the Torah as the revelation of God ... the law cursed him wrongly, thus demonstrating that it no longer represented God's will' (1981: 274–75). Cf. Schweitzer, 1931: 72; Beker, 1980: 185–86. Martyn goes further, speaking of God making things right 'by entering into combat against the Law, in so far as it enacts its curse' and 'by acting in Christ against real enemies' such as the law (1993a: 147 = 1997: 155).

ramifications of cosmic proportion.[45] This curse was the zenith of the law's activity within its valid and proper era of purpose.

Can it be said, however, that the law's curse upon Christ was also God's curse? Many interpreters assert that this would have been impossible for Paul to think,[46] while others suggest that this is precisely Paul's point.[47] It is true that in 2 Cor. 5.21 Paul can speak of Christ having been made sin by God ('God made him to be sin');[48] by analogy, the same divine activity might be in Paul's mind as he talks about Christ becoming a curse. On the other hand, in his citation of Deut. 21.23 in 3.13, Paul omits the significant phrase 'by God' (ὑπὸ θεοῦ).[49] Since this omission is unlikely to have been accidental, it appears that Paul wants to avoid the unqualified conclusion that God cursed Jesus – probably the very conclusion that Paul himself held in the days before his commitment to the Christian gospel.

Had Paul taken the time to enlarge his meaning in this verse, he might have argued that, although the curse was the law's curse, it could not have been so without God's consent. After all, despite being an inferior revelation of God than the sending of the son (cf. 3.19 and 4.4–6), the law was nonetheless God's law. The Judaeo-Christian tradition has often made use of categories distinguishing God's active will and God's permissive, assenting will – categories that Paul might have put to good use to explain some of the ambiguity that he permits in 3.13. While the curse was the law's, the transfer of the curse from 'those of works of law' to Christ involved the consent of the sovereign

---

[45] See esp. Räisänen, 1983: 249–50; Wright, 1991a: 152; N. Elliott, 1994: 145. For this reason, it is also inappropriate to speak, as does Bligh, of the curse being only apparent and not real, with Jesus being merely 'accused in the opinion of men' (1969: 270).

[46] Barrett, 1985: 30; Koch, 1986: 125; Burton, 1921: 174; Oepke, 1973: 107.

[47] E.g., Dunn: 'no distinction between the curse of the law and the curse of God is intended ... the crucified Jesus was cursed by God' (1993a: 177–78); cf. his 1993b: 86. So too, H. A. W. Meyer writes: 'The idea of κατάρα as the curse *of God* [is] obvious of itself to every reader ... And if Paul had not meant the curse *of God*, ... he would have been practising a deception' (1884: 153–54).

[48] The ἁμαρτίαν of 2 Cor. 5.21 is best interpreted to mean 'sin' rather than 'sin offering'. See Hooker, 1990: 13–14; McLean, 1996: 108–109.

[49] The Hebrew (כי־קללת אלהים תלוי) can mean either that the hanged one is cursed by God or that he is a curse (or insult) to God.

God, whose saving purposes were to be served in the process. Paul probably omitted the phrase 'by God' when speaking of Christ's curse because it did not do justice to his understanding of the intricate dynamics of the relationship between God and his faithful son. To speak of Christ being cursed by God in such an unqualified manner might have perpetuated further confusion in the Galatian churches. In the end, the cursing of Jesus by God's law was not 'wrong', nor could it have been in contradiction to God's will. Nonetheless, neither can it be said to have been God's final word on the subject of the crucified Christ.

In each section of this chapter, we have seen that one constant pervades Paul's explanations of the nature and purposes of the law, as well as his interpretation of scripture: namely, the disqualification of nomistic observance as a necessary feature of salvation in Christ. But why should Paul's estimate on these matters carry weight among his Galatian hearers? What makes his interpretative efforts authoritative, as opposed to those of the agitators? Questions of this sort lead to a consideration of Paul's presuppositions about the supra-human power that an interpreter embodies, about whether or not the Spirit of Christ is at work in the life of the one(s) expounding scripture. Such matters are included in the focus of the next chapter.

7

Eschatological Transformation Embodied

In chapter 4 above, we saw how Paul envisages God's eschatological power as transforming the moral character of Christians, whose lives are advertisements of God's invading sovereignty; in Paul's purview, moral lifestyle is caught up in the cosmic drama of God's invading triumph over competing forces. This is especially clear in Gal. 5.17, where Paul locates the sphere of the Spirit as locked in an all-encompassing conflict with the sphere of the flesh. A battle is raging, as the two spheres of influence wage war on each other. Human beings cannot escape the battlefield, but are caught up in the conflict in one way or another, being enlisted to advance the purposes of one sphere or the other.

This backdrop of a great cosmic drama lends added force to the way that Paul characterises the three parties in the Galatian situation: the Galatians, the agitators, and Paul himself. This chapter seeks to give a finer point to what we have already seen concerning Paul's association of moral identity and suprahuman forces. In particular, it highlights Paul's characterisation of himself as embodying Christ (§7.1), in contrast to his characterisation of the agitators as those through whom demonic spirits are at work (§7.2). Moreover, we will see that this same matrix of thought informs Paul's understanding of the Galatians' past and present situations (§7.3). Finally, we will explore the relationship assumed in Galatians between transformed character and scriptural interpretation (§7.4). Each of these matters attests to the way that Paul envisages human life caught up within the orb of suprahuman power of one sort or another, with concrete effects for good or ill.

1. Paul's Embodiment of Christ

The theological thread that unites the whole of Paul's letter to
the Galatians is perhaps best summed up in the phrase 'the
singularity of the gospel',[1] referring to the exclusive claim of
Christ upon the lives of believers, resulting in the complete
transformation of their individual and corporate identity and
the renunciation of all competing loyalties.

Of special significance is the fact that the singularity of the
gospel does not float about in Paul's letter as some disembodied
principle or maxim. It is developed first and foremost in relation
to Paul himself, his own life being set up as the paradigmatic
embodiment of the transforming power of God. This is part of
the rationale behind Paul's self-portrait of Galatians 1–2.
Although the pressing point that Paul addresses in the two opening chapters is the legitimacy of his apostolic ministry, an important component of that matter is Paul's own paradigmatic mod-
elling of Christian transformation.[2] Some interpreters find
Paul's autobiographical account in Galatians 1–2 to function as
an apologetic defence of his apostolic legitimacy, while others
find it to serve as an instructive model of Christian transformation. These two matters are not mutually exclusive, however, but
are integrally related and reinforce each other: No one provides
a better model of Christian transformation than an authentic
apostle, whose life can and should be imitated. Accordingly,
Paul's first moral imperative of his letter in 4.12, 'Become like
me', draws its force from his autobiographical sketch of the first
two chapters, where his own life is presented as an example of
the singularity of the gospel.[3] While Galatians 1–2 serve to
defend Paul's apostolic credentials, and while the specifics mentioned there are exclusive to his apostolic ministry, they also
demonstrate the quality of Christian resilience in the face of
mounting pressure, a quality that Paul expects to be replicated in

---

[1] To borrow the title of Gaventa's 1991 article.

[2] See, for instance, W. P. de Boer, 1962: 188–96; Stowers, 1986: 109 (cf.
100–102); Gaventa, 1986; Lyons, 1985: 123–76; R. N. Longenecker, 1990:
cxvi; Hansen, 1994b; Sampley, 1996: 125.

[3] Lyons exaggerates the case, however, when he claims that 'the major *raison
d'être* of the autobiographical narrative is to be found in Gal. 4.12–20, where
Paul calls for the Galatians to imitate him' (1985: 136; cf. 165).

the lives of all Christians – not least the Galatians as they face increased pressure to be circumcised.

Significant in this regard is the way that Paul's autobiographical reconstruction in Gal. 1.11–2.21 is framed at the beginning and the end in terms of Christ's indwelling of him. So, as Paul says in 1.16, Christ had been revealed ἐν ἐμοί, a phrase that is usually translated 'to me'. Although there is an objective revelation given *to* Paul, the preposition ἐν is under-interpreted if it is restricted to mean simply 'to'. Paul is doing more in this verse than simply describing an initial encounter between himself and the Son of God. Such would be subject to the view that Paul's encounter left him with little more than a first impression of Christ and his significance. And such a view might lead to further denigration of Paul's particular gospel, since first impressions are often poorly founded and in need of some correction. Perhaps deliberately to dodge a misconstrual of this sort (e.g., Paul may have met the risen Jesus on one occasion, but Peter and the Jerusalem apostles were associated with him throughout his earthly ministry), Paul incorporates the preposition ἐν to signify an intensive encounter of an all-embracing and all-encompassing nature. In the revelation of Christ to him, Paul's own identity became caught up in a process of transformation whereby Christ himself invaded Paul's own person. In this way, the chance of a misinformed first impression is ruled out altogether. Accordingly, the sense of ἐν ἐμοί of 1.16 is best conveyed by the phrase 'in me'.[4] Paul speaks of his encounter with the risen Christ as the occasion when his own identity was transformed to such an extent that he himself became a vehicle through which Christ is revealed among the gentiles (ἐν τοῖς ἔθνεσιν).[5] God's eschatological invasion of Paul's world (ἀποκαλύψαι) resulted not just in 'enlightenment' ('revealed to me') but in 'enlivenment'

---

[4] Although Smith goes too far in saying that 'the centre of Paul's concern is not any revelation to Paul, but the revelation *in* Paul' (1979: 15). The two aspects are to be held together as a single phenomenon.

[5] The ἐν of ἐν τοῖς ἔθνεσιν, with the verb 'preach', introduces a simple dative of indirect object, 'to the gentiles' (cf. similar constructions with verbs of declaration in 1 Cor. 2.6; 7.17), or perhaps a locative of sphere, 'among the gentiles'. But the ἐν ἐμοί, in association with the verb 'reveal', is closer to the

('revealed in me').[6] Implicitly Paul is claiming that everything that transpires in his controversial ministry (described in brief in Galatians 1–2) takes place as a consequence of this enlivenment by Christ.

A similar note is struck at the end of Galatians 2, where Paul completes his autobiographical presentation. As we have seen in previous chapters, in 2.20 Paul, who claims to have died with Christ (2.19), describes Christ as living 'in' him (ἐν ἐμοί), animating his own existence so that Christ's own faithful life before God marks out Paul's life as well. Accordingly, Paul's defence of his apostolic credentials throughout Galatians 1–2 is set within the context of Christ's own indwelling of Paul; his ministry and gospel emerge from that fundamental fact. When Paul paints his own self-portrait, it is Christ that appears on the canvas.

2. Demonic Manipulation by the Agitators

The embodiment of Christ is not, however, the form of suprahuman embodiment that Paul sees at work in the Galatian situation. If Paul believed that Christ had taken over his own life to the extent that Christ was the spiritual force at work and alive in him, he portrays the agitators in precisely the opposite manner, metaphorically depicting them as manipulators of demonic suprahuman forces. This is clear from two passages in Galatians where he likens them to wielders of the evil eye and to those who engage in demonic sorcery. In order to demonstrate the impact of the former imagery, consideration needs to be given to the evil eye phenomenon as it was understood in Paul's day.

THE EVIL EYE PHENOMENON
Widespread in the Graeco-Roman culture of Paul's day was the

---

locative of sphere than a simple dative of indirect object, although both aspects are no doubt included. To read ἐν ἐμοί as a dative of indirect object exclusively, in view of ἐν τοῖς ἔθνεσιν, is to apply the rules of grammar slavishly, especially when the governing verbs are taken into consideration. Similarly, compare Paul's flexible use of ἐν in Gal. 4.19–20. In 4.19, ἐν ὑμῖν is a locative of place ('in you') or of sphere ('among you'), while the same phrase in 4.20 involves a dative of reference or respect ('concerning you').

[6] 'Enlivenment' is entered in the *Oxford English Dictionary* (Murray, Bradley, *et al.*: 1933: 3. E192).

belief that the world is populated by a multitude of suprahuman powers in constant conflict with each other. Human beings could become pawns and players in the rivalry and struggles that marked out the other-worldly realm. The spirit world could envelop the concrete world, as demonic powers and mysterious forces impacted upon human affairs. Gods, demons, and spiritual forces were thought to be alive and well, and influencing human circumstances and destiny. Their power could be tapped into for one's own personal gain and benefit; the more divinities one could favourably court, or the more spirits of the dead one could access, the better one's chances in life, love, business and the overall pursuit of happiness. So too, their power might be sought to disadvantage others; one could manipulate a demonic spirit or request a favourably disposed god to bring curses upon other people who might be considered business competitors or rivals in any way. Accordingly, a distinction between 'magic' and 'religion' is all too often an anachronistic and ahistorical abstraction when considering ancient Mediterranean practices devised to enhance one's chances in the competition for survival, advantage and dominance.[7] In the end, the world of the supernatural was one to be feared as much as manipulated.[8]

Belief in the evil eye phenomenon was a popular component of this general worldview.[9] It held a powerful place in hellenistic and Jewish imagination, just as it remains a part of popular worldview in many cultures today. It involves the belief that individuals of certain types possess the power to bring misfortune to things animate and inanimate simply through their glance.[10] An evil eye injury could prove ruinous to one's physical

---

[7] See Segal, 1982; Gager 1992: 24–25; Crossan, 1991: 304–10; somewhat similarly, Betz, 1991. According to Crossan, a socio-political nuance is all that can distinguish the two: 'Religion is official and approved magic; magic is unofficial and unapproved religion' (1991: 305).

[8] See, for example, Aune, 1980.

[9] See esp. J. H. Elliott, 1988, where extensive documentation is provided. Also Blau, 1903; Noy, 1972.

[10] In his *Moralia*, Plutarch records the popular conviction that injury can frequently be sustained 'by a mere look', since the eye provides the most active form of contact between people and can communicate disease more easily than other forms of contact (*Quaest. conviv.* 681A-D).

wellbeing, financial fortunes and/or social stature. Several categories of people were thought to be prime suspects of evil eye perpetrators: social outsiders, deviants, or simply those who suffered from physical disabilities and deformities. Children[11] and those who had avoided misfortune or who were held in high esteem[12] were thought to be most at risk from the evil eye, although all people and things were potentially exposed to its effects. Various strategies would be employed to guard against the evil eye and offer protection, including amulets, hand gestures and spitting.

The moral portrait of those who wielded the evil eye was usually negative, rooting their harmful effects in deficient inner qualities, such as jealousy, covetousness and especially envy ($\varphi\theta\acute{o}\nu o\varsigma$).[13] Moreover, it was popularly thought that malignant moral character could provide the occasion for invisible spiritual forces to become operative through evil eye practitioners. In this way, the effective evil eye could be attributed to the influence of the suprahuman and the demonic.[14]

This brief survey of common convictions about evil eye practitioners provides the context that lends force to Paul's charge against the agitators in Gal. 3.1, as is shown below.

---

[11] Plutarch speaks of the 'susceptible, vulnerable constitutions' of children (*Quaest. conviv.* 680D). For the same in epistolary papyri and Jewish traditions, see Spicq, 1994: 275; Blau, 1903: 280–81; Noy, 1972: 999–1000. Esler gives a modern version of the same (1994: 19).

[12] Cf. Plutarch, *Inv. et od.* 7; Philo, *Flacc.* 143; Josephus, *Ant.* 10.250–57; *Vita* 425; Demosthenes, *C. Lept.* 24.

[13] Cf. Plutarch, *Quaest. conviv.* 681E–682D; *Inv. et od.* 7; Deut. 28.54–56 (LXX); Sir. 14.6–10; Philo, *Flacc.* 29; Josephus, *Ant.* 10.250–57; Demosthenes, *C. Lept.* 24. See too the LXX of Prov. 23.6 and 28.22. Envy is likened to a disease of the eyes in Plutarch (*Inv. et od.* 2). We learn from him that all such evil desires, 'having been a long time in the mind, produce evil conditions' (*Quaest. conviv.* 682C). See too Wis. Sol. 2.23–24, where 'the devil' is depicted as the one who first exhibited envy when he jealously saw how humanity had been blessed, having been created in the image of God; as a consequence, death has come into the world. For further examples, see Spicq, 1994; Elliott, 1988.

[14] Plutarch's extended discussion of the evil eye (*Quaest. conviv.* 680C–683B) closes with the hint that the evil eye was often associated with invisible spiritual forces. Cf. Delling, 1964; J. H. Elliott, 1988: 52; Spicq, 1994: 275.

THE EVIL EYE AND GALATIANS 3.1

In the Graeco-Roman world, an effective way of undermining the stature of other persons or groups was to accuse them of practising malicious magic. Propaganda of this sort is not absent from Paul's letter to the Galatians. This is especially clear from 3.1 where, according to the NRSV, he writes, 'Who has bewitched (ἐβάσκανεν) you?' The verb βασκαίνειν, occurring only here in the New Testament, is a well-established technical term for the evil eye, just as the evil eye practitioner is a βάσκανος, the protective amulet is a βάσκανιον, and the evil eye itself is ὀφθαλμὸς βάσκανος or simply βάσκανια (or ὀφθαλμὸς πονηρός; cf. Mk. 7.22; Mt. 6.23; 20.15).

The metaphor of the evil eye carries forceful connotations that Paul is capitalising on – connotations easily lost in modern cultures. Unlike some reputable scholars of the past,[15] contemporary scholars have for the most part undervalued the rhetorical and theological importance of this passage, which clearly rings with an accusation against the agitators as envious wielders of the evil eye. We do not need to assume, of course, that in Paul's view the agitators were literally practising magical arts, reciting curse formulas and casting demonic spells in order to influence the Galatian Christians; Paul's evil eye imagery is metaphorical on that score. But nonetheless, Paul employs the imagery precisely because he envisaged the Galatians' situation to involve some realities that were typically aligned with the practice of the evil eye, especially the influence of suprahuman forces and the flawed moral character of the agitators.

The possibility of having been 'injured with the evil eye' (as 3.1 might best be translated) involved an alarming, fearful and threatening prospect. First, the imagery of the evil eye is suggestive of a change in the spiritual power influencing the Galatians. Paul describes their previous experience as having been marked out by the Spirit, whom they had received (3.2), whom their Christian life had 'begun with' (3.3), and who had

[15] See Luther, 1963a: 26.190–97; 1963b: 27.244–45; Lightfoot, 1896: 133. Lightfoot writes: 'St Paul's metaphor is derived from the popular belief in the power of the evil eye', implying both the 'baleful influence on the recipient [the Galatians]' and the 'envious spirit of the agent [the agitators]'. Cf. Neyrey, 1988.

been supplied to them, as evidenced by the miracles that occurred among them (3.5). The suggestion of an evil eye injury among the Galatians insinuates the presence of other spiritual forces at work in them more recently, and seems intended to solicit from the Galatians an inventory of the spiritual forces with which they have become aligned, in contrast to the Spirit. Whereas the demonic forces behind evil eye practitioners would bring ruin of one sort or another, the Galatians' early experience of the Spirit was evidence that God had been at work among them (ἐν ὑμῖν), even bringing about miracles in their midst.

The Galatians' experience of the Spirit was the result, says Paul, not of any 'works of law' but solely of their faith (3.2, 5). Paul also suggests in 3.1 that his ministry had been instrumental in their reception of the Spirit, describing the Galatians as those 'before whose eyes Jesus Christ was vividly portrayed as having been crucified'. No doubt Paul is referring here to his own preaching which presented Christ to them in terms that spelt out clearly the exclusive salvific significance of Christ[16] – something he has just emphasised again in the previous verse of Galatians: 'For if righteousness is through law, then Christ died for no purpose' (2.21). The gospel of Christ crucified ensures that the spiritual power at work in the Galatians will not be that of the spirits of the deceased, but the Spirit of the living Christ.

Second, the evil eye imagery is suggestive of a serious flaw in the moral character of those agitators who were promoting circumcision, since perpetrators of the evil eye were frequently thought to be morally defective. The charge of moral deficiency is one that Paul makes repeatedly and explicitly elsewhere in his letter when characterising the agitators (4.17; 6.12–13; cf. 2.4–5). Moreover, it is important to note that Paul includes 'envious attitudes and behaviour' (φθόνοι, 5.21) in his list of 'the works of the flesh' (5.19–21), in close combination with the practices of the law (5.18) which were being advocated by the agitators. So too, just as Paul contrasted the influence of the Spirit with that of the demonic evil eye in 3.1–5, in 5.25–26 he contrasts walking by the Spirit with self-conceit, provocation and

---

[16] See especially Hays, 1983: 196–98.

envy (φθονεῖν, 5.26). These references to envy are significant, since envy was the moral attribute thought particularly to characterise wielders of the evil eye. Paul's inclusion of φθόνοι in these passages is not likely to be merely incidental. His depiction of degenerate moral character highlights on two occasions the quality most associated with the evil eye (5.21, 26) – the second of these occasions rounding off his analysis of degenerate character in contrast to Spirit-filled character. We cannot be sure whether Paul intended an explicit connection between these texts in Galatians 3 and Galatians 5, or whether his perception of the situation as involving the evil eye influences in 3.1 has subtly affected his inventory of character in 5.21–26. Either way, however, the evil eye imagery of 3.1 seems to have played an important role in determining Paul's lexical choices in Gal. 5.21–26.

Notably, Paul also includes mention of 'sorcery' (φαρμακεία, 5.20) in his list of the 'works of the flesh'. This entry too, which appears in no other Pauline catalogue of vices,[17] may not simply be a randomly chosen item for the catalogue, but is itself suggestive of the way that Paul envisages the Galatian situation to involve spiritual realities that run contrary to the ways of God. Paul's reference to sorcery here resonates with his likening of the agitators as wielders of the evil eye in 3.1.

In contrast to his own gospel and its effects, Paul establishes in a single verse (3.1) an implied association between (1) those who would perpetuate interest in observing the law, (2) malicious character, and (3) the influence of malevolent spiritual forces. As we have seen, a strong convergence of these same features appears again in Gal. 5.19–26.

FURTHER POLEMIC OF DEMONIC INVOLVEMENT

A similar strain of polemic might be evident in Gal. 4.12–20. There, Paul not only contrasts his own high moral character (ἐν καλῷ, 4.18) with the agitators' disreputable motivation (οὐ

---

[17] Cf. the vice-lists of Rom. 1.29–31; 13.13; 1 Cor. 5.10–11; 6.9–10; 2 Cor. 12.20–21; Eph. 4.31; 5.3–5; Col. 3.5, 8; 1 Tim. 1.9–10; 2 Tim. 3.2–5; Tit. 3.3. It is not clear from a comparison of Gal. 3.1 and 5.21 whether sorcery is a product of works of flesh or vice versa; Paul seems simply to associate the two in interrelated fashion, rather than setting out a definitive causal relationship.

καλῶς, 4.17), but he may also be likening the agitators to those who cast separation spells upon others.[18] In Paul's day, hatred spells and separation curses were frequently employed as means of dissociating persons from others by the power of demonic spirits or gods of chaos. Separation curses introduced enmity between previously allied parties, and promoted the interests of the one inducing the curse.[19]

This scenario of demonically manufactured enmity between parties profitably informs Gal. 4.16–17, where Paul suggests that he has been made the Galatians' enemy (ἐχθρός, related to 'enmity', ἔχθρα), presumably due to the influence of the agitators, who are trying to separate the Galatians from association with him. When informed by the magical practices of the day, such a depiction suggestively associates the agitators with demonic manipulation for personal gain. Moreover, just as Paul includes 'sorcery' and 'attitudes and practices of envy' in his list of the works of the flesh, so too he includes in that list 'attitudes and practices of enmity' (ἔχθραι, 5.20). This entry too may have been included in the list due to its particular relevance to the situation in Galatia (it appears in no other Pauline catalogue of vices), referring to the effects of the agitators' influence.

In this fashion, the charge of sorcery levelled against the agitators in 3.1 is imaginatively extended into other passages in Galatians, suggestively linking degenerate character with the activity of demonic spirits. While Paul would no doubt grant that the agitators are not literally reciting chants and intentionally conjuring up malicious suprahuman forces (and in this regard his charges work metaphorically), he nonetheless seems to envisage the end result to involve grave concrete realities (and in this regard his charges are not metaphorical): the

---

[18] For a fuller defence of this view, see B. W. Longenecker, 1998.

[19] The following separation curse is exemplary: 'Charm for causing separation: ... "I call upon you, god ... , you who love disturbances and hate stability and scatter the clouds from one another ... Give to him, NN, the son of her, NN, strife, war; and to him, NN, the son of her, NN, odiousness, enmity (ἔχθραν)"' (*Papyri Graecae Magicae* XII.365–75, cited from Betz, 1992: 166). So too there were numerous counter-spells that protected against the anger of, in the words of one papyrus, 'enemies' (ἐχθρούς) and 'accusers' (*PGM* X.24–25).

Galatians are susceptible to spiritual realities other than the Spirit of God, due to the malevolent influence of the agitators.

Galatians 4.12–20 is a compact passage that is pervaded with this connection between suprahuman forces and moral character. In fact, the agitators are not the only ones whose lifestyle is assessed in the light of this connection; so too are the Galatians, as is shown below.

3. The Spirit, Christian Character, and the Galatians

The success of Paul's case in Galatians depends upon the connection that he establishes between (1) one's pattern of life and (2) the suprahuman powers with which one is inevitably aligned. The contrast between opposing types of suprahuman powers is most clearly articulated in 4.1–11, where Paul sets out two categories of spiritual influence. On the one hand, there is the Spirit of Christ who lives in the hearts of Christians (4.6). On the other hand, there are the 'elements of the world' (4.3, 9), 'beings that by nature are no gods' (4.8) – spiritual forces who lead their underlings away from true knowledge of God, who enslave them and who, in contrast to the sovereign God, are weak and beggarly. Paul, of course, associates his ministry with the Spirit (e.g., 3.1–5), and associates the influence of the agitators with the world overseen by the enslaving 'elements'.[20] But a third party, the Galatians themselves, are also assessed in terms of the influences of suprahuman forces, and in this Gal. 4.12–20 plays a significant role.

It is important to note the way in which 4.12–20 is framed at its beginning and close by a singular focus on Christian resilience and lifestyle. We have already suggested above that when Paul writes his first imperative of the letter, 'Become like me' (4.12a), he has his autobiographical sketch of Galatians 1–2 primarily in mind, where his own life is presented as a demonstration of Christian commitment and resilience. What he means in 4.12a is best paraphrased as, 'Become resilient in your commitment to the gospel, just as I am.' Paul urges the

---

[20] There is a close relationship between Paul's description of the agitators in 4.17 and his description of the spiritual forces in 4.8–9, whose influence directs people in ways contrary to those of God.

Galatians to imitate him in wholehearted commitment to the gospel.[21] This same context of thought comes to expression in 4.19 as well, where Paul declares his hope that Christ will become formed 'in' or 'among' them (ἐν ὑμῖν, 4.19; cf. 4.6; Phil. 2.1–11).[22] Whether this is interpreted individualistically ('in each one of you') or corporately ('in the interactions of your corporate life together') or both, the point is the same: those whose lives are invaded by the eschatological power of God become the living embodiment of the indwelling Christ. This is simply a variation on the Pauline theme concerning the intimate union of Christ and the believer – a theme elaborated by images of Christ's indwelling (2.20; 1.16), of Christ being 'put on' (3.27), and of the Spirit nurturing Christ-like character in the lives of those in Christ (5.22–25). The self-portrait of the Galatians is to be identical to the self-portrait of Paul, with only the figure of Christ appearing within the frame.

The whole of Gal. 4.12–20, then, is enclosed by Paul's understanding of Christian lifestyle in relation to resilient commitment and the blossoming of Christ-likeness within the lives of his followers (4.12a, 19). This focus on Christian character provides the conceptual framework for the passage; Paul's comments emerge from this theological context, as he presents two contrasting situations and evaluates them with reference to Christ-likeness. In this way, Gal. 4.12–20 undertakes an inventory of moral character – itself an indicator of the influence of suprahuman forces.

THE INITIAL MANIFESTATION OF CHRISTIAN CHARACTER IN THE GALATIANS

In 4.12–15, Paul recalls the manner in which the Galatians first welcomed him. His comments here are not some nostalgic pondering about the good things that used to be. Instead, they act principally as the beginning of a testament to the Christ-like

---

[21] See Hansen, 1994a: 130–31; 1994b: 200. This resilient commitment to the gospel is evident in Paul's becoming 'like' the Galatian gentiles (4.12b) in order to portray Christ crucified to them.

[22] On the maternal imagery of this verse and its theological significance, see Gaventa, 1990.

qualities exhibited by the Galatians in the initial stages of their relationship with Paul.

The Galatians' welcome of Paul is introduced by the leading statement, 'You did me no wrong' (4.12). Their lack of harm did not simply involve the absence of malice, but included a positive initiative towards Paul, as described in 4.13–14. Paul came to them with a physical 'weakness'. In Paul's day, of course, physical deformities and illnesses were commonly thought to be the result of the influence of demonic or malicious suprahuman forces.[23] Yet despite this physical condition and the dangers it might have been thought to pose to their own wellbeing, the Galatians failed to take the course of action thought to be prudent in such cases. That is, they did not spit in order to protect themselves (ἐξεπτύσατε, 4.14), thereby warding off illness and its demonic manufacturers.[24] Instead, they made themselves vulnerable and received him.

This is not to be interpreted simply as a sign of friendship, as some have suggested.[25] Paul's analysis of his cherished association with the Galatians is informed primarily by something other than the social codes of friendship. His understanding of their acceptance of him is rooted in an underlying theological conviction about the nature of Christian social behaviour. Paul's mention of the extraordinary reversal of values evident in the Galatians' behaviour serves not simply as a personal reminiscence of better days, nor as a demonstration of a responsible handling of friendship. Instead, Paul considers it to have been a clear demonstration of Christian character already within the Galatians even at that early stage. It evidenced the Spirit at work within them already when encountering Paul; they received him as one in need, and bore the burdens of another, even at great risk to themselves. Much like Paul's own dramatic transformation by God (Galatians 1–2), the Galatians' reception, worthy even of Christ Jesus, can only be credited to divine transformation, resulting in attitudes and behaviour at

---

[23] Paul himself might assume as much in 2 Cor. 12.7–10, even if ἐδόθη there is a divine passive.

[24] Cf. Pliny, *Nat. Hist.* 28.26, 29; Theocritus, *Id.* 6, 39.

[25] E.g., Betz, 1979: 224 and 224 n. 46.

odds with the patterns of life that characterise the present evil age.[26]

Rather than exhibiting attitudes characteristic of this age, the Galatians' relationship with Paul had initially exhibited a quality of life that attested to God's 'blessing' (μακαρισμός),[27] his transforming work in their lives. This theological conviction underlies Gal. 4.15b as well, where Paul recalls the extent of God's work in them: they would have gone so far as to give their own eyes to him, had it been possible. This attitude of sincere concern and generosity is (for Paul) not simply a demonstration of friendly devotion and affection, but an attestation of the Galatians' transformation in Christ by the power of God, a testimony to the working of the Spirit of the Son whose own life was marked out by love and self-giving. Their own actions were embodiments of the gospel, manifestations of the Spirit.

In all this, Paul's presentation does not fall neatly into the tidy categories of (initial) 'justification' and (ensuing) 'sanctification'. The initial behaviour of the Galatian Christians towards Paul was thought by him simply to be a concrete demonstration of the primary Christian ethic stated throughout Galatians: 'through love, become servants of each other' (5.13); 'Bear one another's burdens' (6.2).[28] These exhortations are themselves

---

[26] With this we might compare the acts of hospitality and care bestowed upon Paul as a consequence and demonstration of Christian conversion in Acts 16.15 (Lydia; see Richter Reimer, 1992: 147–56) and 16.33–34 (the jailer). Or, in the imagery of Matthew 25, unlike those (the 'goats') who fail to welcome strangers and care for those in need, the Galatians' treatment of Paul replicates the behaviour of those acceptable to God (the 'sheep') who risk vulnerability to invading dangers by showing hospitality and by caring for the needy (25.31–46; cf. Isa. 58.7, 10).

[27] Unlike most, I give μακαρισμός its full theological meaning. For a defence, see B. W. Longenecker, 1998.

[28] Notice, for instance, how well Dunn's comments on 6.2 amplify Paul's meaning not only there (or 5.6, 13) but also at 4.12–14/15b: '[T]he word "burden" ... is regularly used to denote the burden of suffering, but also the burden of responsibility ... So here Paul is probably thinking of a whole range of illnesses and physical disabilities, of responsibilities borne by [members of the Christian community.] ... At any one time all members of a Christian congregation would have such burdens to shoulder, and when such burdens outgrew the individual's strength, it was important that there should be a supportive family-community to help out. This too and particularly this was the mark of the Spirit-led community' (1993a: 322).

elaborations of Paul's concise remark in 5.6 that what matters is 'faith working practically (ἐνεργουμένη) in love'. In Paul's view, this posture of responsible self-giving and loving service to others should be one of the defining marks of the Christian community enlivened by the Spirit of the Son of God – a quality manifest already in the Galatians' early reception of Paul. Paul's epistles demonstrate that he consistently envisages relationships between Christians to be the sphere in which the eschatological power of God is (to be) evident, manifesting Christ-like relationships and social character. We should not be surprised to find the same in Gal. 4.12–15, where Paul reflects on the state of the initial stages of his relationship with the Galatians, finding within that early relationship evidence of the transforming power of God, just as he had done in 3.1–5.

CHRISTIAN CHARACTER AT RISK

All this changes in 4.15–17, however, where Paul depicts Spirit-inspired character as endangered by the agitators who are attracting the loyalties of the Galatian Christians. The problem has arisen due to the agitators' own moral deficiency, as evident in attitudes and motivations that run precisely contrary to Christian character. Paul highlights their ignominious designs on the Galatians when in 4.17 he writes: 'They seek (ζηλοῦσιν) you with dishonourable intentions ... in order that you might seek (ζηλοῦτε) them.' Paul here is suggesting that the agitators' motivation is to woo the Galatians in order to gain their compliance and bolster the agitators' own reputation by enlisting the Galatians in a relationship of dependent allegiance.[29] This stands in sharp contrast to the character of Christian self-giving to and service of others. The same idea appears in 6.12–13, where the agitators are said be motivated by self-interestedness in 'making a good show' and 'glorying in your flesh' – by which Paul seems to be referring to the way in which the agitators seek to exercise power over others in order

---

[29] It is fine, says Paul, for the Galatians 'to be sought after' by Christians other than him (4.18), except when the motivation of others is dishonourable, as in the case of the agitators (4.17). Paul's own motivation had been honourable from the start, and he claims the same to be true even when he is not with them (4.18).

to heighten their own influence and standing. The attitude of the agitators, then, is revealed to be charlatan and deceptive, involving self-interestedness and personal gain, in contrast to the true Christian character of self-giving love.[30]

If there was an initial period in which Spirit-induced Christ-likeness permeated the Galatians' social behaviour, it was not a durable Christ-likeness of the sort evident in Paul's life come thick or thin (Galatians 1–2). If initially they had demonstrated character consonant with the gospel and inspired by the Spirit, later events proved that they were not resilient in that character. It is little wonder, then, that Paul finishes this section with the exasperated cry, 'I am perplexed about you' (4.20), urging them a little later to 'stand fast' (5.1).

Paul's strategy in 4.12–20 is structurally similar to the strategy he employed with regard to the evil eye accusations. Having asserted the principle of Christian enlivenment by Christ in 2.20, Paul goes on to contrast this with the current situation of the Galatians, who are potential victims of demonic activity (3.1), due to those whose character is defective. So too in Galatians 4, having affirmed the enlivenment of Christians by the Spirit of Christ in 4.6, Paul goes on to intimate that this enlivenment is in danger of being compromised, due to the influence of the agitators and their self-seeking interests (4.17). The association of moral character and suprahuman forces is the scaffolding for Paul's analysis in each instance.

4. Christian Character and Scriptural Interpretation

It may seem strange to move from considering Paul's understanding of various forms of suprahuman embodiment to considering his understanding of biblical interpretation. In fact, however, the two issues are intricately linked in Paul's theological perspective. Paul assumed that a valid reading of scripture for Christians presupposes the working of the Spirit within

---

[30] Betz finds that Paul in Gal. 4.17 attempts 'to discredit his opponents *emotionally* rather than "*theologically*"' (1979: 231, emphasis added). In fact, however, Paul's discrediting of the agitators is carried out within the theological arena of Christian character.

those who would read scripture for the edification of their Christian life. As Paul well knew, not least from the crisis that beset the Christian communities in Galatia, scripture can be interpreted in any number of ways; a legitimately Christian reading of scripture has the transforming work of the Spirit as a prerequisite.

As we have seen in chapter 5 above, Paul's thinking about the law in Galatians is permeated with a temporal qualification: the law was to be operative only between the times of Abraham and Christ. Nonetheless, in the same letter Paul can talk about the fulfilment of the law in Spirit-induced cruciform existence and, moreover, can use passages of scripture to support his case and to instruct the Galatian Christians. A fundamental dynamic in the Galatian crisis is the matter of scriptural interpretation, and Paul's letter to the Galatians reveals much about his hermeneutic, explicitly and implicitly giving signposts concerning his assumptions about the proper interpretation of scripture.

Paul employs at least two general strategies in his handling of scripture in Galatians. First, on occasion he can be seen to make the text say 'Pauline' things. Perhaps the best example of this is Paul's handling of the word σπέρμα in 3.16, exegeting the 'seed' of the Genesis Abraham-cycle (13.15; 17.8) with exclusive reference to Christ rather than Abraham's physical offspring. In the light of the narrative context of the passage itself, this reading seems far from natural.[31] When anachronistically judged by modern historical-critical standards, Paul is on somewhat better interpretative ground in his handling of Gen. 15.6 in 3.6 or of Hab. 2.4 (LXX) in 3.11. Nonetheless, this matter of legitimacy apart, each of these is an instance of Paul finding scripture to say Pauline things.

But Paul also employs another interpretative strategy in his handling of scripture for Christian purposes: that is, he recognises that the text does not always promote practices or perspectives that accord with the Christian gospel. Instead of giving assurances that the whole of scripture supports his gospel, Paul indicates that not everything in scripture is edifying

---

[31] This is true, even if there is precedent for reading σπέρμα messianically in 2 Sam. 7.12–14; see Hays, 1989: 85.

for Christians, at least at a (so-called) 'literal' level of meaning or in a 'straightforward' fashion.[32]

This interpretative strategy appears clearly in Gal. 3.11–12. The NRSV of 3.11 reads this way: 'Now it is evident that no one is justified before God by the law; for "The one who is righteous will live by faith".' To be contested, however, is the placing of the phrase 'it is evident', which the NRSV puts with the first half of the verse. In so doing, the NRSV suggests that Paul knows something to be obviously true (that no one can be justified by the law), a view that he then goes on to support by citing Hab. 2.4. But it is not clear that this is the best way to translate the verse. At issue is the placing of a single comma in the Greek text. In the Nestle-Aland and United Bible Society editions of the Greek, 3.11 is edited with a comma falling between δῆλον ('it is evident') and the ὅτι ('for') that follows: ὅτι δὲ ἐν νόμῳ οὐδεὶς δικαιοῦται παρὰ τῷ θεῷ δῆλον, ὅτι ὁ δίκαιος ἐκ πίστεως ζήσεται. This way of punctuating the sentence informs the NRSV translation, but it goes against the grain of how δῆλον clauses are normally constructed. The expected construction is not 'ὅτι ... δῆλον', but rather 'δῆλον ὅτι ...' followed by what the author thinks to be obvious.[33] In that case, 3.11 should be punctuated with the comma before δῆλον, not after: ὅτι δὲ ἐν νόμῳ οὐδεὶς δικαιοῦται παρὰ τῷ θεῷ, δῆλον ὅτι ὁ δίκαιος ἐκ πίστεως ζήσεται. This minor difference is significant far beyond initial appearances, since the verse now reads this way: 'For no one is righteous before God by the law, for clearly "The righteous will live by faith".'

In other words, Paul knows that this passage from Hab. 2.4 is 'obviously' instructive of Christian life, and so he can go on in 3.12 to cite Lev. 18.5 as the type of scriptural text that 'obviously' is not instructive of Christian living. For Paul, these two scriptural passages act as ambassadors of two different ways

---

[32] Words like 'literal', 'obvious', 'straightforward' or 'natural' are of course problematic, since what is thought to be literal to one interpreter may not be so for the next.

[33] E.g., Bauer: 'δῆλον (sc. ἐστίν) w. ὅτι foll. *it is clear that*' (1979: 178). I first saw this suggestion in Wright, 1991: 149 n. 42, but have since seen it assumed by Hays, 1983: 207.

of life: a life of nomistic observance is supported by Lev. 18.5, whereas the life of faith is supported by Hab. 2.4. These two scriptural passages are well-suited for comparison, since each puts forward what for Paul are two different ways of life before God, the ζήσεται ('will live') of each passage providing a basis for their respective versions of proper living. But rather than attempting to reinterpret the meaning of Lev. 18.5 in line with his own gospel (as he did with σπέρμα in 3.16), Paul simply relegates it to a position of irrelevance for the Christian life. It is representative of a way of life that has no salvific value now that the eschatological age has been inaugurated. There is no attempt to put a Pauline spin on Lev. 18.5, in which 'doing the law' is somehow interpreted in accord with Christian faith.[34] It is 'obvious', says Paul, that texts such as Hab. 2.4 are valid guides of life in the eschatological age, the consequence being that texts such as Lev. 18.5 are 'obviously' not (cf. Rom. 10.5–8).[35]

So Paul's strategy for interpreting scripture is not always to 'Christianise' (or 'Paulinise') it, at least in the sense of finding its instructive meaning for daily life. Paul is cognisant that not all of scripture can be harmonised in line with his gospel. But he does not imagine the existence of scriptural passages that are 'counter-gospel' to derail his argument, since his eschatological perspective allows for this eventuality. Such passages are not anomalies, since the eschatological divide that separates the ages of history runs throughout scripture itself. With the coming of the eschaton, scripture can be heard to articulate two voices, only one of which is appropriate to those who belong to the new age where 'neither circumcision is anything, only new creation' (6.15; cf. 5.6).

Nor are such counter-gospel passages problematic, since the way that scripture should be appropriated within the new age is,

---

[34] Presumably a vast number of other passages would also be exempt from such reinterpretative efforts.

[35] See especially, Vos, 1992, and the classic study by Dahl, 1977: 159–77 (despite Betz, 1979: 138 n. 8). Dahl argues that in Paul's day, Jewish interpreters resolved apparent tensions within scripture by apportioning the respective texts to different contexts, something analogous to what Paul is doing in Gal. 3.11–12.

for Paul, obvious and clear (δῆλον). Some passages of scripture are made to conform in a literal fashion to his own theological vision; others are forfeited and considered to be relics of a former age which are not to trespass the boundaries of the ages. Paul did not approach every passage of scripture frenetically searching for its hidden significance for Christian living, determined to make it say something edifying no matter what.[36] As Gal. 3.11–12 shows, he was not immune to relegating some passages of scripture to the category of illegitimacy in the eschatological age.[37]

Falling somewhat between these two strategies of rereading scripture on the one hand, and relegating parts of it to a past age on the other hand, is Paul's Sarah–Hagar analogy of Gal. 4.21–31. Although Paul is able to draw Christian meaning from the scriptural text, and while he encourages the Galatians to hear what scripture says (4.21, 30), at the same time he recognises that Christian meaning emerges from this narrative due to factors beyond a concern for its original significance. The voice of scripture that Paul wants his audience to hear speaks in concert with his gospel only by removing it from its original narrative context. The word he uses to explain his interpretation of scripture is 'allegory' – an important signifier which signals how he is reading the text. He does not claim to explicate the literal meaning of the Genesis story of Abraham and his progeny, and rightly so since, for instance, he avoids any mention of the undeniable connection made in the Genesis

---

[36] In this, the Christian Paul is different from his contemporary, Philo of Alexandria. According to Barclay, Philo 'based his life's work on the conviction that *everything* in the sacred text is worthy and profound . . . He will not accept a hermeneutical strategy which discriminates between text and text; it has to be all or nothing' (1996b: 169, emphasis his).

[37] It is this aspect of Paul's hermeneutic that is missing from Hays' otherwise stimulating work on the importance of scripture to Paul's theological argument (1989). Beker aptly questions whether Hays has paid 'enough attention . . . to the fact that Paul's interpretation of the Old Testament rejects the ethnocentricity of the law (as inherent in the Jewish understanding of the law) for the sake of the inclusion of the Jewish heritage? In other words, the fusion of law and gospel in Paul does not seem to be as smooth as Hays suggests' (1993b: 68). This same deficiency frequently appears in talk about Paul's use of scripture.

narrative between Abrahamic offspring and the requirement of circumcision (Genesis 17).[38] By introducing his reading as an allegory, he invites his audience to perform an imaginative act along non-contextual lines in order to allow their faith to be nourished in their own situation by this ancient text.

Paul's allegory of Hagar and Sarah is not, then, in any way a form of prooftexting. The allegory simply provides a way of looking at the text from an already-established point of view, allowing that text to resonate with new meaning within the parameters of that perspective. Signalling his interpretation to be an allegory, Paul suggests that his meaning goes beyond the constraints of the narrative context of the scriptural text, even if the text remains the occasion and vehicle for his interpretative activity. In this case, the goal of Paul's scriptural interpretation is not the discovery of a text's 'literal' meaning in its original context; instead, scriptural interpretation is here put in the exclusive service of nurturing and enhancing Christian lifestyle, a goal achieved by an imaginative reading strategy that by-passes any concerns for a literal reading. Paul's aim is not to 'refute' the agitators' reading of the same Hagar–Sarah narrative by means of a head-on reinterpretation of the passage's 'surface level' of meaning. Instead, assuming their reading to be an unwise and unhealthy reading for Christian identity, he simply applies another interpretative method to the narrative in order to nurture Christian identity in accordance with a prior understanding of the gospel.

Allegorical interpretation allows Paul to find meaning (for him, true meaning) beyond the confines of the straightforward scriptural narrative. In fact, in this case Paul's allegorical reading is advanced in order to negate the simple meaning of the text, thereby ensuring that the Galatian Christians do not adopt the lifestyle advocated by the agitators.[39] Paul's near contemporary, Philo of Alexandria, also considered allegorical readings of scripture to reveal the deep mysteries of God in a way that a literal reading did not. But Philo did not consider the literal sense of the text to be in fundamental tension with the

---

[38] See, e.g., Martyn, 1990: 172–73.
[39] On allegory as a strategic means of social revision, see Dawson, 1992.

allegorical sense, at least in matters of halakah and lifestyle.[40] Nor did he advocate that in these matters the literal meaning could and should be disregarded. In Gal. 4.21–31, however, Paul resorts to an allegorical reading in order to counter a reading more in accord with its narrative context. Although he can weave a web of meaning from the Hagar–Sarah narrative that is aligned with his gospel, he is well aware that this is due not to an explication of the original narrative meaning. Instead, it arises as an imaginative act from within a Christian perspective in relation to the scriptural text. In Paul's allegory, the scriptural text is interpreted by means of extra-textual factors, and Paul expects the Galatians to join him in this imaginative re-configuration of the story in order to nurture their Christian commitment.[41]

We have seen, then, how Paul employs various strategies when reading scripture. In places, he reads Christian meaning into a scriptural text, intimating that that meaning is natural to the text in its original context (e.g., Gen. 15.6 in 3.6; Gen. 12.3 and 18.18 in 3.8). In other places he does the opposite, either abandoning the effort to find Christian meaning in a scriptural text (Lev. 18.5 in 3.12), or engaging in an allegorical interpretation which creates new meaning for his Christian converts at a non-literal level and which counters the kind of interpretation that might more naturally arise from it (4.21–31).

But this begs the question, by whose reading of scripture

---

[40] Of course, he was not one to enjoy the application of anthropomorphisms to God within scripture. In such cases, allegorical readings alone were definitive.

[41] Paul seems to assume that, if his audience will ever be in a position to hear new tones of meaning in the Hagar–Sarah narrative, it is at this point in the letter. This is significance, since presumably such would not have been the case at the outset of the letter. In this regard, Paul's plea that they become like him (4.12) continues to resound even throughout the interpretative exercise in 4.21–31. Cf. Cosgrove: 'in antiquity allegorizing was employed most typically to bring a revered tradition in line with accepted views ... [T]he interpreter would make points via allegorical exegesis with which his audience was already in sympathy' (1987: 220). Accordingly, Betz's view that Paul assumes that all his arguments in the preceding chapters of Galatians have had little effect on his audience (1979: 239–40) is not wholly compelling, despite 4.20.

should the Galatians be persuaded? Paul's reading sets important passages of scripture aside, reinterprets them playfully, and
might well have seemed quite forced, even by the interpretative
standards of the first century.[42] No doubt the agitators would
have been the first to dispute the meaning that Paul's snatches
out of the scriptural text. What is it that legitimates Paul's
exegetical results when his hermeneutical methods appear so
arbitrary? Why should the Galatians be persuaded by an
allegorical reading of the Hagar–Sarah narrative instead of a
more literal interpretation? What interpretative basis do they
have to determine between Paul's claims and those of the
agitators?

Paul never claims that his gospel is simply founded on the
basis of stringing a few texts together into a package. Instead, he
claims its source to be an 'apocalyptic' revelation from God
(1.15–16; cf. 1.1, 11–12), resulting in a transformation of Paul's
life to such an extent that the very enterprise of scriptural
interpretation has itself been reconstituted for him. Paul seems
to assume that a valid reading of scripture presupposes a
cruciform, Christ-like character embodied within the reader (or
community of readers). Of course, on the face of it, his
hermeneutic of 'obviousness' appears simplistic, unsophisti-
cated and naive. The history of scripture-based religions is filled
with examples of the misuse of scripture by the random picking
and choosing of texts to bolster the standing, authority and
prestige of some and to influence others. But Paul seems to
presume that his various methods of interpreting scripture are
valid if only because of the embodiment of Christ in his life,
invading every aspect of him including his understanding of
scripture. Paul's presentation of his own life in Galatians 1–2,
then, functions as an important hermeneutical premise to his
scriptural interpretations in Galatians 3–4; his reading of
scripture emerges from the performance of the gospel and

---

[42] Chilton and Neusner: 'Judged from the point of view of the scriptural texts he
cites, Paul's argument at various stages seems tenuous' (1995: 103). Sanders
finds Paul's use of scripture in Galatians to involve a view of scripture in which
'*its words are true*; they just have to be arranged and orchestrated so that they
give the right conclusion' (1996: 119).

embodiment of Christ within his own life by the transforming power of God.[43]

At the most basic level, problems have arisen in Galatia due to a defect on the part of those whose Christian character was being compromised (even Peter and Barnabas are accused of 'hypocrisy', 2.13). This defect of Christian character has resulted in a compromise of the gospel itself, fuelled first and foremost by an unwise handling of scripture. In Paul's view, the 'hermeneutical debate' between himself and the agitators was not simply about which scriptural passages are normative and which are not, but about Christian character. The agitators read scripture incorrectly not simply because they prefer some passages of scripture that differ from those preferred by Paul. Instead, their errant interpretation arises from a perversion within their character, a character that has not been continuously nurtured by the Spirit. The compromise of Christian character jeopardises reading scripture for Christian edification, allowing scripture itself to become an instrument for the promotion of things that run contrary to the will of God, and for the enhancement of human reputations rather than the reputation of God.

In this way, central to Paul's hermeneutic in Galatians is the issue of character. Paul's own character contrasts with that of those who would interpret scripture to support conclusions that run contrary to the gospel. The development of Christian character through the power of the Spirit is the prerequisite for the proper reading of scripture in the Galatian communities. Without a mature, Christian character nurtured by the Spirit, Paul knows that scripture can be read to support and justify ways of life that oppose the gospel. The issue at Galatia, then, is not simply about matters of circumcision and nomistic observance, but fundamentally about the way one reads scripture in accordance with Christian character. Paul is all too well aware that scripture can be read in ways that support different definitions of identity and lifestyle. For this reason, his hermeneutical programme is rooted in the more fundamental issue of character, with Christ-like, cruciform character as a presupposi-

---

[43] On this general approach, see Fowl, 1994.

tion for proper readings of scripture.[44] This, for Paul, is the prerequisite for valid Christian readings of scripture, a hermeneutical priority that results from God's triumphant power transforming people by the Spirit to conform to the likeness of the son of God.

[44] This is reminiscent of Luther's view of allegory, who found it to 'seemly ... when the foundation is well laid' (1953: 417).

8

Concluding Observations

'I am astonished that you are so quickly deserting the one who called you in the grace of Christ and are turning to a different gospel', says Paul by way of rebuking Galatian Christians (1.6). The gospel that Paul proclaims but which is being perverted by the agitators is, as his letter demonstrates at key points, driven by a clear discernment of the implications of God's triumphal invasion in Christ. Divine sovereignty has penetrated an age of evil, provided a means of release from the oversight of lesser suprahuman forces, and established a sphere marked out by unprecedented intimacy with God and multi-racial association. Those whose lives have been caught up in this sphere embody the triumph of God in their transformed patterns of life. By means of the Spirit, the pattern of self-giving that characterised the faithful son of God eradicates self-referential patterns of life that mark out the age of evil.

We have seen how Paul elaborates the intricacies of this perspective in relation to a number of issues in Galatians, including: suprahuman competitors of various sorts; the mechanics of participation in the eschatological age; the fulfilment of the law by Christians; the nature and purposes of the law; the enhancement of society by Christians; and presuppositions for reading scripture properly from a Christian perspective. But two other issues in particular have set much of the agenda of this study: the place of salvation history in Galatians, and Paul's presentation of God's triumph in Christ in relation to what we know of the nature and character of prominent forms of Early Judaism. Since these two matters are deserving of more than cursory attention, two sections of this final chapter are given to their consideration (§§8.1

and 8.2). The last section of this chapter (§8.3) has a different character, however. It arises not out of a concern to pin down the historical and theological features of Paul's presentation in Galatians, but out of a consequent interest to explore the interface of that presentation and matters of contemporary significance. To that end, I offer some preliminary reflections on Paul's social vision in relation to contemporary Christian theology.

1. The Triumph of Abraham's God and the History of Israel

Provoked by the situation in Galatia, Paul's heated, stern and uncompromising letter deals with the matter most pressing in Galatian Christian communities: the identity of Abraham's offspring in relation to God's eschatological initiative in Christ. The agitators' position on this matter focused on what God had done in history with the corporate people of Israel, Abraham's descendants; God had long been at work with them, God's eschatological promises had been directed to them, and God would bring redemption to the world through them. For the agitators, it went without saying that to be associated with God's eschatological triumph was to be associated with Abraham's true offspring – ethnic Israel, the covenant people of God. In his rebuttal of the practical consequences of this view (i.e., the salvific necessity of circumcision and nomistic practice), Paul reconfigures the issue, keeping the focus on Abraham but defining Abrahamic heritage in relation to Christ. In so doing, however, Paul dislodges God's dealings with Israel from occupying centre stage.

Contemporary study of Galatians has focused some attention on the verb 'dislodge' in the previous sentence, since there is a world of difference between dislodging something by eliminating it and dislodging it by repositioning it in a different context. As we saw in the first chapter of this book, J. C. Beker and J. L. Martyn argue that Paul, restrained by the Galatian situation, has eliminated in his letter any notion of a salvation historical linearity in relation to the people of Israel.

With this view we largely concur (although in §5.1 a different form of salvation history was noted; see below). It would go against the grain of Paul's case in Galatians to speak of 'the giving of the law to the corporate seed of Abraham',[1] since Paul reserves the designation 'corporate seed of Abraham' for those in Christ (3.29), who is the single seed of Abraham (3.16). In Galatians, unlike Romans 4, Abraham has no direct, positive relationship with ethnic Israel; that relationship is forged only in Christ. One looks in vain in Galatians for anything about God working in and throughout Israel's history in order that the Messiah might arrive as the capstone of the whole process. The time between Abraham and Christ is not a time of salvation-historical progress, and Abraham and Christ are not presented as two ends of an elongated, historical continuum of God's dealings with ethnic Israel. The new creation has no organic connection to Israel's past history other than the God of that history (a crucial point, lest Paul be guilty of the mistakes of Marcion a century later).

This immediately raises methodological issues concerning the interpretation of Paul's letters – in particular, the inevitable interplay between Paul's situational writings and the elusive construct called 'Pauline theology'. If, for instance, on the basis of other extant Pauline texts, we assume a linear process of salvation history in relation to ethnic Israel to be a crucial aspect in Pauline theology, there is an inherent danger of introducing that same aspect illegitimately when reading Galatians. Such would result in a misreading of a contingent text due to the controlling force of a theological construct (i.e., 'Pauline theology') amalgamated from other Pauline texts.

Consequently, we must choose between one of two options. First, it may be that Galatians represents an exception to the rule in Pauline theological expressions, since it lacks a fully-blown form of salvation-historical linearity; it is exceptional due to the effects of the situational needs of Paul's Galatian audience. In this case, Paul might be said to have defended one aspect of his gospel by eliminating another aspect of it. Second, it may be that, on the basis of Galatians, a notion of linear salvific history that stretches from the early Hebrews at one end and includes Christian believers at the other must be relegated to the position of a peripheral extra in Pauline theology; the unfolding story of ethnic Israel as the context into which believers have been

---

[1] As does Braswell, 1991: 83.

included is not a central, essential, irreplaceable feature of Paul's theology. Although (in my view) the second is more likely, full consideration of such matters falls beyond the scope of this project, requiring the assessment of data drawn from a broader sampling of the Pauline material. The point is made here only to signal the way that our findings on salvation history in Galatians engenders further issues and impacts on larger matters relating to Pauline theology in general.[2]

If the position adopted here agrees in large measure with the positions of Beker and Martyn, it also differs from the positions of J. D. G. Dunn and N. T. Wright. As was shown in chapter 1 above, Dunn and Wright argue (in different ways) that, according to Paul's presentation in Galatians, gentiles have been included in the continuing story of Israel's unfolding history. Such a view, while possibly in accord with other Pauline letters (esp. Romans), goes beyond the evidence of Galatians itself. True, Paul seems to identify the Christian community as the 'Israel of God' in Gal. 6.16, but what rationale lies behind the attribution? What theological convictions led him to attribute this title to the Christian community? It would be surprising if the title arose out of some idea that the Christian community embodied the final expression of Israel's corporate history, since such a view has no precedent earlier in Galatians. The fact that Paul's letter has afforded no theological underpinning to associate this title with the ethnic group serves precisely the rhetorical purpose of the letter; that is, Paul's strategy is to retain many of the terms and titles favoured by the agitators within his own programme (e.g., the offspring of Abraham, Israel, fulfilment of the law), while at the same time infusing them with new content that accords with his eschatological convictions. In this way, the title 'Israel of God' is

---

[2] The relationship between the theology of particular letters in relation to a larger construct of 'Pauline theology' has been the object of considerable analysis in recent years; see, for instance, the project undertaken by the Pauline Theology Group of the Society for Biblical Literature, whose findings appear at present in three volumes: Bassler, 1991; Hay, 1993; Johnson and Hay, 1996. See too Dunn, 1994. The issue of salvation history in Galatians has played an important role in discussion of this point; see especially Dunn, 1991a; Gaventa, 1991; and Martyn, 1991.

stripped of any potential to signify an ethnic group that took pride of place throughout salvation history in the run-up to the coming of Christ.

Nonetheless, with that said, even in Galatians it seems impossible for Paul to envisage God's eschatological redemption in Christ without also articulating how that same event has afforded the long-awaited redemption of ethnic Israel. Here we differ from Beker and Martyn. Galatians 3.13–14 and 4.4–5 indicate that divine triumph could not become implemented universally apart from the restoration of ethnic Israel in particular (or at least providing the means for her restoration). That such a view should appear in Galatians seems suggestive. Even on this occasion, when enthusiasm for practices that marked out Israel's history was causing so much of a problem, Paul maintains a firm focus on God's responsibilities to the people of Israel as a necessary precondition for the implementation of divine sovereignty in the eschatological age. As was argued above, Paul has here tapped into a theology of God in relation to Israel that circulated widely in early Christianity, a tradition that he incorporated in other letters as well (e.g., Rom. 15.8–9; 3.25; §§5.1 and 5.3 above). Inherent in this tradition is the combination of a particularistic focus on the people of Israel with a universalistic focus on the whole of humanity in relation to the establishment of divine sovereignty over creation.

A central feature of this tradition is the faithfulness of Christ, a motif that plays a crucial role in Paul's theology of the redemption of Israel. For Paul, the motif of Christ's faithfulness includes an implicit negation of faithfulness in connection with the people of Israel, for whom faithfulness remained elusive. And precisely this contrast between faithfulness and unfaithfulness lies behind Paul's charge in 3.13 that Christ redeemed 'us' (Jewish Christians) from the curse of the law. Since, in Paul's view, the people of Israel (and any others) are unable to do the law, the law pronounces a curse upon them; since Christ stands in a different category from them as one who is faithful to God, so the curse of the law is able to be redirected on to him, with salvific consequences for Israel. Without the faithfulness of Christ, the curse could not be transferred; without the transfer of the curse, Israel could not be redeemed; without the redemption of Israel, the new creation could not be inaugurated.[3]

It is telling that even in Galatians Paul grants to ethnic Israel a unique place before God. The redemption of ethnic Israel is one feature of this, but there are others as well. The law was given to Israel, and to Israel alone (3.19). Although Paul gives various suggestions as to the purpose of this giving (see §6.3 above), he assumes that the giving itself testifies to a special relationship between God and Israel that falls outside of the immediate Abraham–Christ line of blessing. Although the law was mediated and therefore, in Paul's mind, produced a less intimate form of relationship with God than is found in Christ, this should not undermine the significance of the law having been given to Israel in the first place. The same feature seems to be assumed in the imagery of the law as Israel's pedagogue, keeping her under supervisory restraint until the coming of Christ (3.24–25; cf. the imagery of the child under 'guardians and trustees' in 4.1–3). In all this, it seems that, despite the agitators' heavy emphasis on salvation history and Israel as God's covenant people, Paul maintained a keen awareness of Israel's distinctiveness before God in the period between Abraham and Christ. The God of eschatological triumph appears even in Galatians as the covenant God of Israel. If in Galatians Paul does not defend a line of salvation-historical continuity leading from the covenant people of Israel and

---

[3] In Galatians the 'faithfulness of Christ' is unpacked in two distinct ways. On the one hand, it operates implicitly at 3.13 in relation to the redemption of ethnic Israel. On the other hand, in 3.22–25 it is depicted as the frontispiece of the new age. No doubt, the two images could easily be configured as two parts of a single salvation-historical phenomenon. For instance, Paul could have argued that the redemption of Israel afforded by the faithfulness of Christ advanced Israel's history to its eschatological stage wherein gentiles could be included by faith. But in Galatians (arguably unlike Romans), Paul does not advocate such a view. He pivots on the motif of Christ's faithfulness in order to take it this way, then that way, and articulates views that disallow a coupling of the two significations given to Christ's faithfulness. So, for instance, in Gal. 2.15–21 Christian participation in the faithfulness of Christ is not to be seen as inclusion in the full-flowering of Israel's covenant faithfulness (perhaps the view advocated by the agitators); instead, it is the means of entry in the sphere of eschatological obedience. The potential to interpret it in the former fashion is negated by Paul's case in Galatians 3–4.

culminating in Christ, neither does he intend to repudiate that a form of covenant relationship existed between God and ethnic Israel prior to Christ.[4]

2. Paul in Perspective

Professional Pauline interpreters continue to debate whether the perspective that Paul seeks to correct in texts like Galatians and Romans is (1) a type of self-referential 'legalism' (the view maintained by advocates of the traditional view, often called the 'Lutheran perspective') or (2) a type of ethnically-focused 'covenantalism' (the view maintained by advocates of the 'new perspective').[5] The former, of course, involves the acquisition of righteousness before God by means of one's own efforts, while the latter envisages nomistic obedience as the means whereby ethnic Israel was responsive to the merciful God who established her to be a special, distinct and beloved people.

Advocates of the two approaches continue to make claims which suggest that if one approach has merit, the other does not.[6] From what we have seen, however, there is good reason to think that the situation may not be so clear cut, and that the 'either-or' that marks out current polemic in Pauline scholarship might best be laid to rest.[7] On the one hand, Paul gives plenty of indications that problems repeatedly arose in his congregations as a result of a covenantal motivation, in which

[4] Contra Martyn: Galatians gives 'no indication of a covenant-created people of God during the time of the Law' (1991: 174).

[5] These terms may be somewhat unhelpful, however, by reason of their imprecision. The adjectives 'Lutheran' and 'new' disguise a great diversity of interpretation within each general approach, so that the noun that accompanies them might be represented better in plural form ('perspectives'). Moreover, the perspectives that are termed 'new' have strong roots in the work of Baur, who was influential already in the early to mid-nineteenth century (Baur, 1875: 44–152, a translation of a 1854 German original). At the same time, it is far too simplistic to attribute legalistic approaches solely to the influence of Luther. Despite these weaknesses, however, these terms have been adopted within the academy of scholars as handy signifiers of two general approaches when considering the matter of Paul and the law.

[6] Perhaps the reader will forgive me if I refrain from giving examples. Instead of identifying culprits, I hope here to play a more eirenic role.

[7] This possibility is entertained somewhat by Ziesler, 1991.

the practices of the law were seen to be a means of participation in the covenant people of God. While this social function of the law is usually underplayed in more traditional approaches, it has been helpfully brought to the forefront by the new perspective, which gives greater clarity to the issues Paul was facing and greater depth to many Pauline passages. Within Galatians, for instance, the social function of the law helpfully illuminates the dynamics of the following features: Paul's zeal to preserve the covenant identity of Israel (1.14); the problem of Jewish and gentile association in Antioch, raising the issue of Jewish identity and social integration (2.11–14);[8] the phrase 'works of law', referring to the legal stipulations placed upon Israel as a demonstration of her covenant fidelity before God (2.16; 3.2, 5); the law portrayed as Israel's pedagogue and the like, imagery that associates the law closely with Israel as God's specially chosen people (3.23–25; cf. 4.1–3); and not least, the debate about Abrahamic descent and circumcision (throughout Galatians), matters traditionally associated with the identity of Israel as a distinct social group. Fundamentally, then, what was of concern among the Galatians is not whether one is able to earn salvation through works, but whether intimate relationship with God can be assured through faith in Christ alone, apart from observing the law given to the covenant people of Israel. The focus was primarily upon the issue of community identity rather than personal merit; to be excluded was a form of ethnocentrism rather than self-righteousness.

On the other hand, however, it seems also to be the case that Paul portrays covenantal forms of lifestyle in ways that run contrary to the way their practitioners seem to have perceived them. Paul's texts often require us to distinguish between how adherents of more traditional forms of Jewish covenantalism understood their practice on the one hand, and how Paul understood it in the light of what God has done in Christ on the other. The latter often includes features quite at home with traditional 'legalistic' interpretations.[9]

So, for instance, it seems that Paul depicted the law to be

---

[8] For a sober reconstruction of the issues involved in this event, see Sanders, 1990.

[9] See, for instance, Hagner, 1993.

inappropriate as a means to life since human inability rendered it impossible to do the law perfectly, and since the law is powerless to correct that situation (e.g., 3.10, 21–22; see §§6.2 and 6.5). Such a view is common stock in 'Lutheran' approaches to Paul, just as it represents a distortion when judged in the light of views typically articulated in the Jewish traditions and scriptures. Similarly, a concern for the salvific necessity of nomistic observance is characterised by Paul as one form of 'fleshly' existence since the coming of Christ, an advertisement on a national level of self-referentiality and self-promotion – the age-old feature of human rebellion against God (§§4.1 and 4.2). Again, such a view is a mainstay of legalistic interpretations of Paul, just as it flies in the face of mainstream forms of ethnocentric covenantalism, in which nomistic observance marks out a life dedicated to God.[10]

Moreover, for Paul, apart from Christ all humanity is enslaved without distinction 'under' (ὑπό) suprahuman forces of one kind or another. Thus at the forefront of Paul's gospel is reliance on God's gracious invasion and invading grace, breaking the bondage of enslavement to inferior forces of influence. Accordingly, against this all-encompassing backdrop of the invasion of God, human activity comes to nought, even if it is well-meaning and is carried out on the basis that God is in fact gracious. This aspect of Paul's thought, so central to 'Lutheran' interpretations, lies at the heart of Paul's theology of divine transformation in Galatians.

Paul also articulates the same feature throughout Romans.[11] In Romans 7, for instance, Paul depicts Jewish attempts to keep the law to be ineffectual, a feature that results from his belief that divine grace operates in and through Christ alone.[12] This is not at all in keeping with a traditional covenantal theology of law. A typical understanding of what doing the law entailed included the view that acts of repentance and atonement were

---

[10] Moreover, it is important to emphasise that Jewish covenantal particularism often included a universalistic dynamic and vision; see, for instance, Levenson, 1996; Urbach, 1981.

[11] See especially Westerholm, 1996.

[12] Although Paul has some unexpected things to say about this grace in Rom. 11.25–32.

the means wherein transgressions were met by divine grace. In Paul's theology of divine grace through Christ, such a view is undermined altogether, and nomistic observance is thereby shown to be salvifically fruitless. Moreover, elsewhere in Romans, Paul explicitly distinguishes divine grace from human works, as if the two were in fundamental opposition (Rom. 9.32; 11.5–6; cf. 9.11–12; 4.4–5).

Features of this sort, so at home within traditional interpretations, need not be an embarrassment to the view that a form of ethnocentric covenantalism is what Paul is concerned to undermine. Instead, they show the extent to which Paul's theology is itself marked out by a new perspective, so much so that many traditional categories of Jewish thought have consequently been left behind. (This is clearly the case in Rom. 2.25–29, where the practice of circumcision falls outside the definition of what it means to keep the law.) These untraditional features of Paul's perceptions emerge due to a fundamental reconfiguration of his worldview. They should not be seen, as some have done, as evidence that Paul was unaware of the great covenantal traditions of Judaism, or that he suffered from a fundamental misunderstanding of mainstream forms of covenantal Judaism.[13] Instead, his texts demonstrate repeatedly that Paul had good knowledge of those forms and traditions. So, for instance, in Galatians his portrait of the law as a pedagogical guide for corporate Israel in accordance with the will of God (3.23–25; cf. 4.1–3) is wholly in keeping with the traditional understanding of the law in Early Judaism. To this, however, Paul adds a temporal qualification, in which the pedagogical nature of the law (i.e., its function in relation to the ethnic people of Israel) is seen to have no salvific import in the eschatological sphere of existence. The target of Paul's attack in Galatians and elsewhere is precisely a Christian form of traditional Jewish ethnocentric covenantalism, but Paul frequently depicts and engages with that phenomenon in ways that are determined more by his Christian convictions than by the terms thought to be appropriate in traditional forms of Jewish theology.

[13] So, for instance, Schoeps, 1961.

It is difficult to chart precisely how this reconfiguration of Paul's perceptions of ethnocentric covenantalism came about. It may be that, as a consequence of his encounter with Christ, Paul comprehended the weakness of the law to bring life (e.g., Gal. 3.21), resulting in his sustained attempts to undermine forms of ethnocentric covenantalism within Christianity. Or it may be that, as a consequence of his ministry among the gentiles in obedience to the risen Christ, Paul recognised the eschatological Spirit to be at work among gentile Christians in a profound fashion, thereby implying the salvific irrelevance of any kind of ethnocentric covenantalism. Either way, it seems that, chronologically speaking, in Paul's theology the solution preceded the plight.[14] Most likely, Paul's stance against nomistic observance resulted primarily from his anxieties about the social function of the law in distinguishing and separating Jew from gentile. By undermining the attraction of observing the law, Paul sought to ensure the preservation of a socially-united community which thereby testified to the eschatological trans-formation of God. In the process, his strategy included undermining the law's attractiveness by portraying it in ways that went against the grain of covenantal traditions altogether – ways that often coincide with traditional interpretations of Paul's letters.

The suggestion being made here is not that the 'Lutheran' and 'new' perspectives are really one and the same thing. Nonetheless, there is a large area where the two can and should be seen to overlap. The sooner we can move beyond the present 'either-or' that has some professional students of Paul's letters at loggerheads, the sooner real progress can be made in facilitating a better understanding of Paul's theological vision and corporate enterprise.

3. Paul's Vision of God's Transforming Power

Anxiety runs rampant in many sectors of modern society. Part of this can be attributed to the tremendous rate of change that marks out our era on a global scale – change that is more

---

[14] The modern articulation of this point is best found in Sanders, 1977, a position that has received strong support from others.

comprehensive and profound than in any prior period in world history. But modern disquiet cannot be reduced exclusively to the fast pace of progressive development. Most of us enjoy a great many advances and benefits brought by the techno-scientific age. More fundamental to the modern form of anxiety is the ever-increasing sense that the fabric of contemporary society is beginning to wear thin, showing signs of inability to cope with the stresses of unrelenting abuse.

The ancients feared the up-swell of chaotic forces emerging from the sea and plummeting the whole of the created world into a morass of swirling confusion. While we moderns may not share the particulars of their mythology, our anxieties may be nothing more than the first cousins of ancient anxieties about the potential overthrow of order and the removal of structures that promote goodness. The stability of our society often appears to be threatened in one way or another.

Few of us have not considered the prospects of fearful and alarming scenarios, such as the burgeoning of war, the increase of terrorism, the possibility of destabilisation of the world banking organisations by computer fraud, and the like. But such grand, catastrophic scenarios, whether fanciful or not, are not the main source of modern anxiety. More significant is the apparent breakdown of patterns of lifestyle that promote the health and wellbeing of society. Individual offences of this kind might appear to be relatively insignificant in the grand course of things, and they may touch the lives of some of us less frequently than others. But these less-than-earthshaking incidents, when taken together, tend to inspire a more general and far-reaching sense of foreboding. A geometry of cancerous self-referentiality (at both personal and corporate levels) lies configured within the very structures of modern society.[15]

---

[15] Stibbe has argued that the hallmark of contemporary society is 'addiction' in one form or another (1996). Stibbe finds addiction to spring from underlying pain (65–66), and suggests that addicts *become* self-oriented (99). While he is certainly correct to find forms of personal or corporate addiction to be pervasive in contemporary society, these seem to me to be surface features of a more fundamental phenomenon, identified here as malignant self-referentiality, or labelled 'flesh' by Paul; it is not that addicts *become* self-oriented in their addiction, but that self-orientation leads to addictions.

Incidents of moral abuses, social violence and civic crime are advertised every day in the media, specifically in the form of flagrant disregard for others, sometimes to the extent where the perpetration of harm and injury appears as a form of pleasurable enjoyment and a vehicle of self-advancement.

With this in mind, Paul's words written to Christians in Galatia seem to have an extended significance as a resource for consideration about modern society. In Paul's analysis, the 'present age of evil' is sponsored by what he calls the 'flesh', which he characterises as 'self-conceit' resulting in the provocation of others (5.26). A community or society motivated by the 'flesh' ends up devouring and consuming its own members and destroying itself (5.15). A dysfunctional, threadbare moral fabric within society is, then, not without precedent in Paul's theological imagination.

Against this background, Paul urges his readers to be enlivened by character that runs contrary to all this. He holds out a formula that he expects will infuse health and wellbeing within the Christian communities in Galatia, as well as spilling over with beneficial effect on society as a whole (6.10). In contrast to the human propensity towards self-referentiality (whether ego- or ethno-centrism), Paul posits a scenario where social relationships are characterised by the volunteering of self for the benefit of others, the offering of one's resources and energies for the nurturing of others. In contrast to our modern times when freedom, social liberties and personal rights have become the mainstay of so much of the western developed world, Paul's theology of freedom translates into the practice of responsibility towards and love for others in a network of mutual care and support.

If Paul's corporate vision has attraction, it is not the case that it simply translates into, or corresponds with, any particular socio-political equivalent in contemporary society. While his corporate imagings may be a welcome corrective to many modern versions of the same, and while it may help to enhance our own social visualisation and interpretative awareness, Paul's vision is first and foremost theological. Paul's programme in Galatians has nothing to do with hope for the betterment of society simply for the sake of society. It has everything to do with the belief that corporate hope lies exclusively in the power of God, who according to Paul can transform individual and collective identity in ways that ensures the wellbeing of all. In Paul's mind, personal and corporate identity cannot be defined apart from relation both to God and to others. In contrast to the rampant individualism of our day, Paul understands person-hood to be fundamentally relational; he cannot envisage relatedness to God without social cash-value, nor can he analyse social relationships without considering what they advertise in terms of the presence or absence of divine transformation.

A vision of this sort challenges some deeply-rooted and pervasive societal values, values not absent within the contemporary Christian church. For Paul, Christian social interaction is to be the stage upon which God's transforming power is performed and advertised. Accordingly, Paul calls his Galatian hearers not simply to a life unfettered by nomistic practice, but to a life of transformed existence through the power of the Spirit. Paul expects Christian lifestyle to embody eschatological existence, in conformity to the pattern of faithfulness expressed by Christ in loving and self-giving service. For the people of Christ today, such a vision is not simply challenging; all too often it serves as a humbling critique.

Paul does not offer his Galatian audience a recipe for Christian behaviour other than the pattern of cruciform existence. Prescriptive ethical regulations delimiting specific practices and behaviour have little to do with this text.[16] Instead, Paul seeks to exercise the imagination of the Galatians in order that they, enlivened by the Spirit of Christ, might be conformed to the model of Christ. Paul's imagings regarding Christian identity offer a vision which might have personal and corporate relevance even in contexts vastly different from the original context of this letter. Our world is not Paul's world, and the structures of our society differ from those of his society; Christian theology becomes a static enterprise if it seeks

---

[16] This is true even of Gal. 6.1–10, which is not prescription but description; Paul sets out his vision of a community enlivened by the Spirit, where responsibility is enacted in personal and social matters in a context of love and support under the auspices of a righteous God.

merely to replicate forms of life appropriate to a past day, as if some ancient social construct could simply be 'downloaded' into successive generations. Nostalgic anachronism is a world away from faithfulness to Christ,[17] though the two are often confused. But prescriptive regulations are not on offer in Galatians. Instead, Paul crafts a vision of Christ-modelled identity that might be readily transferable into other contexts as well.

Although Paul might have been surprised to learn that his text to the Galatians would be read by the Christian church for millennia to come, he would not have been surprised in the least to think that his vision of cruciform identity could and should shape Christian identity in innumerably diverse situations. He himself introduces the same vision repeatedly in his letters.[18] In Romans 12–15, his vision of cruciform identity informs the matter of Jewish Christian and gentile Christian relations; in 1 Corinthians 1–4, it guides his reflections on Christian ministry; in 1 Corinthians 8–10, it animates his advice concerning food sacrificed to idols (especially chapter 9); in 1 Corinthians 11, it functions to correct abuses of the Lord's Supper (especially 11.23–26); in 1 Corinthians 12–14, Paul allows it to instruct on the matter of spiritual gifts (especially chapter 13); in Philippians, it appears at the heart of his remarks concerning Christian corporate identity (2.6–11).

In the light of this, Paul's theology is perhaps best grasped by taking account of the social function of his theological language, arguments, and concepts – all of which are intended to foster a cruciform ethos and practice within his communities. Things like Paul's doctrine (so-called) of 'justification by faith', terms such as 'redemption' or 'in Christ', and salvific models such as 'participation' or 'sacrifice' are all to be translated into a distinctive personal and corporate lifestyle within the Christian communities spread throughout the Graeco-Roman world. Concern to nurture that distinctiveness of Christian identity is what unites the Pauline corpus in a way that no doctrine or

---

[17] So, Meeks, 1993: 215; see too R. N. Longenecker, 1984.
[18] On this, see further Hays, 1996b: 16–46.

motif does.[19] And Paul would no doubt assume that the same transformed identity should be the hallmark of Christians throughout the world and years, as the character of Christ is continuously replicated and embodied within the individual lives and corporate life of his people.[20]

Of course, it would be wrong to suggest that Paul is simply offering 'insights', or calling his audience to a vision of how things could and should be. Paul's vision is informed by his experience and understanding of the God who transforms identity. In this way, the account of Paul's own encounter with the risen son of God (1.12–16) serves as a paradigm for the whole of Paul's theology of Christian identity in Galatians. The experience of Christ's enlivenment within Paul informs his theology of transformation and crafts his vision of corporate cruciform existence. For Paul, this cruciform vision cannot take shape in concrete form apart from the Spirit of Christ sent into the hearts of Christians. Without the latter, the former remains at the level of the conceptual, the ethereal and the hypothetical; but where the latter occurs, Paul expects the former to transpire naturally. And it is in this transformed identity of God's people that Paul locates the hope for communal and societal health, the advertisement of God's sovereignty, and the embodiment of God's emerging triumph.

---

[19] Tomson writes: 'the basic coherence in Paul's thought is not in any particular theme but in the organic structure of practical life' (1990: 265; cf. 55–58). See too Beker, 1986b: 597.

[20] Meeks aptly writes: 'Paul's most profound bequest to subsequent Christian discourse was his transformation of the reported crucifixion and resurrection of Jesus Christ into a multipurpose metaphor with vast generative and transformative power – not least for moral perceptions ... Paul's use of the metaphor of the cross resists its translation into simple slogans. Instead he introduces into the moral language of the new movement a way of seeking after resonances in the basic story for all kinds of relationships of disciples with the world and with one another, so that the event-become-metaphor could become the generative center of almost endless new narratives, yet remain a check and control over those narratives' (1993: 196–97).

Bibliography

Arnold, C. E.
1996:   'Returning to the Domain of the Powers: *Stoicheia* as Evil Spirits in Galatians 4:3, 9', *Novum Testamentum* 38, 55–76.

Aune, D. E.
1980:   'Magic in Early Christianity', in W. Haase (ed.), *Religion (Vorkonstantinisches Christentum: Verhältnis zu römischem Staat und heidnischer Religion).* ANRW II. 23.1; Berlin/New York: De Gruyter, 1507–57.

Baasland, E.
1984:   'Persecution: A Neglected Feature in the Letter to the Galatians', *Studia Theologica* 38, 135–50.

Bandstra, A. J.
1964:   *The Law and the Elements of the World: An Exegetical Study in Aspects of Paul's Teaching.* Kampen: J. H. Kok.

Barclay, J. M. G.
1988:   *Obeying the Truth: A Study of Paul's Ethics in Galatians.*   ✓
        Edinburgh: T. & T. Clark.
1995:   'Paul among Diaspora Jews: Anomaly or Apostate?', *Journal for the Study of the New Testament* 60, 89–120.
1996a: '"Neither Jew nor Greek": Multiculturalism and the New Perspective on Paul', in M. G. Brett (ed.), *Ethnicity and the Bible.* Leiden: Brill, 197–214.
1996b: *Jews in the Mediterranean Diaspora: From Alexander to Trajan (323 BCE–117 CE).* Edinburgh: T. & T. Clark.

Barrett, C. K.
   1982:   'The Allegory of Abraham, Sarah and Hagar in the
             Argument of Galatians', in his *Essays on Paul.*
             London: SPCK, 118–31.
   1985:   *Freedom and Obligation: A Study of the Epistle to the
             Galatians.* London: SPCK.
   1994:   *Paul: An Introduction to His Thought.* London:
             Geoffrey Chapman.

Bassler, J. M. (ed.)
   1991:   *Pauline Theology, volume 1: Thessalonians, Philippians,
             Galatians, Philemon.* Minneapolis: Augsburg For-
             tress.

Bauer, W.
   1979:   *A Greek-English Lexicon of the New Testament and Other
             Early Christian Literature.* Trans. W. F. Arndt and
             F. W. Gingrich; 2nd edn; Chicago: University of
             Chicago Press.

Baur, F. C.
   1878:   *The Church History of the First Three Centuries*, vol. 1.
             London: Williams & Norgate.

Becker, J.
   1989:   *Paulus: Der Apostel der Völker.* Tübingen: J. C. B. Mohr
             (Paul Siebeck).

Beker, J. C.
   1980:   *Paul the Apostle: The Triumph of God in Life and
             Thought.* Philadelphia: Fortress Press; Edinburgh:
             T. & T. Clark.
   1982:   *Paul's Apocalyptic Gospel: The Coming Triumph of God.*
             Philadelphia: Fortress Press.
   1986a: 'The Faithfulness of God and the Priority of Israel in
             Paul's Letter to the Romans', *Harvard Theological
             Review* 79, 10–16.
   1986b: 'The Method of Recasting Pauline Theology: The
             Coherence-Contingency Theme as Interpretive
             Model', in K. H. Richards (ed.), *Society of Biblical
             Literature 1986 Seminar Papers.* Atlanta: Scholars
             Press, 596–602.

√ 1990:   *The Triumph of God: The Essence of Paul's Thought.*
           Minneapolis: Augsburg Fortress.

1993a: 'The Promise of Paul's Apocalyptic for Our Times',
           in A. J. Malherbe and W. A. Meeks (eds.), *The Future
           of Christology: Essays in honor of Leander E. Keck.*
           Minneapolis: Augsburg Fortress, 152–59.

1993b: 'Echoes and Intertextuality: On the Role of Scrip-
           ture in Paul's Theology', in C. A. Evans and J. M.
           Sanders, (eds.); *Paul and the Scriptures of Israel.*
           JSNTS 83/SSEJC 1; Sheffield: JSOT Press, 64–69.

Betz, H. D.
1979:   *Galatians: A Commentary on Paul's Letter to the Churches
           in Galatia.* Hermeneia; Philadelphia: Fortress Press.

1991:   'Magic and Mystery in the Greek Magical Papyri', in
           C. A. Faraone and D. Obbink (eds.), *Magika Hiera:
           Ancient Greek Magic and Religion.* Oxford/New York:
           Oxford University Press, 244–59.

Betz, H. D. (ed.)
1992:   *The Greek Magical Papyri in Translation, Including the
           Demotic Spells.* 2nd edn; Chicago: University of
           Chicago Press.

Blau, L.
1903:   'Evil Eye', in *The Jewish Encyclopaedia*, vol. 5. Lon-
           don/New York: Funk & Wagnalls, 280–81.

Bligh, J.
1969:   *Galatians: A Discussion of St. Paul's Epistle.* London:
           Saint Paul Publishing.

Blinzler, J.
1961:   'Lexikalisches zu dem Terminus τὰ στοιχεῖα τοῦ
           κόσμου bei Paulus', *Analecta Biblica* 18, 429–42.

Boers, H. W.
1988:   'The Foundation of Paul's Thought: A Methodo-
           logical Investigation – The Problem of the Coherent
           Center of Paul's Thought', *Studia Theologica* 42,
           55–68.

1994:   *The Justification of the Gentiles: Paul's Letters to the
           Galatians and Romans.* Peabody: Hendrickson.

Bolt, P.
 1994:   'What were the Sadducees Reading? An Enquiry
         into the Literary Background of Mark 12:12–23',
         Tyndale Bulletin 45, 369–94.

Bornkamm, G.
 1974:   'The Heresy of Colossians', in F. O. Francis and
         W. A. Meeks (eds.), *Conflict at Colossae*. SBLSBS 4;
         Chico: Scholars Press.

Bousset, W.
 1906:   *Die Religion des Judentums im neutestamentlischen
         Zeitalter*. Berlin: Reuther & Reichard.

Boyarin, D.
 1994:   *A Radical Jew: Paul and the Politics of Identity*. Berkeley:
         University of California Press.

Braswell, J. P.
 1991:   '"The Blessing of Abraham" versus "The Curse of
         the Law"; Another Look at Gal 3:10–13', *Westminster
         Theological Journal* 53, 73–91.

Bring, R.
 1969:   *Christus und das Gesetz*. Leiden: Brill.

Bruce, F. F.
 1982:   *The Epistle of Paul to the Galatians*. NIGTC; Grand
         Rapids: Eerdmans; Exeter: Paternoster Press.

Bultmann, R.
 1952:   *Theology of the New Testament*, vol. 1. London: SCM
         Press.
 1956:   *Primitive Christianity in its Contemporary Setting*. Phil-
         adelphia: Fortress Press [1980].

Bundrick, D. R.
 1991:   '*Ta Stoicheia tou Kosmou* (Gal 4:3)', *Journal of the
         Evangelical Theological Society* 34, 353–64.

Burton, E. de W.
 1921:   *A Critical and Exegetical Commentary on the Epistle to
         the Galatians*. International Critical Commentary;
         Edinburgh: T. & T. Clark.

Callan, T.
  1980:   'Pauline Midrash: The Exegetical Background of
          Gal. 3.19b', *Journal of Biblical Literature* 99, 549–67.

Calvert, N.
  1993:   'Abraham and Idolatry: Paul's Comparison of
          Obedience to the Law with Idolatry in Galatians
          4.1–10', in C. A. Evans and J. M. Sanders (eds.), *Paul
          and the Scriptures of Israel.* JSNTS 83/SSEJC 1;
          Sheffield: JSOT Press, 222–37.

Camara, D. H.
  1971:   *Spiral of Violence.* London: Sheed & Ward.

Campbell, D. A.
  1992:   *The Rhetoric of Righteousness in Romans 3.21–26.*
          JSNTS 65; Sheffield: JSOT Press.

Campbell, R. A.
  1996:   '"Against such things there is no law"? Galatians
          5:23b Again', *The Expository Times* 107, 271–72.

Caneday, A.
  1989:   '"Redeemed from the Curse of the Law": The Use
          of Deut. 21:22–23 in Gal. 3:13', *Trinity Journal* 10,
          185–209.

Carlson, R. P.
  1993:   'The Role of Baptism in Paul's Thought', *Inter-
          pretation* 47, 255–66.

Carroll, J. T. and Green, J. B.
  1995:   *The Death of Jesus in Early Christianity.* Peabody:
          Hendrickson, 1995.

Charlesworth, J. H.
  1988:   *Jesus within Judaism: New Light from Exciting Archaeo-
          logical Discoveries.* New York/London: Doubleday.

Chilton, B. and Neusner, J.
  1995:   *Judaism in the New Testament: Practices and Beliefs.* New
          York/London: Routledge.

Collins, J. J.
1991: 'Genre, Ideology and Social Movements in Jewish Apocalypticism', in J. J. Collins and J. H. Charlesworth (eds.), *Mysteries and Revelations: Apocalyptic Studies since the Uppsala Colloquium.* JSPS 9; Sheffield: JSOT Press, 11–32.

Cook, D.
1992: 'The Prescript as Programme in Galatians', *Journal of Theological Studies* 43, 511–19.

Cosgrove, C. H.
1987: 'The Law Has Given Sarah No Children (Gal. 4:21–30)', *Novum Testamentum* 29, 219–35.

Cranford, M.
1994: 'The Possibility of Perfect Obedience': Paul and an Implied Premise in Galatians 3:10 and 5:3', *Novum Testamentum* 36, 242–58.

Crossan, J. D.
1991: *The Historical Jesus: The Life of a Mediterranean Jewish Peasant.* Edinburgh: T. & T. Clark.

Dahl, N. A.
1977: *Studies in Paul: Theology for the Early Christian Mission.* Minneapolis: Augsburg Fortress.

Dalton, W. J.
1990: 'The Meaning of "We" in Galatians', *Australian Biblical Review* 38, 33–44.

Davies, W. D.
1980: *Paul and Rabbinic Judaism.* 4th edn; Philadelphia: Fortress Press.
1984: *Jewish and Pauline Studies.* Philadelphia: Fortress Press.

Dawson, D.
1992: *Allegorical Readers and Cultural Revision in Ancient Alexandria.* Berkeley: University of California Press.

de Boer, M. C.
1988: *The Defeat of Death: Apocalyptic Eschatology in 1*

Corinthians 15 and Romans 5. JSNTS 22; Sheffield: JSOT Press.

de Boer, W. P.
1962:   *The Imitation of Paul.* Kampen: J. H. Kok.

Delling, G.
1964:   'βασκαίνω', in G. Kittel (ed.), *Theological Dictionary of the New Testament,* vol. 1 (trans. and ed. G. W. Bromiley). Grand Rapids: Eerdmans, 594–95.

Dibelius, M.
1934:   *From Tradition to Gospel.* London: Ivor Nicholson & Watson.

Dodd, B. J.
1996:   'Christ's Slave, People Pleasers and Galatians 1.10', *New Testament Studies* 42, 90–104.

Dodd, C. H.
1968:   '"Εννομος Χριστοῦ', in his *More New Testament Studies.* Manchester: Manchester University Press.

Donaldson, T. L.
1986:   'The "Curse of the Law" and the Inclusion of the Gentiles: Galatians 3.13–14', *New Testament Studies* 32, 94–112.

Drane, J. W.
1975:   *Paul: Libertine or Legalist? A Study in the Major Pauline Epistles.* London: SPCK.

Duncan, G. S.
1934:   *The Epistle of Paul to the Galatians.* New York: Harper.

Dunn, J. D. G.
1975:   *Jesus and the Spirit.* London: SCM Press.
1980:   *Christology in the Making: An Inquiry into the Origins of the Doctrine of the Incarnation.* London: SCM Press.
1985:   'Works of the Law and the Curse of the Law (Galatians 3:10–14)', *New Testament Studies* 31, 523–42.
1988:   *Romans.* WBC; Dallas: Word.

1990:   'Pharisees, Sinners and Jesus', in his *Jesus, Paul and the Law*. London: SPCK; Louisville: Westminster, 61–88.

1991a: 'The Theology of Galatians: The Issue of Covenantal Nomism', in J. M. Bassler (ed.), *Pauline Theology, volume 1: Thessalonians, Philippians, Galatians, Philemon*. Minneapolis: Augsburg Fortress, 125–46.

1991b: 'Once More, ΠΙΣΤΙΣ ΧΡΙΣΤΟΥ', in E. H. Lovering, Jr. (ed.), *Society of Biblical Literature 1991 Seminar Papers*. Atlanta: Scholars Press, 730–44.

1991c: *The Partings of the Ways Between Christianity and Judaism and their Significance for the Character of Christianity*. London: SCM Press; Philadelphia: Trinity Press International.

1993a: *The Epistle to the Galatians*. Black's New Testament Commentaries; London: A. & C. Black.

1993b: *The Theology of Paul's Letter to the Galatians*. Cambridge: Cambridge University Press.

1993c: 'Echoes of Intra-Jewish Polemic in Paul's Letter to the Galatians', *Journal of Biblical Literature* 112, 459–77.

1994:   'Prolegomena to a Theology of Paul', *New Testament Studies* 40, 407–32.

1996a: 'In Search of Common Ground', in J. D. G. Dunn (ed.), *Paul and the Mosaic Law*. WUNT 89; Tübingen: J. C. B. Mohr (Paul Siebeck), 309–34.

1996b: '"The Law of Faith", "the Law of the Spirit" and "the Law of Christ"', in E. H. Lovering, Jr. and J. L. Sumney (eds.), *Theology and Ethics in Paul and His Interpreters: Essays in Honor of Victor Paul Furnish*. Nashville: Abingdon, 62–82.

Dunnam, M. D.
1982:   *Galatians, Ephesians, Philippians, Colossians, Philemon*. Waco: Word.

Elliott, J. H.
1988:   'Fear of the Leer: The Evil Eye from the Bible to Li'l Abner', *Forum* 4, 42–71.

1990:   'Paul, Galatians and the Evil Eye', *Currents in Theology and Mission* 17, 262–73.

Elliott, N.
1994:   *Liberating Paul: The Justice of God and the Politics of the Apostle.* Maryknoll: Orbis; 1995 reprint, Sheffield: Sheffield Academic Press.

Esler, P. F.
1994:   *The First Christians in their Social Worlds.* London/New York, Routledge.
1996:   'Group Boundaries and Intergroup Conflict in Galatians: A New Reading of Galatians 5:13–6:10', in M. G. Brett (ed.), *Ethnicity and the Bible.* Leiden: Brill, 215–40.

Faraone, C. A.
1991:   'The Agonistic Context of Early Greek Binding Spells', in C. A. Faraone and D. Obbink (eds.), *Magika Hiera: Ancient Greek Magic and Religion.* Oxford/New York: Oxford University Press, 3–32.

Fee, G. D.
1987:   *The First Epistle to the Corinthians,* Grand Rapids: Eerdmans.
1994a: 'Freedom and the Life of Obedience (Galatians 5:1–6:18)', *Review and Expositor* 91, 201–17.
1994b: *God's Empowering Presence: The Holy Spirit in the Letters of Paul.* Peabody: Hendrickson.

Fowl, S.
1994:   'Who can read Abraham's Story? Allegory and Interpretive Power in Galatians', *Journal for the Study of the New Testament* 55, 77–95.

Fredriksen, P.
1991:   'Judaism, the Circumcision of Gentiles, and Apocalyptic Hope: Another Look at Galatians 1 and 2', *Journal of Theological Studies* 42, 532–64.

Fung, R. Y. K.
1988:   *The Epistle to the Galatians.* NICNT; Grand Rapids: Eerdmans.

Furnish, V. P.
1993:   '"He Gave Himself [Was Given] Up ... "': Paul's
          Use of a Christological Assertion', in A. J. Malherbe
          and W. A. Meeks (eds.), *The Future of Christology:
          Essays in honor of Leander E. Keck*. Minneapolis:
          Augsburg Fortress, 109–21.

Gager, J. G. (ed.)
1992:   *Curse Tablets and Binding Spells from the Ancient World*.
          Oxford: Oxford University Press.

García Martínez, F.
1994:   *The Dead Sea Scrolls Translated*. Leiden: Brill.

Garlington, D. B.
1991:   'Burden Bearing and the Recovery of Offending
          Christians (Galatians 6:1–5)', *Trinity Journal* 12
          (1991) 151–83.

Gaston, L.
1987:   *Paul and the Torah*. Vancouver: University of British
          Columbia Press.

Gaventa, B. R.
1986:   'Galatians 1 and 2: Autobiography as Paradigm',
          Novum Testamentum 28, 302–26.
1990:   'The Maternity of Paul: An Exegetical Study of
          Galatians 4:19', in R. T. Fortna and B. R. Gaventa
          (eds.), *The Conversation Continues: Studies in Paul and
          John in Honor of J. Louis Martyn*. Nashville: Abingdon,
          189–201.
1991:   'The Singularity of the Gospel: A Reading of
          Galatians', in J. M. Bassler (ed.), *Pauline Theology,
          volume 1: Thessalonians, Philippians, Galatians, Phile-
          mon*. Minneapolis: Augsburg Fortress, 147–59.

George, T.
1994:   *Galatians*. Location not cited: Broadman & Hol-
          man.

Goddard, A. J. and Cummins, S. A.
1993:   'Ill or Ill-Treated? Conflict and Persecution as the
          Context of Paul's Original Ministry in Galatia

(Galatians 4.12–20)', *Journal for the Study of the New Testament* 52, 93–126.

Gordon, T. D.
1989: 'A Note on ΠΑΙΔΑΓΩΓΟΣ in Galatians 3.24–25', *New Testament Studies* 35, 150–54.

Hagner, D. A.
1993: 'Paul and Judaism. The Jewish Matrix of Early Christianity: Issues in the Current Debate', *Bulletin of Biblical Research* 3, 111–30.

Hall, R. G.
1996: 'Arguing Like an Apocalypse: Galatians and an Ancient *Topos* Outside the Greco-Roman Rhetorical Tradition', *New Testament Studies* 42, 434–53.

Hamerton-Kelly, R. G.
1990: 'Sacred Violence and "Works of Law"; "Is Christ Then an Agent of Sin?" (Galatians 2:17)', *Catholic Biblical Quarterly* 52, 55–75.

Hansen, G. W.
1989: *Abraham in Galatians: Epistolary and Rhetorical Contexts.* JSNTS 29; Sheffield: JSOT Press.
1994a: *Galatians.* IVPNT 9; Downers/Leicester Grove: IVP.
1994b: 'A Paradigm of the Apocalypse: The Gospel in the Light of Epistolary Analysis', in L. A. Jervis and P. Richardson (eds.), *Gospel in Paul: Studies on Corinthians, Galatians and Romans for Richard N. Longenecker.* JSNTS 108; Sheffield: Sheffield Academic Press, 194–209.

Harvey, G.
1996: *The True Israel: Uses of the Names Jew, Hebrew and Israel in Ancient Jewish and Early Christian Literature.* Leiden: Brill.

Hay, D. M. (ed.)
1993: *Pauline Theology, volume 2: 1 & 2 Corinthians.* Minneapolis: Augsburg Fortress.

Hays, R. B.
1983: *The Faith of Jesus Christ.* SBLDS 56; Chico, CA: Scholars Press.

1987:   'Christology and Ethics in Galatians: The Law of Christ', *Catholic Biblical Quarterly* 49, 268–90.

1989:   *Echoes of Scripture in the Letters of Paul.* London/New Haven: Yale University Press.

1991a: 'Crucified with Christ: A Synthesis of the Theology of 1 and 2 Thessalonians, Philemon, Philippians, and Galatians', in J. M. Bassler (ed.), *Pauline Theology, volume 1: Thessalonians, Philippians, Galatians, Philemon.* Minneapolis: Augsburg Fortress, 227–46.

1991b: 'ΠΙΣΤΙΣ and Pauline Christology', in E. H. Lovering, Jr. (ed.), *Society of Biblical Literature 1991 Seminar Papers.* Atlanta: Scholars Press, 714–29.

1992:   'Justification', in D. N. Freedman *et al.* (eds.), *Anchor Bible Dictionary*, vol. 3. New York: Doubleday, 1129–33.

1996a: 'Three Dramatic Roles: The Law in Romans 3–4', in J. D. G. Dunn (ed.), *Paul and the Mosaic Law.* WUNT 89; Tübingen: J. C. B. Mohr (Paul Siebeck), 151–64.

1996b: *The Moral Vision of the New Testament: Community, Cross, New Creation.* New York: HarperCollins.

Hendriksen, W.
1968:   *A Commentary on Galatians.* London: Hendriksen.

Hengel, M.
1990:   'Der vorchristliche Paulus', *Theologische Beiträge* 21, 174–95.

Hofius, O.
1996:   'Die Adam-Christus-Antithese und das Gesetz: Erwägungen zu Röm 5,12–21', in J. D. G. Dunn (ed.), *Paul and the Mosaic Law.* WUNT 89; Tübingen: J. C. B. Mohr (Paul Siebeck), 165–206.

Hong, I.-G.
1993:   *The Law in Galatians.* JSNTS 81; Sheffield: JSOT Press.

1994:   'Does Paul Misrepresent the Jewish Law? Law and

Covenant in Gal. 3:1–14', *Novum Testamentum* 36, 164–82.

Hooker, M. D.
1990: *From Adam to Christ: Essays on Paul.* Cambridge: Cambridge University Press.
1994: *Not Ashamed of the Gospel: New Testament Interpretations of the Death of Christ.* Carlisle: Paternoster Press.

Howard, G.
1979: *Crisis in Galatia.* Cambridge: Cambridge University Press.

Hübner, H.
1975: 'Das ganze und das eine Gesetz: Zum Problemkreis Paulus und die Stoa', *Kerygma und Dogma* 21, 239–56.
1984: *Law in Paul's Thought.* Trans. J. C. G. Greig; Edinburgh: T. & T. Clark.

Hultgren, A. J.
1980: 'The *Pistis Christou* Formulation in Paul', *Novum Testamentum* 22, 248–63.

Janzen, J. G.
1996: 'Coleridge and *Pistis Christou*', *The Expository Times* 107, 265–68.

Jeremias J.
1967: *The Prayers of Jesus.* ET: London: SCM Press.

Jervis, L. A.
1991: *The Purpose of Romans: A Comparative Letter Structure Investigation.* JSNTS 55; Sheffield: JSOT Press.
1993: '"But I want you to know ... ": Paul's Midrashic Intertextual Response to the Corinthian Worshippers (1 Cor 11:2–16)', *Journal of Biblical Literature* 112, 231–46.

Jewett, R.
1971: 'The Agitators and the Galatian Congregation', *New Testament Studies* 17, 198–212.
1979: *Dating Paul's Life.* London: SCM Press. Also

appeared as *A Chronology of Paul's Life*. Philadelphia: Fortress Press.

Johnson, E. E.
1989:   *The Function of Apocalyptic and Wisdom Traditions in Romans 9–11*. SBLDS 109; Atlanta: Scholars Press.

Johnson, E. E. and Hay, D. M (eds.)
1996:   *Pauline Theology, volume 3: Romans*. Minneapolis: Augsburg Fortress.

Käsemann, E.
1969a: 'The Beginnings of Christian Theology', in his *New Testament Questions of Today*. London: SCM Press, 82–107.
1969b: 'On the Subject of Primitive Christian Apocalyptic', in his *New Testament Questions of Today*. London: SCM Press, 108–37.
1971:   *Perspectives on Paul*. London: SCM Press.
1980:   *Commentary on Romans*. Trans. G. W. Bromiley; Grand Rapids: Eerdmans.

Keck, L. E.
1984:   'Paul and Apocalyptic Theology', *Interpretation* 38, 229–41.
1990:   'Christology, Soteriology, and the Praise of God (Roman 15:7–13)', in R. T. Fortna and B. R. Gaventa (eds.), *The Conversation Continues: Studies in Paul and John in Honor of J. Louis Martyn*. Nashville: Abingdon, 85–97.

Kertelge, K.
1984:   'Gesetz und Freiheit im Galaterbrief', *New Testament Studies* 30, 382–94.
1989:   'Freiheitsbotschaft und Liebesgebot im Galaterbrief', in H. Merklein (ed.), *Neues Testament und Ethik*. Freiburg: Herder, 326–37.

Kim, S.
1981:   *The Origin of Paul's Gospel*. Tübingen: J. C. B. Mohr (Paul Siebeck).

Koch, D. -A.
1986:   *Die Schrift als Zeuge des Evangeliums.* BHT 69; Tübingen: J. C. B. Mohr (Paul Siebeck).

Kraus, W.
1991:   *Der Tod Jesu als Heiligtumsweihe: Eine Untersuchung zum Umfeld der Sühne-verstellung in Römer 3,25–26a.* WMANT 66; Neukirchen-Vluyn: Neukirchener Verlag.
1996:   *Das Volk Gottes: Zur Grundlegung der Ekklesiologie bei Paulus.* Tübingen: J. C. B. Mohr (Paul Siebeck).

Kruse, C. G.
1996:   *Paul, the Law and Justification.* Leicester: Apollos.

Kümmel, W. G.
1975:   *Introduction to the New Testament.* ET: London: SCM Press.

Lagrange, M. -L.
1925:   *Saint Paul Épître aux Galates.* 2nd edn; Paris: Gabalda.

Lambrecht, J.
1991:   'Transgressor by Nullifying God's Grace: A Study of Galatians 2.18–21', *Biblica* 72, 217–36.
1996:   'Paul's Reasoning in Galatians 2:11–21', in J. D. G. Dunn (ed.), *Paul and the Mosaic Law.* WUNT 89; Tübingen: J. C. B. Mohr (Paul Siebeck), 53–74.

Lategan, B.
1988:   'Is Paul Defending His Apostleship in Galatians?', *New Testament Studies* 34, 411–30.

Levenson, J. D.
1996:   'The Universal Horizon of Biblical Particularism', in M. G. Brett (ed.), *Ethnicity and the Bible.* Leiden: Brill, 143–69.

Lichtenberger, H.
1996:   'Das Tora-Verständnis im Judentum zur Zeit des Paulus', in J. D. G. Dunn (ed.), *Paul and the Mosaic Law.* WUNT 89; Tübingen: J. C. B. Mohr (Paul Siebeck), 8–23.

Lightfoot, J. B.
  1896:   *Saint Paul's Epistle to the Galatians.* London: Macmillan.

Longenecker, B. W.
  1989:   'Different Answers to Different Issues: Israel, the Gentiles and Salvation History in Romans 9–11', *Journal for the Study of the New Testament* 36, 95–123.
  1991:   *Eschatology and the Covenant: A Comparison of 4 Ezra and Romans 1–11.* JSNTS 57; Sheffield: JSOT Press.
  1993:   'ΠΙΣΤΙΣ in Romans 3.25: Neglected Evidence for the "Faithfulness of Christ"?', *New Testament Studies* 39, 478–80.
  1995:   *2 Esdras.* GAP; Sheffield: Sheffield Academic Press.
  1996a: 'Defining the Faithful Character of the Covenant Community: Galatians 2.15–21 and Beyond', in J. D. G. Dunn (ed.), *Paul and the Mosaic Law.* WUNT 89; Tübingen: J. C. B. Mohr (Paul Siebeck), 75–97.
  1996b: Review of J. R. W. Stott, *The Message of Romans, Anvil* 13, 70–71.
  1997:   'Contours of Covenant Theology in the Post-Conversion Paul', in R. N. Longenecker (ed.), *The Road from Damascus: The Impact of Paul's Conversion on His Life, Thought and Ministry.* Grand Rapids: Eerdmans, 125–46.
  1998:   '"Until Christ is formed in you": Suprahuman Forces and Moral Character in Galatians', *Catholic Biblical Quarterly* (forthcoming).

Longenecker, R. N.
  1982:   'The Pedagogical Nature of the Law in Galatians 3.19–4.7', *Journal of the Evangelical Theological Society* 25, 53–61.
  1984:   *New Testament Social Ethics for Today.* Grand Rapids: Eerdmans.
  1990:   *Galatians.* WBC; Waco: Word.

Luck, G.
  1985:   *Arcana Mundi.* London: Johns Hopkins University Press.

Lüdemann, G.
1983:   *Paulus der Heidenapostel. II. Antipaulinismus im frühen Christentum.* Göttingen: Vandenhoeck & Ruprecht.
1984:   *Paul Apostle to the Gentiles: Studies in Chronology.* London: SCM Press.
1989:   'Paul and the Law, with Special Attention to his Founding Proclamation', in D. A. Knight and P. J. Paris (eds.), *Justice and the Holy: Essays in Honor of Walter Harrelson.* Atlanta: Scholars Press.

Lührmann, D.
1978:   *Der Brief an die Galater.* Zurich: Theologischer Verlag.

Lull, D. J.
1980:   *The Spirit in Galatia: Paul's Interpretation of Pneuma as Divine Power.* SBLDS 49; Chico: Scholars Press.
1986:   '"The Law was our Pedagogue": A Study in Galatians 3.19–25', *Journal of Biblical Literature* 105, 481–98.
1991:   'Salvation History: The Theological Structure of Paul's Thought (1 Thessalonians, Philippians, and Galatians)', in J. M. Bassler (ed.), *Pauline Theology, volume 1: Thessalonians, Philippians, Galatians, Philemon.* Minneapolis: Augsburg Fortress, 247–65.

Luther, M.
1953:   *A Commentary on the Epistle to the Galatians.* Trans. and ed. P. S. Watson; London: James Clarke.
1963a: 'Lectures on Galatians (1535)', in J. Pelican (ed.), *Luther's Works,* vols. 26 and 27. Saint Louis: Concordia.
1963b: 'Lectures on Galatians (1519)', in J. Pelican (ed.), *Luther's Works,* vol. 27. Saint Louis: Concordia.

Lyons, G.
1985:   *Pauline Autobiography: Toward a New Understanding.* SBLDS 73; Atlanta: Scholars Press.

Malina, B. and Neyrey, J. H.
1996:   *Portraits of Paul: An Archaeology of Ancient Personality.* Louisville: Westminster/John Knox.

Martin, T.
  1996:   'Pagan and Judeo-Christian Time-Keeping Schemes
            in Gal 4.10 and Col 2.16', *New Testament Studies* 42,
            105–119.

Martyn, J. L.
  1985a: 'Apocalyptic Antinomies in Paul's Letter to the
            Galatians', *New Testament Studies* 31, 410–24; re-
            printed in Martyn, 1997: 111–23.
  1985b: 'A Law-Observant Mission to Gentiles: The Back-
            ground of Galatians', *Scottish Journal of Theology* 38,
            307–24; reprinted in Martyn, 1997: 7–24.
  1990:   'The Covenants of Hagar and Sarah', in J. T. Carroll
            et al. (eds.), *Faith and History: Essays in Honor of Paul
            W. Meyer.* Atlanta: Scholars Press, 160–92; reprinted
            in Martyn, 1997: 191–208.
  1991:   'Events in Galatia: Modified Covenantal Nomism
            versus God's Invasion of the Cosmos in the Singular
            Gospel: A Response to J. D. G. Dunn and B. R.
            Gaventa', in J. M. Bassler (ed.), *Pauline Theology,
            volume 1: Thessalonians, Philippians, Galatians, Phil-
            emon.* Minneapolis: Augsburg Fortress, 160–79.
  1993a: 'On Hearing the Gospel Both in the Silence of the
            Tradition and in its Eloquence', in M. C. de Boer
            (ed.), *From Jesus to John: Essays on Jesus and New
            Testament Christology in honour of Marinus de Jonge.*
            JSNTS 84; Sheffield: JSOT Press, 129–47; reprinted
            in Martyn, 1997: 141–56.
  1993b: 'Covenant, Christ and Church in Galatians', in A. J.
            Malherbe and W. A. Meeks (eds.), *The Future of
            Christology: Essays in honor of Leander E. Keck.* Min-
            neapolis: Augsburg Fortress, 137–51; reprinted in
            Martyn, 1997: 161–75.
  1995:   'Christ, the Elements of the Cosmos, and the Law in
            Galatians', in L. M. White and O. L. Yarbrough
            (eds.), *The Social World of the First Christians: Essays in
            Honor of Wayne A. Meeks.* Minneapolis: Augsburg
            Fortress, 16–39; reprinted in Martyn, 1997:
            125–40.

1996: 'The Crucial Event in the History of the Law (Gal 5:14)', in E. H. Lovering, Jr. and J. L. Sumney (eds.), *Theology and Ethics in Paul and His Interpreters: Essays in Honor of Victor Paul Furnish*. Nashville: Abingdon, 48–61; reprinted in Martyn, 1997: 235–50.

1997: *Theological Issues in the Letters of Paul*. Edinburgh: T. & T. Clark.

Matera, F. J.
1988: 'The Culmination of Paul's Argument to the Galatians: Gal. 5.1–6.17', *Journal for the Study of the New Testament* 32, 79–91.

1992: *Galatians*. SP 9; Collegeville, MN: Liturgical Press (Michael Glazier).

1996: *New Testament Ethics: The Legacies of Jesus and Paul*. Louisville: Westminster/John Knox.

Matlock, R. B.
1996: *Unveiling the Apocalyptic Paul: Paul's Interpreters and the Rhetoric of Criticism*. JSNTS 127; Sheffield: Sheffield Academic Press.

McLean, B. H.
1996: *The Cursed Christ: Mediterranean Expulsion Rituals and Pauline Soteriology*. JSNTS 126; Sheffield: Sheffield Academic Press.

Meeks, W. A.
1974: 'The Image of the Androgyne: Some Uses of a Symbol in Earliest Christianity', *History of Religions* 13, 165–208.

1983: *The First Urban Christians: The Social World of the Apostle Paul*. New Haven/London: Yale University Press.

1993: *The Origins of Christian Morality: The First Two Centuries*. New Haven/London: Yale University Press.

Mell, U.
  1989:   *Neue Schöpfung: eine traditionsgeschichtliche und exege-
            tische Studie zu einem soteriologischen Grundsatz pauli-
            nischer Theologie*. BZNW 56; Berlin/New York: de
            Gruyter.

Meyer, H. A. W.
  1884:   *Critical and Exegetical Handbook to the Epistle to the
            Galatians*. CECNT 7; Edinburgh: T. & T. Clark.

Meyer, M. and Smith, R. (eds.)
  1994:   *Ancient Christian Magic*. San Francisco: Harper.

Meyer, P. W.
  1990:   'The Worm at the Core of the Apple: Exegetical
            Observations on Romans 7', in R. T. Fortna and B.
            R. Gaventa (eds.), *The Conversation Continues: Studies
            in Paul and John in Honor of J. Louis Martyn*. Nashville:
            Abingdon, 62–84.

Mitchell, S.
  1993:   *Anatolia: Land, Men, and Gods in Asia Minor*, 2 vols.
            Oxford: Clarendon Press.

Moore, G. F.
  1927:   *Judaism in the First Centuries of the Christian Era, the Age
            of the Tannaim*, 3 vols. New York: Schocken Books;
            vols. 1–2, 1927; vol. 3, 1930.

Moore-Crispin, D. R.
  1989:   'Galatians 4:1–9: The Use and Abuse of Parallels',
            Evangelical Quarterly 60, 203–23.

Morland, K. A.
  1995:   *The Rhetoric of Curse in Galatians: Paul Confronts
            Another Gospel*. Emory Studies in Early Christianity;
            Atlanta: Scholars Press.

Murray, J. A. H, Bradley, H. *et al.*
  1933:   *Oxford English Dictionary*. 12 vols.; Oxford: Claren-
            don Press.

Mussner, F.
  1974:   *Der Galaterbrief.* HTKNT 9; Freiburg: Herder.

Neyrey, J. H.
1988: 'Bewitched in Galatian: Paul and Cultural Anthropology', *Catholic Biblical Quarterly* 50, 72–100.

Nickelsburg, G. W. E.
1991: 'The Incarnation: Paul's Solution to the Universal Human Predicament', in B. A. Pearson (ed.), *The Future of Early Christianity*. Minneapolis: Ausburg Fortress, 348–57.

Noy, D.
1972: 'Evil Eye', in *Encyclopaedia Judaica*, vol. 6. Jerusalem: Keter, 997–1000.

Oepke, A.
1973: *Der Brief des Paulus an die Galater*. THKNT; Berlin: Evangelische Verlagsanstalt.

Onesti, K. L. and Brauch, M. T.
1993: 'Righteousness, Righteousness of God', in G. F. Hawthorne *et al.* (eds.), *Dictionary of Paul and His Letters*. Downers Grove/Leicester: IVP, 827–37.

Percy, E.
1964: *Die Probleme der Kolosser- und Epheserbriefe*. Lund: Gleerup.

Pluta, A.
1969: *Gottes Bundestreue: Ein Schlüsselbegriff in Röm 3:25a*. SBS 34; Stuttgart: Katholisches Bibelwerk.

Preisendanz, K. and Henrichs, A. (eds.)
1928: *Papyri Graecae Magicae: Die griechischen Zauberpapyri*. 3 vols.; Leipzig: Teubner; vol. 1, 1928; vol. 2, 1931, vol. 3, 1941.

Quarles, C. L.
1996: 'The Soteriology of R. Akiba and E. P. Sanders' *Paul and Palestinian Judaism*', *New Testament Studies* 42, 185–95.

Räisänen, H.
1983: *Paul and the Law*. Tübingen: J. C. B. Mohr (Paul Siebeck); reprinted, Philadelphia: Fortress Press, 1986.

Reicke, B.
1951: 'The Law and This World According to Paul: Some Thoughts Concerning Gal. 4:1–11', *Journal of Biblical Literature* 70, 259–76.

Richter Reimer, I.
1992: *Frauen in der Apostelgeschichte des Lukas: Eine feministisch-theologische Exegese.* Gütersloh: Mohn.

Ridderbos, H. N.
1953: *The Epistle of Paul to the Churches of Galatia.* NICNT; Grand Rapids: Eerdmans.

Röhser, G.
1987: *Metaphorik und Personifikation der Sünde.* WUNT 2. 25; Tübingen: J. C. B. Mohr (Paul Siebeck).

Rowland, C. C.
1982: *The Open Heaven: A Study of Apocalyptic in Judaism and Early Christianity.* London: SPCK.
1985: *Christian Origins.* London: SPCK.

Rudolph, K.
1984: *Gnosis: The Nature and History of Gnosticism.* Trans. and ed. R. McL. Wilson; Edinburgh: T. & T. Clark, 1984; San Francisco: Harper & Row, 1987.

Rusan, D.
1992: 'Neue Belege zu den στοιχεῖα τοῦ κόσμου (Gal 4,3. 9; Kol 2,8. 20)', *Zeitschrift für die neutestamentliche Wissenschaft* 83, 119–25.

Sampley, J. P.
1996: 'Reasoning From the Horizons of Paul's Thought World: A Comparison of Galatians and Philippians', in E. H. Lovering, Jr. and J. L. Sumney (eds.), *Theology and Ethics in Paul and His Interpreters: Essays in Honor of Victor Paul Furnish.* Nashville: Abingdon, 114–31.

Sanders, E. P.
1976: 'The Covenant as a Soteriological Category and the Nature of Salvation in Palestinian and Hellenistic

Judaism', in R. Hammerton-Kelly and R. Scroggs (eds.), *Jews Greeks and Christians: Religious Cultures in Late Antiquity*. Leiden: Brill, 11–44.

1977:   *Paul and Palestinian Judaism*. Philadelphia: Fortress Press.

1983:   *Paul, the Law, and the Jewish People*. Philadelphia: Fortress Press.

1990:   'Jewish Association with Gentiles and Galatians 2:11–14', in R. T. Fortna and B. R. Gaventa (eds.), *The Conversation Continues: Studies in Paul and John in Honor of J. Louis Martyn*. Nashville: Abingdon, 170–88.

1992:   *Judaism: Practice and Belief: 63 BCE–66 CE*. London: SCM Press; Philadelphia: Trinity Press International.

1996:   'Paul', in J. Barclay and J. Sweet (eds.), *Early Christian Thought in its Jewish Context*. Cambridge: Cambridge University Press.

Sandmel, S.
1978:   *Judaism and Christian Beginnings*. Oxford: Oxford University Press.

Schlier, H.
1949:   *Der Brief an der Galater*. Göttingen: Vandenhoeck & Ruprecht.

Schnelle, U.
1996:   *The Human Condition: Anthropology in the Teachings of Jesus, Paul, and John*. Edinburgh: T. & T. Clark.

Schoeps, H. J.
1961:   *Paul*. Philadelphia: Westminster.

Scholer, D. N.
1990:   '"The God of Peace Will Shortly Crush Satan Under Your Feet" (Romans 16:20a): The Function of Apocalyptic Eschatology in Paul', *Ex Auditu* 6 (1990) 53–61.

Schweitzer, A.
1931:   *The Mysticism of Paul the Apostle*. London: A. & C. Black.

Scott, J. M.
1992:   *Adoption as Sons of God.* WUNT 2.48; Tübingen:
        J. C. B. Mohr (Paul Siebeck).
1993:   ' "For as Many as are of Works of the Law are under
        a Curse" (Galatians 3.10)', in C. A. Evans and J. A.
        Sanders (eds.), *Paul and the Scriptures of Israel.* JSNTS
        83/SSEJC1; Sheffield: JSOT Press, 187–221.
1995:   *Paul and the Nations.* WUNT 84; Tübingen: J. C. B.
        Mohr (Paul Siebeck).

Scroggs, R.
1972:   'Paul and the Eschatological Woman', *Journal of the
        American Academy of Religion* 40, 283–303.
1974:   'Paul and the Eschatological Woman: Revisited',
        Journal of the American Academy of Religion 42,
        532–37.

Segal, A. F.
1982:   'Hellenistic Magic: Some Questions of Definition',
        in R. van den Broek and M. J. Vermaseren (eds.),
        Studies in Gnosticism and Hellenistic Religions. Leiden:
        Brill, 349–75.
1995:   'On the Nature of Magic: A Report on a Dialogue
        between a Historian and a Sociologist', in L. M.
        White and O. L. Yarbrough (eds.), *The Social World of
        the First Christians: Essays in Honor of Wayne A. Meeks.*
        Minneapolis: Augsburg Fortress, 16–39.

Seifrid, M. A.
1992:   *Justification by Faith: The Origin and Development of a
        Central Pauline Theme.* NovTS 68; Leiden: Brill.
1993:   'In Christ', in G. F. Hawthorne and R. P. Martin
        (eds.), *Dictionary of Paul and His Letters.* Downers
        Grove/Leicester: IVP, 433–36.

Smith, C. C.
1996:   'Ἐκκλεῖσαι in Galatians 4:17: The Motif of the
        Excluded Lover as a Metaphor of Manipulation',
        Catholic Biblical Quarterly 58, 480–99.

Smith, M.
1979:   'On the History of ΑΠΟΚΑΛΥΠΤΩ and

Bibliography 213

ΑΠΟΚΑΛΥΨΙΣ', in D. Hellholm (ed.), *Apocalypticism in the Mediterranean World and the Near East*. Tübingen: J. C. B. Mohr (Paul Siebeck), 9–20.

Soards, M. L.
1987: *The Apostle Paul: An Introduction to his Writings and Teaching*. New York: Paulist Press.
1989: 'Seeking (ZÊTEIN) and Sinning (HAMARTÔLOS & HAMARTIA) according to Galatians 2.17', in J. Marcus and M. L. Soards (eds.) *Apocalyptic and the New Testament: Essays in Honor of J. Louis Martyn*. Sheffield: JSOT Press, 237–54.

Spicq, C.
1994: 'βασκαίνω, *baskainō*', in his *Theological Lexicon of the New Testament*, vol. 1. Trans. and ed. J. D. Ernest; Peabody: Hendrickson, 272–76.

Stanley, C. D.
1990: '"Under a Curse": A Fresh Reading of Galatians 3.10–14', *New Testament Studies* 36, 481–511.
1992: *Paul and the Language of Scripture*. SNTSMS 69; Cambridge: Cambridge University Press.

Stanton, G.
1996: 'The Law of Moses and the Law of Christ: Galatians 3:1–6:2', in J. D. G. Dunn (ed.), *Paul and the Mosaic Law*. WUNT 89; Tübingen: J. C. B. Mohr (Paul Siebeck), 99–116.

Stern, M.
1974: *Greek and Latin Authors on Jews and Judaism*, 3 vols. Jerusalem: Israel Academy of Sciences and Humanities; vol. 1, 1974; vol. 2, 1980; vol. 3, 1984.

Stibbe, M.
1996: *O Brave New Church: Rescuing the Addictive Culture*. London: Darton, Longman & Todd.

Stowers, S. K.
1986: *Letter Writing in Greco-Roman Antiquity*. Philadelphia: Westminster.

Stuhlmacher, P.
  1994:   *Paul's Letter to the Romans: A Commentary.* Trans. S. J.
            Hafemann; Edinburgh: T. & T. Clark.

Talbert, C. H.
  1987:   *Reading Corinthians: A Literary and Theological
            Commentary on 1 and 2 Corinthians.* New York:
            Crossroad.

Thielman, F.
  1989:   *From Plight to Solution: A Jewish Framework for Under-
            standing Paul's View of the Law in Galatians and
            Romans.* NovTS 61; Leiden: Brill.

Thrall, M. E.
  1982:   Review of J. C. Beker, *Paul the Apostle, Journal of
            Theological Studies* 33, 268–70.

Tomson, P. J.
  1990:   *Paul and the Jewish Law: Halakah in the Letters of the
            Apostle to the Gentiles.* Assen: van Gorcum; Minneapo-
            lis: Augsburg Fortress.

  1996:   'Paul's Jewish Background in View of his Law
            Teaching in 1 Cor 7', in J. D. G. Dunn (ed.), *Paul
            and the Mosaic Law.* WUNT 89; Tübingen: J. C. B.
            Mohr (Paul Siebeck), 251–70.

Urbach, E. E.
  1981:   'Self-Isolation or Self-Affirmation in Judaism in the
            First Three Centuries: Theory and Practice', in E. P.
            Sanders *et al.* (eds.), *Jewish and Christian Self-Defini-
            tion, Volume Two: Aspects of Judaism in the Greco-Roman
            Period.* Philadelphia: Fortress, 269–98.

van Dülmen, A.
  1968:   *Die Theologie des Gesetzes bei Paulus.* Stuttgart: Katho-
            lisches Bibelwerk.

van Henten, J. W.
  1993:   'The Tradition-Historical Background of Romans

3.25: A Search for Pagan and Jewish Parallels', in M. C. de Boer (ed.), *From Jesus to John: Essays on Jesus and New Testament Christology in honour of Marinus de Jonge.* JSNTS 84; Sheffield: JSOT Press, 101–28.

Vermes, G.
1995:   *The Dead Sea Scrolls in English.* 4th edn; Sheffield: Sheffield Academic Press.

Verseput, D. J.
1993:   'Paul's Gentile Mission and the Jewish Christian Community: A Study of the Narrative in Galatians 1 and 2', *New Testament Studies* 39, 36–58.

Vos, J. S.
1992:   'Die hermeneutische Antinomie bei Paulus (Gal 3.11–12; Röm 10.5–10)', *New Testament Studies* 38, 254–70.

Wallace, D. B.
1996:   *Greek Grammar Beyond the Basics: Exegetical Syntax of the New Testament.* Grand Rapids: Zondervan.

Watson, F.
1986:   *Paul, Judaism and the Gentiles.* SNTSMS 56; Cambridge: Cambridge University Press.

Weima, J. A. D.
1993:   'Gal. 6:11–18: A Hermeneutical Key to the Galatian Letter', *Calvin Theological Journal* 28, 90–107.
1994:   *Neglected Endings: The Significance of the Pauline Letter Closings.* JSNTS 101; Sheffield: JSOT Press.

Westerholm, S.
1988:   *Israel's Law and the Church's Faith.* Grand Rapids: Eerdmans.
1996:   'Paul and the Law in Romans 9–11', in J. D. G. Dunn (ed.), *Paul and the Mosaic Law.* WUNT 89; Tübingen: J. C. B. Mohr (Paul Siebeck), 215–37.

Wilckens, U.
1978:   *Der Brief an die Römer,* 3 vols. EKK 6.1–3; Neukirchen-Vluyn: Neukirchener Verlag; vol. 1, 1978; vol. 2, 1980; vol. 3, 1982.

Williams, S. K.
  1975:   *Jesus' Death as Saving Event: The Background and Origin of a Concept.* HDR 2; Missoula: Scholars Press.
  1980:   'The "Righteousness of God" in Romans', *Journal of Biblical Literature* 99, 241–90.
  1987:   'Again *PISTIS CHRISTOU*', *Catholic Biblical Quarterly* 49, 431–47.

Wink, W.
  1984:   *Naming the Powers: The Language of Power in the New Testament.* Philadelphia: Fortress Press.
  1986:   *Unmasking the Powers: The Invisible Forces that Determine Human Existence.* Philadelphia: Fortress Press.
  1992:   *Engaging the Powers: Discernment and Resistance in a World of Domination.* Philadelphia: Fortress Press.

Winter, B. W.
  1993:   'The Entries and Ethics of Orators and Paul (1 Thessalonians 2.1–12)', *Tyndale Bulletin* 44, 55–74.
  1994:   *Seek the Welfare of the City: Christians as Benefactors and Citizens.* Grand Rapids: Eerdmans.

Witherington, B.
  1992:   *Jesus, Paul and the End of the World: A Comparative Study in New Testament Eschatology.* Downers Grove/Leicester: IVP.
  1994:   *Paul's Narrative Thought World: The Tapestry of Tragedy and Triumph.* Louisville: Westminster/John Knox.

Wright, N. T.
  1978:   'The Paul of History and the Apostle of Faith', *Tyndale Bulletin* 29, 61–88.
  1991a: *The Climax of the Covenant: Christ and the Law in Pauline Theology.* Edinburgh: T. & T. Clark.
  1991b: 'One God, One Lord, One People: Incarnational Christology for a Church in a Pagan Environment', *Ex Auditu* 7, 45–58.
  1992a: *The New Testament and the People of God.* London: SPCK.
  1992b: 'The World, The Church, and the Groaning of the

Spirit', in his *The Crown and the Fire: Meditations on the Cross and the Life of the Spirit.* London: SPCK, 67–78.

1994:   'Gospel and Theology in Galatians', in J. A. Jervis and P. Richardson (eds.) *Gospel in Paul: Studies on Corinthians, Galatians and Romans for Richard N. Longenecker.* JSNTS 108; Sheffield: Sheffield Academic Press, 222–39.

1996:   'The Law in Romans 2', in J. D. G. Dunn (ed.), *Paul and the Mosaic Law.* WUNT 89; Tübingen: J. C. B. Mohr (Paul Siebeck), 131–50.

Young, N. H.
1987:   '*Paidagôgos:* The Social Setting of a Pauline Metaphor', *Novum Testamentum* 29, 150–76.

Ziesler, J.
1991:   'Justification by Faith in the Light of the "New Perspective" on Paul', *Theology* 94, 188–94.

Index of Ancient Sources

Biblical References

219

Apocrypha

Old Testament Pseudepigrapha

Dead Sea Scrolls

Philo

Index of Modern Authors